HEKATE HER SACRED FIRES

With beautiful Blessings,

[signature]

*"Having spoken these things, you will behold a fire leaping skittishly
Like a child over the aery waves,
Or a fire without form, from which a voice emerges"*

*Chaldean Oracles,
from The Epiphany of Hekate, in S.I. Johnston*

THIS BOOK IS DEDICATED TO ALL THOSE WHO READ
'HEKATE KEYS TO THE CROSSROADS'
AND TOLD ME SO.

HEKATE

HER SACRED FIRES

EXPLORING THE MYSTERIES OF THE
TORCHBEARING GODDESS OF THE CROSSROADS

WITH ESSAYS, PROSE & ARTWORK FROM AROUND THE
WORLD GIVING UNIQUE INSIGHTS INTO HER MYSTERIES IN
THE 21ST CENTURY

COMPILED & EDITED BY

SORITA D'ESTE

PUBLISHED BY AVALONIA

WWW.AVALONIABOOKS.CO.UK

Figure 1 - Keys to the Keybearers

Published by Avalonia
BM Avalonia
London
WC1N 3XX
England, UK

www.avaloniabooks.co.uk
HEKATE HER SACRED FIRES
Copyright © Avalonia 2010
Individual contributors retain copyright of their essays and artwork.

ISBN-10: 1-905297-35-1
ISBN-13: 978-1-905297-35-1

First Edition, May 2010; Second Edition, September 2010
Design by Satori

Front Cover Art: top left Emily Carding, bottom left by Brian Andrews; centre by Magin Rose; top right by Shay Skepevski, bottom right by Georgi Mishev.

Back Cover Art: Orryelle Defenstrate-Bascule (tattoo of Hekate on Catamara Rosarium) and top right insert by Magin Rose.

British Library Cataloguing in Publication Data. A catalogue record for this book is available from the British Library.

Figure 2 - Hekate as the Keybearing Goddess of the Whole Universe by Georgi Mishev

The following books may also be of interest to readers:

Other Books about The Goddess Hekate:

Historical Studies:
Hekate in Ancient Greek Religion by R.Von Rudloff
Hekate Liminal Rites by Sorita d'Este and David Rankine
Hekate Soteira, by Sarah Iles Johnston
The Goddess Hekate by Stephen Ronan

Other / Modern Pagan:
Bearing Torches (numerous contributors) by Bibliotheca Alexandrina
Crossroads by Greg Crowfoot
Hecate I: Death, Transition and Spiritual Mastery by Jade Sol Luna
Hecate II: The Awakening of Hydra by Jade Sol Luna
Hekate Keys to the Crossroads (numerous contributors) edited by Sorita d'Este
Queen of Hell by Mark Alan Smith
The Rotting Goddess by Jacob Rabinowitz

Other Books by Contributors on related topics:

A Collection of Magical Secrets by Stephen Skinner and David Rankine, translated by Paul Harry Barron
Artemis Virgin Goddess of the Sun and Moon by Sorita d'Este
Beyond the Broomstick by Morgana Sythove
Coagula by Orryelle Defenestrate-Bascule
Conjunctio by Orryelle Defenstrate-Bascule
Defences Against the Witches' Craft by John Canard
Goth Craft by Raven Digitalis
Horns of Power edited by Sorita d'Este (numerous contributors)
Planetary Spells and Rituals by Raven Digitalis
Priestesses Pythonesses Sibyls edited by Sorita d'Este (numerous contributors)
Shadow Magick by Raven Digitalis
The Book of Gold by David Rankine and Paul Harry Barron
The Craft of the Wise by Vikki Bramshaw
The Dance of the Mystai by Tinnekke Bebout
The Guises of the Morrigan by Sorita d'Este and David Rankine
The Isles of the Many Gods by Sorita d'Este and David Rankine
The Shaman's Drum by Jean Marie Feddercke
The Tarot of the Sidhe (cards) by Emily Carding
The Transparent Oracle (cards) by Emily Carding
The Transparent Tarot (cards) by Emily Carding
The Veritable Key of Solomon by Stephen Skinner and David Rankine, translated by Paul Harry Barron
Tubelo's Green Fire by Shani Oates
Underworld by Katherine Sutherland
Visions of the Cailleach by Sorita d'Este and David Rankine
Wicca Magickal Beginnings by Sorita d'Este and David Rankine

Other:
For more information also see:

Hekate Her Sacred Fires (Book Project Website) – www.sacredfires.co.uk
The Covenant of Hekate (International Organisation) – www.hekatecovenant.com

ACKNOWLEDGEMENTS

This project was a labour of love for me, inspired by the flames of Hekate in my temple sanctuary in Powys, Wales during a stormy night in November 2009, and encouraged into its conception by the enthusiasm and love of the contributors and the many others who helped by contributing their time and passion in diverse ways.

Firstly, I would like to thank all those who contributed their knowledge, experiences and understanding of the Goddess Hekate through their essays, prose and artwork. Together your visions provide the most complete glimpse into the modern day mysteries of this ancient Torchbearing Goddess, you are *Her Sacred Fires* burning all over the world today.

In particular I would like to offer my gratitude to Emily Carding, for being a wondrous friend and inspiring visionary, for her support and encouragement throughout the months – and her endless patience with my mutable Sagittarian nature.

Tara Sanchez for her steadfast and unfaltering support with this project, for making the long journey to me in Wales on a rainy Beltane morning to be with me for the first expression of *The Rite of Her Sacred Fires*, and all her help in creating the multi-media productions for the rite.

Thank you to Georgi Mishev for being an inspiration through his dedication in serving the Gods with honour and for sharing so much of his research and ideas with me over the last few months.

Also to Catamara Rosarium for being an incidental Muse, just when I needed it and to Stuart Inman for providing the avenues to the last piece which made this project that much more complete.

My gratitude also to the team of proofreaders who assisted me with the final editing, especially Kim Huggens, Yuri Robbers, Jill Lake, Jonathan Sparrow, Sophia Martin, Soror Lina and Sue Bowman; and to those who shared research with me including August Hunt, Douglas Blowe, Peter Ferne and Nina Lazarus.

To Karagan my appreciation for permission to use the beautifully haunting track "*Hymn to Hekate*" from his album *Chants of Old* for the *Rite of Her Sacred Fires,* and for his support in helping raise awareness of the project through WitchTalk Radio. Likewise, to Magin Rose for the use of her recording of her beautifully haunting *Hekate Star and Centre* and to Jade Sol Luna for his generous permission to use his salient and powerful musical offerings from his albums *Scorpio Invocatio* and *Queen of the Crossroads* to Hekate for the *Rite of Her Sacred Fires.*

I would also like to thank Damon Zacharias Lycourinos of the *Temple of Iakkhos*, for providing many hours of astute debate and discussion on the Western Occult Tradition, as well as on philosophy, mysticism and religion. It is a delight to know someone who understands and shares a passion for both the stars and the stones.

Then finally, I would like to thank David Rankine, for his help with some of the research and for all the help and support he has given me throughout this project. For putting up with my nocturnal habits, my crazy never-ending aesthetic obsessions, my interminable demands and enchanting requests for more fresh coffee at all hours of the day and night. For being my friend and priest over the many years when we lit Her fires, and many others. I love you.

You are the *Lightbearers in Darkness, the Harbingers of Change*. You are the Torchbearers and the keepers of Her Sacred Flames.

Figure 3 - Three Formed Hekate from The Mythology of Greece & Rome, 1887

TABLE OF CONTENTS

Figure 4 - Torchbearing Priestess of Threskeia

LIST OF IMAGES

EDITORIAL NOTES

With a project as unique as this, involving more than 50 individuals from all over the world, it is necessary to clarify a few minor editorial issues regarding the contents before we continue.

Very few of the contributors are professional writers, with many writing in second or third languages. As this project is about personal experiences, as editor I was keen to where possible preserve the individual voice of the contributor, so please keep this in mind as you read through the essays.

There are particular points which I should highlight here:

Hekate or Hecate?

The Greek transliteration of Hekate (with a 'k') and Roman transliteration of Hecate (with a 'c') have been left unaltered reflecting the authors' preferences in the essays. Both are taken to mean the same deity, who is the subject of this book.

Pronounciation:

There are many debates about the correct pronounciation of the name "Hekate" and it is impossible to provide a conclusive answer. Today many native English speakers pronounce her name as "he-ka-tee", whilst some prefer the pronounciation as "e-ka-tay" which has been suggested as being correct when based on Greek pronounciation. However, taking into account that Hekate's name has been recorded since at least the 8th or 7th century BCE and that there is no conclusive evidence (only theories) on how the Ancient Greek language was pronounced during the Archaic period, together with the fact that we know that this Goddess originated outside of Greece, a conclusive argument for a specific pronounciation is not possible. Taking therefore into account that in the ancient world, like the modern one we live in, there would have been regional accents, so the best advice is probably to pronounce it in the way you feel most comfortable with.

Capitalisation:

The individual choices of contributors to capitalise particular words for emphasis, such as *Goddess, She, Her,* etc, have been respected.

Words as artistic expression:

Practitioners of some traditions like Chaos Magick sometimes use the spelling of words as a form of magical expression and when this occurs the words have been left in their original form to ensure the flow of consciousness effect created by the authors is not altered.

"If you call upon Me often you will perceive everything in lion-form.
For then neither does the curved mass of Heaven appear, nor the stars shine.
The light of the moon is hidden, and the earth is not firmly secured.
But all things are seen by flashes of lighting. "

From: Chaldean Oracles, C2nd CE (Ronan trans.)

Figure 5 - Hekate Triformis by Ellis

Before we begin...

Foreword by Sorita d'Este

To the Reader,

Her Sacred Fires was born in the fires of my temple sanctuary in November 2009, when during a ceremony in which I explored the mysteries of the *Seven Wandering Stars* I invoked the god Dionysos. Chanting his name and epithets, I implored him to give me a vision for a query I had about the work I was undertaking and in which he would play a central role. I continued the invocation vibrating divine names and then hearing a rhythm which sounded both familiar and extraordinarily alluring, I started moving, dancing and spinning myself into a frenzied state of reverie. I am not sure how long I was dancing for, but I continued until I eventually dropped to the ground both exhausted and elated, my eyes transfixed on the flames of the fire burning next to my altar which continued the dance I had started.

Those flames seemed much larger than they could possibly have been, or maybe it was that I had become smaller in that moment, which it is I will never really know. Perspective and discernment thereof, at moments such as those never really seem to be important. The dancing flames intensified, moving with purpose and with intelligence, flickering beings of red, white and black, beckoning me to look and see.

Before me formed an image of the world as a map and marked upon it were numerous markers in the form of small torches marking numerous locations. Instantaneously I comprehended that these torches represented the torches of the goddess Hekate, and the *"small torches"* which it was said would burn with the cakes left for her at the crossroads as offerings at the Hekate Suppers. Then I knew, that the exploration of her mysteries would once again take centre stage in my life, even though I had planned to do something else for the year ahead of me.

By the time I had returned to the house and my office that night, I knew what I had to do. A project that would follow on from *Hekate Keys to the Crossroads* which I had compiled and published in 2006, but this time instead of bringing together the voices and experiences of people who all came from one country, I had to find individuals who represented the flames of Hekate all over the world.

I knew this project would have to be something unique and completely different from my previous efforts, reflecting the fact that Hekate stands at a global crossroads of traditions and people from all over the world.

My aim was thus to try and present a cross-section of the views currently held around the world in different pagan, spiritual and magical traditions in regards to the goddess Hekate. As such, my own views on Hekate do not necessarily concur with those of the contributors included here. Through diversity I hope to challenge all the readers into gaining not only a wider perspective on the mysteries of this one goddess, but also of magic and mysticism as a whole. It is in our differences that the beauty of new experiences and knowledge can be found.

Books are magical things. They have the ability to change your world, in ways which can be of earth shaking magnitude – or often in more subtle ways. How much, if at all this book will change you, is not for me to say, but it is my hope that you will allow yourself to approach each contribution with an open mind and allow yourself to step across the thresholds between worlds known and unknown, to experience the goddess Hekate from the perspective of the contributors.

The men and women who contributed to this book are extraordinary people who have all, in one way or another encountered the Torchbearing Goddess of the Crossroads in their lives. Their views are as unique as they are, reflections of their individual experiences, and sometimes also cultural, social and educational differences. Indeed, it would be a great disappointment to me as the editor of this volume if I found out that everyone who read it, agreed with absolutely all the ideas and visions expressed herein.

When back in 2006 I decided to put together a collection of material related to the goddess Hekate, the work was mainly drawn from individuals I knew worked closely with the goddess Hekate and from folk who were members of one the Alexandrian lineaged Craft covens I had founded in London with David Rankine in late 2000. The resulting project *Hekate Keys to the Crossroads* really was something we put together just for us, as a way of sharing our experiences and ideas – and was originally inspired by some of the excellent ritual material and essays several of the initiates created. Over the months and years which followed the publication of *Keys to the Crossroads*, many people asked me when I would be doing another such anthology, but I always dismissed the idea as I wished to focus on my work in other areas and my research into the historical origins of Hekate.

In May 2009 *Hekate Liminal Rites* was published, which contains some of the research David and I had done over the years regarding the magical and ritual practices associated with Hekate from historical sources. This work showed a broader perspective of Hekate through exploring a significant cross-section of the numerous references to her found throughout the ancient world. It is part of a much larger long term project I am working on – but it will likely take many more years of research to complete!

As editor of this and numerous other anthologies, I am acutely aware of the fact that some of the contributors are more skilled with written words than others. This is very understandable when taking into consideration that many of the contributors to this volume have written in their second or even third languages in order for their visions and views to be included in this project. I have made only essential changes, and in all instances I tried to preserve the "*voice*" of the writer, after all that is what this project is about – expressing diversity to encourage the expansion of horizons.

What is of the utmost importance to me as the editor and compiler of this book is that you the reader will know and understand that the work presented in this volume was not brought together by me, but by the guiding light of the flaming torches of the goddess Hekate herself. Each contribution helped shape the project into a whole, and the whole could never be complete without all its parts.

It has been a long and challenging few months putting this together, maybe amongst the most interesting, exhausting and testing months of my life. The lesson I have taken away from this is that I should never, ever say *"never ever"* when the gods might be listening, especially not when it comes to Hekate. But really, I knew that already.

What is Her Sacred Fires?

The title of this book was inspired by the vision which ignited it, it also has many additional layers of significance, all of which are equally important.

Her Sacred Fires are also the fires which burn, and have burned in the past or will burn in future, on altars and shrines erected in her honour. They are the fires which will be lit all around the world when the *Rite of Her Sacred Fires* is celebrated on the Full Moon on 27th May 2010 to celebrate the release of this book.

Her Sacred Fires are also the flames of Hekate's Torches, being the light which guides the initiate through the pathways of initiation into the mysteries. The flames from her torches are the light which provides safety in the darkness when travelling from one place to another on roads which are filled with unseen dangers. The fires of her torches are also weapons, because fire burns and can destroy and purify that which is undesired and dangerous to us and can also in this context be used for protection.

Her torches can likewise be seen as possibly representing the Evening and Morning Stars (the planet Venus) which as the first and last star of evening and morning encloses the darkness of night between them, but equally the light of the day. It is even possible to speculate, that the torches are the Sun (Helios) and the Moon (Selene), who provide light in an otherwise dark world and like the Morning and Evening stars, enclose night and day between them in their never ending journeys through the sky.

But most of all, *Her Sacred Fires* are the individuals who understand that the goddess can be perceived through the formless fires, and that hers are the fires which ignite both love and passion, joy and sadness – in equal measures. Whichever way you choose to interpret it, her torches are always fires of illumination.

The mysteries have the ability to diminish artificial boundaries, to reach out beyond that which can be seen and perceived when we restrict ourselves and bind ourselves to the illusions we are subjected to every day. To perceive them is effortless, but entering them by crossing the boundary takes courage and wisdom – to do so with fear and folly is an act only the really foolish would indulge in.

Dancing in Her Flames,
Sorita d'Este

(Wales, April 2010)
www.sorita.co.uk

Figure 6 - The Serpent Flame by Emily Carding

HEKATE'S TORCHBEARERS

Her Sacred Fires is a mosaic of perspectives, providing us with the insights of men and women from all six of the inhabited continents. Together these provide us with a unique 21st century image of the Torchbearing Goddess of the Crossroads. Amongst them are modern Mystics, Philosophers, Magicians, Root Workers, Theurgists, Sorcerors, Enchanters, Witches, Wiccans, Druids, Thelemites and a multitude of other traditions and practices. They are the Torchbearers of Hekate today.

In alphabetical order by first name, the men and women who contributed to *Hekate Her Sacred Fires* are:

AMBER ROSE (AUSTRALIA)

Amber Rose is a Conjure woman of the Vieux Carré /Tsalagi Medicine- Hoodoo with a spicy blend of Vodou & Cherokee Wolf Medicine. She resides in Australia and writes for the Occult Magazine *Opus Magus*. She feels that Hekate is highly recognized as the Patroness of the Crossroads; and rightfully treated so within the Hoodoo tradition and paid homage to at the 'Y' shaped crossroads whereas Hermes represents the 'X. She is also synchronized in Vodou/Voodoo with the Blessed Virgin Mary as a Catholic representation. Amber states that in all words of veneration, Hekate has touched her life in such a profound and multifaceted way from the blossoming rose of a child to that which she is today. She can be contacted via email: zombiecrackers@gmail

AMELIA OUNSTED (ENGLAND, UK)

Amelia Ounsted is a Wiccan High Priestess running an Alexandrian lineage Coven in the London area. She is a priestess of Hekate and previously contributed to the anthologies *Hekate: Keys to the Crossroads* and *Priestesses Pythonesses Sibyls*, having a particular passion for oracular work. She lives in fear that Hekate will demand an exclusivity contract and considers commitment to a Goddess more terrifying than marriage or the M25 motorway on a Friday evening.

ANDREA SALGADO-REYES (CHILE AND SPAIN)

Andrea Salgado Reyes is a Chilean witch and Orixá devotee, blessed by being a daughter of Yemanyá and of Ogún. She has established Comunidad Paganus, a neo-pagan and pagan community in Chile, on a hill within sight of the sea. Her main interests are Wicca, Candomblé and traditional Latin American witchcraft. By profession she is a translator and interpreter. She has previously contributed to *Priestesses Pythonesses Sibyls* and *From a Drop of Water*. You can contact her by email - tierrapagana@gmail.com

BRIAN ANDREWS (ENGLAND, UK)

Brian Andrews is an artist based in South London. He studied design at Croydon Art College and later studied illustration in Hereford. Returning to London he found and was initiated into an Alexandrian Coven that worked with Hekate. Since then Hekate has become a major influence on his work. He contributed an essay and artwork to the anthology *Hekate: Keys to the Crossroads,* and his artwork features in *Artemis: Virgin Goddess of the Sun & Moon, The Guises of the Morrigan*, and *Heka*. Brian is currently bemused by the relationship between mental illness and magick but thinks it's probably part of growing up and being British.

CATAMARA ROSARIUM (U.S.A.)

Catamara Rosarium is an Alchemist, Master Herbalist, and Ritual Artist. She has been a student and practitioner of various Western and Eastern traditions over the past 13 years. Her current studies and practicum include Spagyrics, Wortcunning, Qabalistic Symbolism, Alchemy and Cunning Craft Sorcery. Her newest endeavour is *'Rosarium*

Blends' a business concocting various alchemical creations to enliven the senses. www.rosariumblends.com. Her continuous passions lie in esoteric arts, with an emphasis on cross diversification, working to cultivate networking and community based events wherein diverse belief systems and traditional practices may be shared and to offer deeper understanding and education through these communal experiences. Catamara spends much of her time being co-administrator/book hag of the annual Esoteric Book Conference in Seattle, USA: www.esotericbookconference.com

CONNIA SILVER (U.S.A.)
Connia Silver is a writer and educator who has taught a wide range of intuitive skills and Goddess mysteries. Connia lives with her husband and companion animals in the Sonoran Desert, where they put into practice organic and sustainable living whenever possible. She enjoys learning about the Goddess, the desert and dreamwork, among other subjects. Connia is the founder and director of studies of *In Her Name Temple* and the *Crossroads Lyceum*, which provides spiritual courses and Priestess training through correspondence. She may be reached through the following websites: www.inhername.com and www.crlyceum.com

DAVID RANKINE (WALES, UK)
David Rankine is an occultist, author, and esoteric scholar who has been studying magic since the 1970s. He has written numerous books on magic, of which eleven books to date have been co-authored with his wife Sorita d'Este, including *Practical Qabalah Magick*, *Practical Elemental Magick* and *Hekate Liminal Rites*; and the *Sourceworks of Ceremonial Magic* series with Stephen Skinner, which includes works such as *The Goetia of Dr Rudd* and *The Veritable Key of Solomon*. David has dedicated his life to the exploration and elucidation of magic through history, with his particular passions being for the Qabalah, Grimoires, Greco-Egyptian magic and British folklore. See www.ritualmagick.co.uk

DIANE M. CHAMPIGNY (U.S.A.)
Diane M. Champigny (Thea) is a 3rd Degree High Priestess and Lineage Elder of the Alexandrian Tradition of Witchcraft. She is an active member of the *Society of Elder Faiths* and has served as a Ritualist and Workshop Facilitator for the *Wiccan Educational Society*, a Global Pagan Community. Thea is also a Trance Medium, Occult Bibliophile and contributing author to the books *Priestesses Pythonesses Sibyls* and *From A Drop of Water* published by Avalonia. Inquiries may be directed to PriestessThea@hotmail.com or for more detailed information, visit Thea at http://www.myspace.com/PriestessThea.

DORN SIMON-SINNOTT (IRELAND)
Dorn Simon-Sinnott is a Pagan Witch with eclectic leanings; incorporating Ancient Witchcraft Traditions, with Druidry, Shamanism, Inca, and the Occult Sciences. She considers herself a child and servant of Hekate, Isis, Hermes, Pachamama and Wirococha, and also works with a multitude of other energies. She is an Adept in the *Fellowship Of Isis*, trained in the *Iseum of Aradia*, and is founder of the Iseum *of Hekate, Phosphoros, Soteira & Psychopompus Hermeneus*. For more info see www.wix.com/IseumHekateHermeneus/training. She loves writing in all its forms be it poetry, lyrics, short stories, novels or scripts. Dorn lives in Wexford, Ireland.

EKATERINA ILIEVA (BULGARIA)
Ekaterina Ilieva (Plovdiv, Bulgaria) is a Priestess and co-founder of the *Threskeia* – a pagan tradition based on ancient Thracian beliefs. A devoted explorer of the ancient myths and culture looking forward to getting a degree in History, until that happens she is happy to be a gardener, herbalist and private researcher of magical practices and rituals. You can find out more about *Threskeia* by visiting their website http://threskeia.ucoz.com. She can also be contacted by email - dadaleme@abv.bg

EMILY CARDING (CORNWALL, UK)

Emily Carding is a self-taught artist and author, best known for her Tarot work. Her creations include the groundbreaking *Transparent Tarot*, the *Tarot of the Sidhe*, and the *Transparent Oracle*, a seventy card transparent deck based on the seven directions, which forms circular mandalas when cards are layered. Her work has also featured in magazines and book covers, including Avalonia's *Both Sides of Heaven*, for which she also contributed an essay, and *From a Drop of Water*. She currently has a number of projects on the boil and creative ideas in gestation! For more information, please visit www.childofavalon.com

GEORGI MISHEV (BULGARIA)

Georgi Mishev (Plovdiv, Bulgaria) is a Priest and co-founder of the *Threskeia*, a pagan tradition based on the beliefs of ancient Thrace. Blessed by being a member of family of healers and trained in folk traditional magic, Georgi is a Bachelor in German and Russian language and has a Master's degree in the field of Preservation of cultural heritage. He is also a researcher in ancient history and religion of the Mediterranean world and especially in magic practices, rituals and ancient relics in the modern folklore. See http://threskeia.ucoz.com

HANSA (INDIA AND ENGLAND, UK)

Hansa is a devotee of Hekate and Kali, who spends her year divided between London, England and Kulgachia, India. She was born and raised in India until she was ten, when her parents sent her to live with family in the UK to continue her education there. She works in fashion, and enjoys the freedom to travel this brings her. She feels happiest when she is performing rituals, whether these are Hindu pujas or Wiccan circles, which she sees as both expressing part of the same greater power, that of Sakti, the great goddess.

HENRIK HOLMDAHL (SWEDEN)

Henrik is a jack of all trades, eclectic witch and a mystic of various traditions. He considers himself a servant of Hekate, who has the most prominent role in his life, and acts as his mentor. In his spare time he likes creativity in different forms, especially something he calls the magickal art_art. He also likes travelling, culture, gardening, animals and computer games. He can be reached on Facebook and at Youtube where he sometimes posts videos. http://www.youtube.com/user/Rasputin712

JADE SOL LUNA (U.S.A.)

Hecate devotee and Astrologer, Jade Sol Luna is the first Westerner ever to reconstruct Jyotish (Hindu astrology) into a Greco-Roman format. Jade has travelled to India more than 30 times and spent a great deal of time with various teachers, Saints and Sadhu's in Asia. He was tutored by Bhau Kalchuri (disciple of Meher Baba) and Kal Babji (Khajuraho, India) in advanced mysticism and classical Indian lore during and after his formal Astrological training. His work has featured on many radio shows and in magazines worldwide. Jade is the author of *Hecate I: Death, Transition and Spiritual Mastery* and *Hecate II: The Awakening of Hydra*. He is currently working on a series of books on astrology. Jade is available for private consultations and conducts a number of exclusive seminars around the world each year. For more information see his website www.hiddenmoon.com

JEAN MARIE FEDDERCKE (ENGLAND, UK)

Jean Marie Feddercke is Momma White Cougar, Priestess of Hekate, Sekhmet and Elen, Devotee of Lord Ganesha. She is the author of *The Shaman's Drum* which is her personal journey through poetry and prose. If she could put her philosophy into just one sentence it would be that knowledge is not only for the young, and like a tree, we must continue to grow and send out new shoots, because even in later years we can bear the fruits of latent talents. The entire cycle of life is filled with immense Joy. May you always find your own True Path and may you always Walk in the Light! You can find her on FaceBook and PaganSpace.

JEN RICCI (ENGLAND, UK)
Solitary Witch Jen is based in South London where she typically shares her house with a black cat and two children - hers. She has a background in Reiki healing, complementary therapies and this led her to experience distance healing, opening her mind to the concepts of *'energy'* and *'intention'*, which in turn led her to the use of Witchcraft, spells and subsequently paganism as a way of life. Her first encounter with Hekate began long before her current journey and since meeting the Goddess she describes her path as being filled with a lot more clarity. Jen is a budding writing who has contributed to numerous magazines, and also enjoys writing horror, sensual romance and paranormal fiction – which she likes to make as scary as possible! You can find her on MySpace – writerjenricci.

JOHN CANARD (ENGLAND, UK)
Root magician John Canard misspent most of his youth in the Cambridgeshire fens, where he met the woman of his dreams, who he still believes to be only part human, and subsequently moved with her to Somerset (UK) to live the wild life. They live on a small farm where John spends his time tending a menagerie of animals and growing organic produce. He has always enjoyed writing, with his first book, *Defences Against the Witches' Craft* being published in 2008, and has previously contributed essays to *Hekate: Keys to the Crossroads*, *Horns of Power* and *From A Drop of Water*. He is currently working on a number of other projects related to traditional magick, witchcraft and root cunning.

KATHERINE SUTHERLAND (ENGLAND, UK)
Katherine Sutherland is an occult scholar and practitioner with wide ranging interests. Also a poet and author of fiction, Katherine is currently working on a children's novel focused on a character not dissimilar to Dr John Dee. Her poetic re-working of the Persephone myth, entitled *Underworld* is now available. Katherine is a Priestess in the *Fellowship of Isis*, and a devotee of the flowing spiritual path that her gods have chosen for her. She has previously contributed to *Both Sides of Heaven* and *From A Drop of Water*.

KAY GILLARD (ENGLAND, UK)
Kay is a healer, teacher and writer based in south-east London, UK, running courses and retreats in Kent and Wiltshire. She specialises in combining Reiki, shamanism, sound healing and psychic work to help healers and teachers find their own style and confidence, as well as building personal healing programmes for clients to change physical, emotional and behavioural issues. In her personal life she is a Wiccan and a devotee of Hekate, and her spiritual path as Her priestess is at the core of her life. She previously contributed essays to *Hekate: Keys to the Crossroads* and *Priestesses Pythonesses Sibyls*. See - www.kaygillard.com

LEZLEY FORSTER (ENGLAND, UK)
Lezley Forster lives in Devon with her wonderful husband, where she can indulge her passion for walking the moors and the woods. She is currently interested in healing, shamanic work and using craft as a way of expressing spirituality through creativity (this may of course just be an excuse to play with glue and glitter!) She has developed her work with Hekate for the past 10 years and previously contributed to *Hekate: Keys to the Crossroads*. Just like back then, Lezley still has a mad cat and will still be nice to you if you give her chocolate. See www.theraventree.co.uk

MADRE VAN DER MERWE (SOUTH AFRICA)
Madre is a Hekate priestess who lives on the Wine Route in Cape Town, SA. She loves good wine and it was this that brought her to Hekate, as her work with Bacchus and Dionysos led her to their connection and intrigued her enough to engage her interest. Whilst she is aware that some people see all goddesses as being one, she feels that Hekate is a very unique and powerful goddess who has taken over her life and demands frequent offerings of fynbos on top of Table Mountain.

MAGIN ROSE (ENGLAND, UK)

Magin Rose is a writer, illustrator, priestess, runic practitioner and Wiccan. She has a particular fondness for the Greek and Norse traditions. She loves making things, knocking things down and day dreaming. She lives in London with Mr Magin and their three cats who all do their best to keep her feet on the ground. Magin previously contributed to the anthology *Hekate: Keys to the Crossroads*, providing both an essay and the cover artwork. For more on Magin's work visit www.maginrose.com.

MARK ALAN SMITH (SPAIN)

Mark Alan Smith is a practitioner of Traditional Witchcraft and Hecate devotee. An ex-professional soldier, Mark now lives with his family in Southern Spain where he dedicates everyday of his life to the attainment of the lost and fragmented gnosis of the ancient magickal craft of the Dark Goddess. His recently published book *Queen of Hell* is the first of several volumes which herald the return to the full concept of the spiritual transmutation of the soul that is found within Ancient Witchcraft upon the path of Hecate. www.primalcraft.com

MICHAEL ELLIS (GERMANY)

Micheal Ellis lives in Germany with his partner and their three large black dogs. His magical journey began, as for so many people, during his teens when he developed an interest in Witchcraft and the work of Aleister Crowley. He became immersed in the mysteries of Hekate after attending a ceremony facilitated by Sorita d'Este in 2003, and soon after became a devotee. He threatened to leave us with a sequence of numbers to decipher, but instead concludes that numbers and mathematics are important in magic and should not be ignored!

MORGANA (THE NETHERLANDS)

Morgana is a Gardnerian Wiccan High Priestess, who was born in Britain but has lived in the Netherlands since 1974. She is the International Coordinator for the Pagan Federation, an international Pagan organisation. PFI is an affiliated organisation of the Pagan Federation, a British organisation founded in 1971. In 2005 it became a Foundation – Stichting PFI, registered in the Hague. She has facilitated a variety of Gardnerian Wiccan groups over the years. Morgana is the co-editor of the international bilingual magazine *Wiccan Rede*, which was founded in 1980, and the co-ordinator of *Silver Circle*, a Wiccan network in the Netherlands. She travels extensively attending conferences and presenting lectures at pagan and other spiritual events and gatherings. See www.paganfederation.org /www.silvercircle.org

NAZA COGO (AUSTRALIA)

Naza Cogo was born into a culture of traditional Balkan witchcraft. She is a Priestess of Hekate whose life journey since birth was one which prepared her to walk the path of this goddess, to whom she is extremely devoted. She teaches healing and divination, and has a great passion for the Greek and Egyptian mysteries, as well as Tarot, herbal magick and healing. She has a wonderful husband, Arnel, another Hekate devotee, and four children whom she has raised as part of their magickal world. She is currently studying herbal medicine to aid her further in her service of Hekate, and sees herself as a daughter of the goddess, a wife and a mother. In her spare time she likes to connect with like-minded people, visit fairs and expos and read occult books.

NIKKI CULLEN (U.S.A.)

Nikki Cullen is a 32 year old mother of three beautiful children who was born in Queens, New York. With a Catholic father and Pagan mother her religious upbringing favoured her mother, who practised the old Celtic tradition of the Goddess craft and taught her how to deal with her ability to see and hear things other children could not. Her first meditation was at age 7 in Forest Park in Queens, and as a child she was taught about the medicinal use of herbs, the moon and her phases, the Sabbats and esbats, the power of intent and words. Adulthood brought different occult and goddess teachings to her earlier Celtic roots, and she has since moved her learning to what might be seen as a darker place.

ORRYELLE DEFENESTRATE-BASCULE (AUSTRALIA AND THE WORLD)

Orryelle Defenestrate-Bascule is a globe-trotting barehoof *ChAOrder Magickian*. Director of Australian-based *Metamorphic Ritual Theatre Co.* and creator of *The Book of Kaos Tarot*, he finds Art– whether music, theatre, drawing, sculpture, film, writing or... -effective media for earthing hir sorcery. Current projects are the *Tela Quadrivium* fourfold bookweb being progressively published by Fulgur Limited (*Conjunctio* 2008, *Coagula* 2010...) and a related Alchemical theatre tour of Europe in collaboration with an Austrian glass-blower. Hir devotional journey with Kali and Hecate Moerae and further explorations of the arachnean mysteries of Destiny are explored in greater depth in hir forthcoming (2011) book from *Avalonia, Time, Fate and Spider Magick*. For more of Orryelle's ritual tattoo work see www.crossroads.wild.net.au/pic.htm.

PAUL HARRY BARRON (WALES, UK)

Paul Harry Barron has been interested in holistic healing from a very early age, and for many years from the mid 1990's he was the chairperson of a charity promoting holistic living. He works as an Acupuncturist with a practice split between the heart of Wales and Birmingham. In addition to his work within the field of healing and charity, he is also the translator of magical grimoires, including the French manuscripts which form the core of the highly acclaimed *Veritable Key of Solomon, A Collection of Magical Secrets* (both by Skinner & Rankine) and *The Book of Gold*. He has previous contributed essays to a number of anthologies including *Hekate; Keys to the Crossroads, Horns of Power* and *From A Drop of Water*. To find out more about his work see http://healingcymru.blogspot.com

PETRA SCHOLLEM (MEXICO)

Petra Schollem is a mother, wife and psychic from northern England who now lives in Mexico City with her husband and four children. She loves the Tarot and learning more about the world around her. This includes Hekate, the Aztec gods, Mexican food and culture. With Hekate's aid she helps guide the souls of the departed on to where they should be, a responsibility she takes very seriously and which she find very rewarding, though often bittersweet.

RAVEN DIGITALIS (U.S.A.)

Raven Digitalis (Montana, USA) is the author of *Planetary Spells & Rituals, Shadow Magick Compendium*, and *Goth Craft*, all on Llewellyn. He is a Neopagan Priest and co-founder of the "*disciplined eclectic*" shadow magick tradition and training coven *Opus Aima Obscuræ*, and is a radio and club DJ of Gothic and industrial music. Also trained in *Georgian Witchcraft* and Buddhist philosophy, Raven has been a Witch since 1999 and a Priest since 2003, and an Empath all of his life. Raven holds a degree in anthropology from the University of Montana and is also an animal rights activist, black-and-white photographic artist, Tarot reader, and is the co-owner of *Twigs & Brews Herbs*, specializing in bath salts, herbal blends, essential oils, and incenses. He is a regular contributor to *The Ninth Gate* and *Dragon's Blood* magazines, and has been featured on *MTV News* and *CBS PsychicRadio*. See www.ravendigitalis.com

RICHARD A. DERKS (U.S.A.)

Richard Derks is a Druid of the revival tradition. He is an Ovate with the *Order of Bards, Ovates, and Druids* (OBOD) and a member of *Ancient Order of Druids in America* (AODA). His main spiritual interest is in the Gods of ancient Greece and Britain. He gave his oath to serve Hekate on January 15th, 2010, and has patron relationships with Cernunnos and Dionysos as well. He also worships many of the other Gods of Greece, Egypt, and Britain all merged into a syncretic personal practice that he is constantly struggling to figure out and make sense of. He currently resides in Madison, Wisconsin USA where he happily juggles a life of being a husband, father, working professional in clinical research, and a devout practitioner of as well as adherent to The Old Ways. You can find out more at http://bluedruid.wordpress.com.

SARA CROFT (U.S.A.)

After finding Wicca in her early teens, Sara Croft has grown into a solitary witch and artist who spends her time studying religious history and the history of art. Hekate first touched her life in 2007 and has since led her on a harrowing trek through the wilderness. You can view more of Sara's artwork at http://neheti.deviantart.com

SHANI OATES (ENGLAND, UK)

Shani Oates lives in Derbyshire (UK) where she is a devoted practitioner of the true art, a mystic, a pilgrim, artist, professional photographer and holistic therapist. She is also a life-long student and researcher of theology, philosophy and anthropology intrinsic to all praxes that engage the Mysteries proper. All of these serve to enrich her role and duty as the Maid of the *Clan of Tubal Cain* (see www.clanoftubalcain.org.uk) and her resources as a Conference lecturer and published author within several popular pagan, folklore and occult magazines for over a decade, including *The Cauldron, Pendragon, The White Dragon* and *The Hedge Wytch*. She has recently launched her debut book *Tubelo's Green Fire* through *Mandrake of Oxford*.

SHAY SKEPEVSKI (AUSTRALIA)

Shay Skepevski has been a practicing solitary Witch and devotee of the goddess Hekate for over twelve years. From an early age he was aware of his psychic abilities as a clairvoyant, and his interest in magick and love of nature led him to discover paganism and witchcraft. His practice is an eclectic blend of Shamanic, Feri, and Eleusinian influence, and focuses heavily on the Chthonic Mysteries of Death, Transformation and Rebirth. He is particularly interested in Herbalism, Art, and holds a deep love for Greek Mythology. Born and raised in Sydney, Australia, Shay lives with his partner and their cat Circe, and devotes his time to writing, studying the occult, painting, and giving spiritual counselling as a tarot reader. You can contact Shay at his Facebook profile www.facebook.com/ShayWitch

SORITA D'ESTE (WALES, UK)

Sorita d'Este is the author of numerous books on magic, mythology and spirituality, many of which she co-authored with her occult author husband David Rankine - including *Hekate Liminal Rites, Practical Planetary Magick* and *The Isles of the Many Gods.* She is a Priestess, Enchantress and Theurgist, her personal practices are focused on bringing tradition and history in line with progression. She is the Managing Director of Avalonia, a publishing company dedicated to producing publications which contribute towards the expansion of the esoteric horizons into the 21st century, whilst keeping its roots firmly in the magical and spiritual traditions of the past. See www.sorita.co.uk

SOROR BASILISK (AUSTRALIA)

As a child, Soror Basilisk was aware of spirits and other energies but it was not until she was in her 20s that she developed an interest in parapsychology and Spiritualism, studying and contributing to groups of both disciplines. At 25, she studied with a UK Qabalistic Order and she commenced professional psychic/Tarot readings, later joining a magickal order in Australia and developing an interest in mediumship. During her 30s, Soror Basilisk joined a Chaos Magick temple in Australia, assisted in the formation of 2 magickal groups. Since then, she has focused on magickal studies including Vodou, Sabbatical Witchcraft, Luciferian Magick, and Hoodoo. Communication with the spirits of the Dead, as well as Deity and other energies, through altered states remains predominant in her practices. She resides in the southern Antipodes with her partner of 15 years. Also see www.between-spaces.com

TARA SANCHEZ (ENGLAND, UK)

Tara began to experience the magick of Hekate in 2004 whilst studying for her OBOD Bardic grade, and after a few years of generally trying to stick her fingers in her ears and go *"la la la I'm not listening"* under the guidance of her then mentor she formalised the relationship in 2007. Things have never been quite the same since. She has given a few talks and written one or two articles and has even been known to run the odd workshop, normally when she is tricked into it by erstwhile friends and other meddling do-gooders. She lives in the North West of England with her husband, daughter and an ever growing collection of cats, some of which she has adopted and some that have adopted her. She has been many things in her life, an apprentice, a student, an electronics engineer, a salesman, a computer scientist and a teacher to name but a few, her titles include, wife, mummy, priestess, miss, friend and she is even occasionally known to respond to *'Oi you'*. For more information see: www.templeofhekate.net

THOMAS STARR (CANADA AND JAPAN)
Renegade Solomonic magician Thomas Star escaped from the turmoil of lodges and old magical orders in the 1980s to find a fresh beginning in Toronto, Canada. Dissatisfied with his experiences of Western magic, he returned to the roots and found Hekate waiting there. He has been working with Her ever since, focusing his efforts on learning from her angels using the skills he learned from the works of Agrippa to good advantage. He now spends all his spare time talking to angels in the wilds or riding horses, his other enduring passion.

TIM FURLOW (U.S.A.)
Tim Furlow is a thirty year old full time graphic design student, who has been an actively practicing Pagan since he was thirteen years old, and a devotee of the Goddess Hekate for more than a decade. He has a very active relationship with Hekate, and credits her with all of the blessings in his life, including his ever inquisitive son Anthony, whom he considers the greatest gift She has ever bestowed upon him. He is engaged to be married to his soul mate Meghan, another Hekate devotee, and they hope to open a Pagan wellness and education centre in the future. He is a legally ordained reverend and considers himself honoured to have held Priest status several times, and hopes to learn and teach Hekate's wisdom for the rest of his life.

TINA GEORGITSIS (AUSTRALIA)
Tina Georgitsis is a hereditary folk witch and an initiated Wiccan priestess who is deeply respectful of the ancient Egyptian and Greek spiritual paths. She runs the Lyceum of Heka within the *Fellowship of Isis* as Priestess Hierophant, and is a Master Mason within Co-Masonry. She operates a spiritually based business which includes readings, healings, magical items and workshops in various metaphysical and occult modalities whilst also working in the corporate world.

TINNEKKE BEBOUT (U.S.A.)
Tinnekke Bebout is a Dianic Witch and Priestess, who has been on her Path for 30 years. She is one of the co-founders of the Michiana Pagan Alliance and is also a co-founder of The Lake Area Goddesses Society and The Mystai of the Moon Dianic Tradition. She is a Mentor Sister of the Mystai and teaches women in a Lunar Mystery tradition that has been recreating the Rites of Hekate for a modern era. She has been published in a variety of magazines including *Goddess, Circle, PanGaia, The Loom*, and *The Goat and Candle*, and is the author of *The Dance of the Mystai*. She is the webmistress for the Mystai and runs her own online Dianic BOS and resource guide. She's also an artist, mom, and nurse - and she makes a really good guacamole. See http://dreamweaver.mystaiofthemoon.com & www.mystaiofthemoon.com

TRYSTN M. BRANWYNN (U.S.A.)
Trystn M Branwynn was born in 1967 in St. Louis, MO. He has served in the United States Marine Corps and travelled extensively in the service. He received admission to a Traditional Witchcraft group in 1987, and achieved his Second Admission in 2000 and currently serves as Magister for his branch of the current. He also currently serves as Education Chair for the Tacoma Earth Religions Revival Association. He is father to a son Kyle, and a daughter Gabrielle, both of whom live in Ohio. Trystn currently resides in Lakewood, WA with his significant other, Damais, and their two pet rabbits, (The Great) Peony Bunny and Mr. Zen Z. Bunzl.

VIKKI BRAMSHAW (ENGLAND, UK)

Vikki Bramshaw is an author and priestess of esoteric initiatory witchcraft. Having trained for 10 years under respected elders, she now runs her own working group near the New Forest in Hampshire. She released her first book, *Craft of the Wise: A Practical Guide* with O-Books (John Hunt Publishing) in 2009. Some of her passions are theurgy, initiatory rites and Hellenic and Sumerian mythology. In addition to her magical training, Vikki successfully completed several courses as part of her ongoing research, including The Origins of Human Behaviour, with Oxford University and is also a trained Holistic Healer with the Scottish Healing Association. She is currently studying counselling and transactional analysis with Peter Symonds College of Winchester. See www.vikkibramshaw.co.uk for more info.

VLASTA MIJAC (CROATIA)

Vlasta Mijac is an Arts Graduate from the *Fine Art School of Split*, who works in a variety of mediums, including macramé, tapestry, painting and digital art. She is a member of the *Emanuel Vidovic Art Society* and her work has been sold to private collections internationally. She lives and works in Croatia.

YURI ROBBERS (THE NETHERLANDS)

Yuri Robbers currently lives in Leiderdorp, the Netherlands. He works as a teacher, scientist and author. It is a rare subject that he doesn't take at least a passing interest in. Since last summer he can officially say that he has spent more than half his lifespan deeply involved in the Western Esoteric Tradition, sometimes as a teacher, and always as a student. His main hope is that he will never stop being first and foremost a student, always learning and experiencing new things. Hekate may not always have been the main influence in his spiritual life, but she has never been wholly absent either, and she has been there since the beginning. She may even turn out to be that which is attained at the end of desire! Surely one could do worse...

Wishing to remain anonymous other than a mention here are Aedos Alala (Turkey), MDL, Anon (UK), Peter (Canada) and Izzy Purplespoon (UK).

Figure 7 - Threskeia

Figure 8 - Library Shrine by MDL
Books are Magical, they have the ability to change your world.

UNFURLING HER MYSTERIES

THIS SECTION PROVIDES A BRIEF OVERVIEW OF THE ORIGINS, ROLES AND POWERS OF THE GODDESS HEKATE THROUGHOUT HER LONG HISTORY. IT EXPLORES HER POSSIBLE ORIGINS WITHIN THE CULTS OF THE GREAT MOTHER GODDESS, AS WELL AS HER OWN ROLES IN MYTHOLOGY AND IN THE MYSTERY TRADITIONS OF THE ANCIENT WORLD THROUGH INTO THE 21ST CENTURY POP-CULTURE AND PAGAN REVIVAL.

Figure 9 - Animal Headed Hekate from Cartari (1571)

THE HEKATE CHRONICLES

BY SORITA D'ESTE

Hekate is a Goddess of great antiquity. She is primordial, powerful and sometimes animalistic - and yet also sophisticated, modern and capable of adapting to different cultures. She is the Torchbearer, the Cosmic World Soul, the Guide and Companion. She is Mistress of the Restless Dead, who rules over the Heavens, Earth and Sea. She is the Keybearer who stands at the crossroads of life, death and initiation. Her devotees today, as throughout the ages, include philosophers, poets, sorcerers, theurgists, witches, root-cutters, enchantresses and ordinary people.

She has been loved, feared and hated throughout the millennia of her known history. Depicted variously as three-formed facing in three directions, as well as sometimes with the heads of animals – and at other times as single bodied standing bearing torches, or enthroned like the depictions of the goddess Kybele, Hekate has and possibly will always remain one of the greatest enigmas amongst the gods.

It is easy to believe that, like many of the other gods, her mysteries were forgotten, only to re-emerge and be reconstructed at the hands of the modern Pagan revival, but even just scratching at the surface of the available evidence soon provides us with a different story. She was never forgotten, and maybe just maybe, there has never been a time in which fires weren't kept burning for her somewhere, nor a time in which offerings were not made in her name.

Today her worship has spread through diverse magical traditions and to all six of the inhabited continents of the world. This magical and geographical diversity is reflected in the essays and other contributions in this work. So what if anything has changed about the Torchbearing Goddess of the Mysteries? Certainly the diversity of practices which have developed during the last few decades, many of which are based on older practices, others created from channelled material, from visions or through enthused creativity, means that Hekate is venerated, invoked and evoked using methods which sometimes would have been quite alien to those who knew her in the ancient world. However this reflects a change in her devotees rather than Hekate herself.

Culturally, and socially we are very different today in comparison to the Hellenic Greeks who honoured her, but then they were also very different from the cultures which preceded them and honoured Hekate, and those which subsequently continued to honour her through the centuries in their own unique and diverse ways. So it is important when considering the history of Hekate to do so with at least some empathy for the social and cultural context from which it emerged.

HISTORICAL ORIGINS

The earliest known literary reference to Hekate is found in the cosmological *Theogony* of Hesiod dating to the eight century BCE. It is widely believed that Hekate's origins are outside of the Greek pantheon, and for us to gain a greater understanding of Hekate we need to consider where she may have originally come from. To fully explore this subject would require a volume of its own. The overview that follows will help expand your appreciation and perception of this extraordinary goddess. All of these possibilities suggest she migrated or expanded her worship from cultures in proximity to Dark Age Greece.

One possible origin for Hekate is from the cult of the Phrygian and Anatolian great mother goddess Kybele, with whom she shared many symbols such as dogs, keys, lions, serpents, torches and caves. As with many ancient deities, her true name is unknown, with Kybele being the popular title for this goddess used by both the Greeks and the Romans. Matar (*'mother'*), another of her titles, fits well with her role as earth goddess and goddess of wild animals. Kybele became a popular goddess in Greece, often being depicted in her lion-drawn chariot flanked by torch-bearing Hekate and Hermes, emphasising the connection between these three deities. She was conflated with the Titan Mother of the Gods Rhea, and her worship continued into the Roman Empire as the Magna Mater (*'Great Mother'*). Kybele was worshipped at Ephesus by the tenth century BCE, and she is a likely precursor to Artemis of Ephesus, whose temple would become one of the Wonders of the World. Kybele herself drew on qualities of the Neo-Hittite goddess Kubaba, whose worship was previously celebrated in Phrygia before the rise of Kybele's cult. Her worship was also popular in other part of Anatolia, and it is possible that her origins are to be found in the depictions discovered in the ancient Anatolian city of Katolhuyuk dating back to the sixth millennia BCE.

Intriguingly however, the Hittites, who ruled Anatolia and the surrounding areas from around 1700-1180 BCE absorbed the Hattian tribes who had been living there in the third millennium BCE. Amongst the deities the Hittites absorbed into their huge official pantheon was the Hattian mother goddess Kattahha, whose name means *'[Divine] Queen'*, and which can also be written as Hatkatta, which is not very far linguistically from Hekate!

The Minoan culture provides us with another possible origin for Hekate. There are some interesting parallels with the Minoan snake goddess from around 1500 BCE, and the Minoan Mistress of the Animals (*Potna Theron*) who was subsumed by Artemis and Kybele. Minoan culture and language influenced some coastal parts of Greece, and a tablet found in the city of Pylos, dating to around 1200 BCE may contain a clue to this connection. This tablet contains the goddess names Iphimedeia, Pereswa and Diwija. These may be early forms of several of the Greek goddesses, with Iphimedeia being an alternative name for Hekate (who was called Iphimede in the eighth century BCE work *Catalogue of Women*, which was attributed to Hesiod), and the other names being possibly linked to the spring and underworld goddess Persephone and her mother the grain goddess Demeter. It is interesting to note that Pylos was abandoned around the eighth century BCE, which coincides with the period that Hekate starts to appear in Greek literature.

The land of Thrace to the north of Greece provides another possible origin for Hekate. Although we have little information on the Thracian lunar goddess Bendis, we know that she was described as two speared, which seems to parallel the two torches of Hekate. The worship of Bendis became accepted in Athens in the mid-fifth century BCE, around the same time that Hekate was becoming increasingly popular there. Furthermore, Hekate was also mentioned as bearing a spear in the lost fifth century BCE Sophocles play *The Root Cutters*. Bendis was conflated with both Hekate and Kybele, and Hekate's worship also expanded into and beyond the Thracian lands of Bendis' origin (to modern Bulgaria and Macedonia). Thrace was influenced by both Indo-European and Middle Eastern cultures, which would explain the diverse nature of Hekate if this was her homeland.

From the evidence provided, it is clear that whilst definite origins for Hekate cannot be categorically stated, they stretch back far before her presence in Dark Age Greece. The power of her presence is clear in the extent to which her cult spread, and the number of other goddesses whose cults and qualities she subsumed in the centuries of her worship in the Greek and then Roman empires.

THE ANCIENT MYSTERY CULTS

The Mystery Cults of the ancient world were initiatory traditions which contained secret experiential and philosophical teachings, often around a core myth. Due to the effectiveness of their secrecy strictures, little is known about the inner workings of these highly organised religions, and there has been a great deal of speculation about them.

One of the best known of these ancient cults is that of the Temple at Eleusis. It is believed that the temple there was built around 1600 BCE, although the evidence suggests that it was built on a much earlier site, which might have been there since the Bronze Age, and maybe even the Neolithic period!

The first literary reference to the Eleusinian Mysteries, which in addition to improved social status were said to ensure its initiates had a good afterlife, is in the seventh century BCE *Homeric Hymn to Demeter*, which formed its core myth. This myth tells of the abduction of the spring goddess Persephone at the hands of the lonely underworld god Hades. The grain goddess Demeter, mother of Persephone, mourned for her daughter, and after ten days Hekate approached her and told Demeter that she had heard Persephone's cries from her cave. Hekate and Demeter spoke to the sun god Helios, who had seen the abduction and he gave a full description of events to Demeter. Demeter stormed off and in her fury withdrew her power to make life grow on the earth. Requests from the gods to allow life to continue on the earth were disregarded by Demeter, which worried the gods, who did not want to lose all their worshippers due to famine. After negotiations between the gods, Hekate with her twin torches went to the underworld to retrieve Persephone, who was constrained to stay there for four months of each year with Hades as his queen due to having eaten some pomegranate seeds there. Hekate agreed to act as Propolos (*'guide'*) to Persephone on her annual descent and ascent to and from the underworld, during which time Demeter would mourn and no plant life would grow on the earth. This is the myth of the creation of the seasons.

From the few written references to the Eleusinian Mysteries, it is known that the initiates were expected to fast beforehand, and to drink kykeon (commonly believed to contain a mixture of barley, pennyroyal and water). The initiates were shown sacred images, led by torch-bearing priestesses (probably representing Hekate Propolos) and the myth of the Abduction of Persephone was enacted. The god Iakkhos (who was sometimes equated with Dionysos) was also part of the rites, with his role (or that of his priest) being to lead the processions with twin torches, paralleling Hekate's role. The three goddesses of the Eleusinian Mysteries were also worshipped at a temple in Selinus on the island of Sicily, where a Greek colony was founded in the mid-seventh century BCE. It has been suggested that similar mysteries to those of Eleusis were celebrated there on a smaller scale. It was here in the fifth century BCE that the philosopher Empedocles created the doctrine of the four elements of air, earth, fire and water. His legendary demise by jumping into the volcano Mount Etna leaving a single bronze sandal (one of her symbols) floating out on the lava, suggests he was a devotee of Hekate.

The Greek island of Samothrace was mentioned by several writers in connection with mystery initiations in the Zerynthian cave, where dogs were sacrificed to Hekate. The torches of Hekate were also part of the ceremonies there, with references made to torch-bearing maids of Hekate thronging on the rocks of the island, recalling the priestesses of Eleusis. It is significant to note that the Korybantes, or priests of Kybele, were also said to perform rites in the cave, further reinforcing the connection between Hekate and Kybele. The island of Aigina was another centre of Hekate worship, with a wooden Hekate statue created by the famous fifth century BCE sculptor Myron housed in the temple there. In his *Description of Greece*, the geographer Pausanias referred to annual mystic rites there which were said to have been founded by Orpheus (founder of the Orphic Mysteries), having been brought from Thrace, one of the possible geographical origins of Hekate. The other great Hekate temple was at Lagina in Caria (now Turkey). The geographer Strabo mentioned great festal assemblies there in the late first century BCE in his epic seventeen volume work *Geography*. The Lagina temple was the only major temple built by the Greeks in the late Hellenistic period, emphasising the importance of Hekate at this time.

The Orphic Mysteries focused on the liberating wine god Dionysos, and like the Eleusinian Mysteries promised advantages in the afterlife. There are several interesting links to Hekate in these mysteries which make it clear she was relevant to their practices. The Orphic goddess Melinoe ('*Dark Mind*') was almost certainly a form of Hekate, as can be seen from the descriptions in the Orphic hymn to her. The Orphic initiates used the name of the goddess Brimo ('*Frightening/Terrifying One*', a title of Hekate) as a password in the underworld, and also introduced the old woman Baubo into the *Homeric Hymn to Demeter*. Baubo, who was seen as a form of Hekate, or sometimes as one of her companions, showed her genitals to Demeter to make her laugh and drink the sacred drink kykeon, helping her to overcome her grief over her lost daughter Persephone and return to the other gods. The lewd Baubo could be viewed as a prototype of the apotropaic Sheela-na-gig figures found on medieval European churches. If this was the case, Hekate even managed to get herself onto churches across Europe at a time when her worship was much less prominent!

There can be no doubt that Hekate's role as initiatrix was part of her enduring popularity. As the torch-bearing guide who had power in all realms, she was a logical choice for inclusion in Mystery Religions. References in the *Greek Magical Papyri* and the *Chaldean Oracles* hint at her connection with initiation in the Roman world, and that function has continued through the ages, with many people and traditions today still viewing her as the great magical initiatrix.

OFFERINGS

It is well known that animals were regularly sacrificed to the gods in ancient Greece, sometimes on a large scale, like the festival of Laphria for Artemis, so the fact that black dogs and other animals were offered to Hekate should not be taken out of context. However, that dogs were sacrificed is unusual, as most sacrifices in ancient Greece were of food animals, i.e. cows, pigs, sheep and goats. Evidence indicates that dogs were only sacrificed to deities with non-Greek origins, such as Hekate and the war god Ares.

All of the Greek philosophers who wrote about Hekate or were her devotees, including Empedocles, Hesiod and Porphyry, were staunch vegetarians and wrote about the negative qualities of animal sacrifice. They emphasised the transmigration of souls and the idea of a fleshless Golden Age where fruits, grains and incense were offered to the gods.

Offerings were a standard part of the veneration of the gods. Chthonic ('*earthly*') gods had their altars on the ground, and offerings were often made into a pit which had been dug, i.e. into the earth. By contrast Ouranian ('*heavenly*') gods had altars which raised their contents into the air, and had their offerings burned in a fire. Hekate falls into both of these categories having a multitude of qualities which link her to both the Chthonic and Ouranian realms.

Hekate Suppers (*Deipna Hekates*) were offerings of food made on the new moon at crossroads to Hekate. These were performed to honour Hekate and request that she control the restless dead, who were attracted to the liminal three way crossroads. Ancient Greek satirists commented on the poor stealing the food offerings from the crossroads, and that some viewed these suppers as a form of charity to the poor. As well as food offering, the remains from sacrifices were taken to the Hekate shrines at crossroads as a liminal place for disposal, as were clay censers which were used to fumigate private houses for protection by burning the house sweepings.

Medieval European Church records show people were penalised for making offerings at crossroads, and such offerings, as well as roadside shrines, have remained a prevalent practice through to the modern day in some Mediterranean countries.

FOOD OFFERINGS

The following table includes types of food and drink which are associated with offerings to Hekate.

FOOD	NOTES
Amphiphon	A flat cheesecake surrounded by torches (candles)
Asphodel	Food for the restless dead
Barley	Both as grain and made into cakes
Basunias	A type of cake
Cheese	As she was sometimes shown with a goat-head, goats cheese would be appropriate
Eggs	Traditionally offered raw, may represent life force
Garlic	A traditional protection from the restless dead since ancient Egypt
Honey	A standard offering to chthonic deities and the restless dead
Magides	A type of loaf or cake of unknown shape and type. Bread could be substituted
Milk	A standard offering to chthonic deities, again goat milk would be appropriate
Mullet	Fish were often included as a sacrifice to her, and mullet was particularly sacred
Olive Oil	A standard offering to chthonic deities
Onion	A traditional apotropaic offering
Psammeta	A sacrificial cake
Sesame	Seeds used in apotropaic Hekate spell
Sprat	Fish were often included in her rites as a sacrifice
Water	A standard offering to chthonic deities
Wine	A standard offering to chthonic deities

AT THE CROSSROADS

One of Hekate's most distinguishing features in the ancient world was her triple nature. This is manifested repeatedly in her forms and symbols, and we see her as Triformis ('*three-bodied*') and Trioditis ('*of the three roads*'), standing guarding the three-way crossroads where she received monthly offerings. In the fifth century BCE, the sculptor Alkamenes created the popular Triformis image, of three identical figures standing forming a triangle around a central pillar, which would become the template for the Hekataion, guarding doorways and crossroads. It has been suggested that her three forms corresponded to the three realms over which she had power, i.e. earth, sea and sky, and also the three liminal moments in life where she had dominion, of birth, initiation and death. As a triple-headed figure she is also depicted with different animal heads, emphasising her primal essence and powerful connection to nature. Her threefold character was expressed in a different form in the Renaissance, with magicians, poets and playwrights alike all referring to her as the triple lunar maiden Hecate-Diana/Luna-Proserpina.

Considering that threefold Hekate was often associated with biform gods such as Dionysos, Hermes, Janus and Sabazius/Zagreus, it is tempting to speculate whether this might have contributed to the Qabalistic attribution of the masculine and feminine divine to the numbers two and three, as see in the Sephiroth of Chokmah (2) and Binah (3) on the Qabalistic Tree of Life. Certainly the modern Pagan movement seems to have embraced and emphasised these attributions, with the masculine two horns of the horned god, or lords of light and darkness for the two halves of the year, and the feminine three forms of the Maiden Mother Crone construct.

The modern *'triple goddess'* construct of *'Maiden Mother Crone'* is a product of the neo-Pagan revival taking its influence from such writers as Aleister Crowley, Dion Fortune, Robert Graves and C.G. Jung, and mixing it with that of classical paganism. Crowley referred to Hekate as a *'Crone'* and the idea spread from there. Considering depictions of her throughout her long history, we find that she is always described and depicted as a woman of indeterminate age, or specifically as a *'maiden'*. For our ancestors the gods were immortal, and as such perfect, immune to ageing and the physical issues it brought. Of course it is true that even in ancient Greece, Hekate was considered to be a very ancient goddess and as such is very very old indeed. However, as you will discover on your journey through *Her Sacred Fires*, Hekate has had many forms over the millennia, and as a deity who has not been forgotten it is clear that she can and has adopted additional symbolism and forms over the centuries.

MYTHOLOGICAL ORIGINS

Whilst Hekate's pre-Greek origins seem to hearken back to great mother goddess figures like Kybele and the Minoan animal goddesses, her roles and origins in Greek mythology are more wide ranging and clearly defined. In the *Theogony*, Hesiod gave the first description of her Greek parentage, stating, *"Also she bare Asteria of happy name, whom Perses once led to his great house to be called his dear wife. And she conceived and bore Hecate whom Zeus the son of Cronos honoured above all."* The stellar Asteria, Titan goddess of astrology and prophetic dreams, and the obscure god Perses are her most frequently mentioned parents. Later writers did suggest alternative parentage for her, with the *Orphic Hymns* suggesting Demeter (Deo) as her mother and the poet Bacchylides suggesting Nyx, the primal goddess of night. The poet and seer Mousaios suggested Zeus as her father with Asteria, and the philosopher Pherecydes gave the god Aristaios as her father. Aristaios was the god of medical herbs, who gave the world several notable gifts, including cheese-making, honey, mead and olives. Although this might seem an obscure connection, it should be noted that Aristaios was the son of Apollo and Cyrene, who had a city named after her. At the Greek city of Cyrene (in Libya) there were temples of Apollo and Hekate, showing that this connection was a significant one.

Zeus as Hekate's father is also seen in the *Orphic Hymn to Melinoe* where he is described as taking Hades' form to seduce his daughter Persephone. Some intriguing Greek coins from the early second century BCE, show Zeus standing or enthroned, holding a sceptre in his left hand, and a smaller figure of Hekate Triformis ('*three-formed*') in his right hand in a gesture of presentation. This resembles the Egyptian practice of the presentation of Maat, the goddess who represented truth, balance and the underlying order of the cosmos which even the gods had to maintain. The Presentation of Maat was a ritual performed by the Egyptian Pharaoh where he offered a small statue of Maat in his right hand to a large statue of one of the creator gods such as Atum or Ra to maintain cosmic order in the land of Egypt. Hekate too would represent the cosmic order and be the power behind the gods, distributing the power of Zeus as the creator in the eyes of the Theurgists who were inspired by the *Chaldean Oracles* several centuries later.

HEKATE AND OTHER GODDESSES

Through the centuries the goddess Hekate subsumed and/or was conflated with many goddesses, both from Greece and other countries in the ancient world. The following table includes some of the key examples of this:

Goddess	Comments
Artemis	Virgin huntress goddess, twin of Apollo. Became conflated with Hekate from C5th BCE, they possibly both originally came from the same source
Baubo	Old woman in the *Orphic Homeric Hymn to Demeter* equated to Hekate around C3rd BCE
Bendis	Thracian lunar goddess of two spears, conflated with Hekate from C5th BCE, possible origin for Hekate
Bona Dea	Roman healing goddess with serpent as cult animal, conflated with Hekate from C2nd CE
Brimo	Thessalian underworld goddess conflated with Hekate, Persephone and Demeter from at least C3rd BCE
Diana	Roman virgin huntress goddess equated with Artemis and conflated with Hekate from around C2nd CE
Enodia	Thessalian road goddess who was conflated with Hekate from C5th BCE
Ereschigal	Babylonian underworld goddess conflated with Hekate from C3rd CE
Isis	Egyptian mother and magic goddess conflated with Hekate from C2nd CE
Kybele	Phrygian/Anatolian great mother goddess conflated with Hekate from around C3rd BCE, possible origin for Hekate
Melinoe	Orphic form of chthonic Hekate from C3rd BCE
Nemesis	Vengeance goddess who was conflated with Hekate at times after C3rd CE

Persephone	Spring and underworld goddess, daughter of Demeter, conflated with Hekate from C4th CE
Rhea	Mother of the gods and earth goddess conflated with Kybele from C1st BCE and with Hekate from C2nd CE
Selene	Lunar goddess and sister of Helios, conflated with Hekate and Artemis from C1st BCE

HEKATE AND MALE GODS

Hekate was often described as being a virgin goddess, but in later times some writers did attribute children to her. The best known of these were the Hekate priestesses Medea and Circe (who was also sometimes called a daughter of Helios). She was also described as having a son Aigialeus by the same father, Aeetes, himself the son of Helios by the Oceanid Nymph Perseis. The sea monster Scylla was also attributed to her as offspring by the sea god Phorkys in the *Argonautica* of Apollonius Rhodius.

Another point worth noting is the conflation of Hekate's cult with that of the mother goddess Isis, with examples of Isis-Hekate being depicted on engraved gems and coins. Some early votive reliefs from several centuries prior to her conflation with Isis show Hekate bearing a child in her arms, in a pose reminiscent of Isis images, or the later Virgin Mary. Such tales and images demonstrate that, to some devotees at least, Hekate also took the role of mother goddess, which is not surprising considering her conflation with mother goddesses like Rhea, Kybele and Isis.

Hermes

Of all the gods, the one most commonly paired with Hekate is the psychopomp Hermes. Like Hekate, he has the ability to move between realms, and is associated with movement and communication, through ruling roads trade, theft, language, writing and many other areas. Hermes was the god of travellers, and piles of stones called Herms were set up at crossroads and other liminal points by travellers in ancient Greece to propitiate him. These herms would later become stylised into a pillar surmounted by a Hermes head, or the heads of other deities including Hekate. Hermes was often to be found at city gates with Hekate in the role of guardian of the city. He also had a chthonic aspect, and was called as Hermes Chthonia with Hekate Chthonia on curse tablets. Furthermore dogs were sacred to Hermes as guardians and his caduceus was serpent entwined, two major cult symbols he shared with Hekate. He played a role in the myth of the Abduction of Persephone as the messenger between the different gods. Like Dionysos, Hermes was portrayed both as a beautiful young man, as well as a bearded mature man.

Dionysos

Phrygia and Thrace are both considered possible homelands for the god Dionysos, who arrived in Greece around the ninth-eight century BCE, at about the same time that Hekate first seems to emerge there. Dionysos was the liberating god of wine and ecstasy. He was known as twice-born due to his first incarnation as Zagreus, only to be killed by some of the Titans, and his heart taken by Zeus and used as the basis of his rebirth as Dionysos. In Thrace Dionysos became equated with Sabazius as the son of the lunar goddess Bendis, as well as being associated with the mother goddesses Kybele or Rhea in some of the myths. Whether or not Dionysos originated in the same homeland as Hekate before they became known in Greece, and the full extent of their association, is a subject which raises many interesting questions and possibilities and deserves a study of its own. However, it is surely no coincidence that Hekate had a significant role in the Orphic Mysteries, a tradition which was centred on Dionysos. Furthermore, the torch-bearing god Iakkhos, who was sometimes portrayed with Hekate has also been equated with Dionysos, or is sometimes described as one of the daimons in his retinue. The name Iakkhos is derived from the ritual cry *Iakkhe*, made by his priests when they bore the twin torches in the procession at Eleusis.

Poseidon

When it is recalled that Hekate had a share of the sea, it is easy to see why she should have a strong connection with the sea god Poseidon. The *Theogony* links these two, and fish was offered as a sacrifice in some of Hekate's rites. Additionally, a temple to Poseidon and Hekate Propylaia (*'before the gate'*) at Ephesus emphasises their connection. Although Pausanias described it as a temple of Artemis Propylaia, the evidence does not support this, and the title is one of Hekate's, not Artemis. The presence of Hekate in the Eleusinian Mysteries would also indicate that it was her temple with Poseidon.

Zeus

Zeus and Hekate have a distinctive connection, which is unusually asexual for the predatory Zeus. In the *Theogony* he honoured her above all other gods and increased her existing share of the three realms of earth, sky and sea. Around a thousand years later this strong connection was re-emphasised when Zeus and Hekate were portrayed as the supreme god and goddess in the *Chaldean Oracles*. The Romans sometimes equated Zeus with their liminal god Janus, as can be seen in Proclus' *Hymn to Hekate and Janus*. In the text he described Hekate as Mother of the Gods (i.e. she had subsumed Rhea/Kybele) and Zeus as the forefather, implying a stronger relationship between them.

POST-GREEK HEKATE

Although some Roman writers portrayed Hekate as the threatening goddess called upon for malefic magic by sorcerors and witches, this was completely contrasted and overshadowed by the *Chaldean Oracles*. This collection of fragments emphasised Hekate in a more powerful role than she had ever been seen before, that of saviour (*Soteira*) and cosmic soul. She was described as the supreme goddess figure, subsuming the Titan Rhea who had been the Greek Mother of the Gods, and who had been combined with Kybele, with whom Rhea shared this title and symbols like lions and mountains, as the Roman Magna Mater (*'Great Mother'*). The connection between Hekate and Rhea had been hinted at nearly a thousand years earlier, when they were both described in the *Homeric Hymn to Demeter* as *'bright-coiffed'*. In the *Chaldean Oracles* Hekate became the source of souls and virtues, bestowing her power on the theurgists who approached her appropriately. Theurgists concentrated on union with the gods to achieve perfection, and emphasised the spiritual development of the practitioner, rather than the mundane concerns of the witch or sorceror. This text also expanded her already extensive retinue, which had previously included the restless dead, torch-bearing nymphs and various monstrous creatures, to now also contain hordes of daimones and three orders of angelic beings to do her will.

Juxtaposed with the *Chaldean Oracles* was the combination of practices which have become known collectively as the *Greek Magical Papyri*. These texts blended magic from Egyptian, Greek, Hebrew and Gnostic sources, and as a result called on a wide range of deities and beings. The most popular goddess in the spells and charms is Hekate-Selene, and the most popular god Apollo-Helios. Amongst the many descriptions of Hekate in the *Greek Magical Papyri* were a number of references to triple-formed Hekate with animal heads, an unusual expression recalling the ancient Egyptian gods at a time when deities were commonly viewed in fully human forms. The *Greek Magical Papyri* also conflated her with other goddesses, subsuming them into her, including the Babylonian underworld goddess Ereschigal, the Greek underworld goddess Persephone and Mene, the Greek lunar goddess (either as Selene or her daughters).

As Christianity became the dominant religion in Europe, Hekate's presence was less obvious. Early Church scholars and theologians often demonised her in their attempts to diminish her influence, as can be seen in the works of such significant church fathers as Origen, Eusebius, Arnobius and St Augustine between the third-fifth centuries CE. Of course this did not stop the Church from borrowing useful material from Hekate's worship to include in their practices. Thus we see the term Lampades, originally used for Hekate's torch-bearing nymphs, being used to refer to the seven archangels who stand in the presence of God, and who interestingly are often depicted as flames! Likewise the title of Kleidouchos (*'key-bearer'*) which could represent Hekate as the guardian of the entrance to the paradisiacal Elysian Fields in the underworld was appropriated for Saint Peter as holding the keys to heaven. The Gnostics joined the Church in demonising Hekate, calling her one of the five demonic archons (*rulers*) who tormented souls, in her case by burning them.

An intriguing and largely unknown survival of her presence may have occurred in fourteenth-fifteenth century Bosnia and Herzegovina. Between the third century BCE and the third century CE votive funerary tablets representing a woman between two male riders were popular in the region around the Danube which would become these countries. The males may represent the Rider God, and the woman has been identified in some images as Artemis, Hekate or Kybele. Many centuries later such images reappeared on tombstones, often with a crescent over the woman's head, suggesting a resurgence of Artemis-Hekate.

The sixteenth century saw Hekate re-emerging with a vengeance. In Europe the Italian magician Giordano Bruno and the German magician Cornelius Agrippa both referred to her in their writings in her association with the Moon, conflated with the Roman goddesses Diana and Prosperina (the Roman equivalent of Persephone). In Britain Hekate was being described in literature as the fairy queen and the queen of hell, recalling her roles as witch goddess and underworld goddess with her retinue of assorted spiritual creatures. This cascaded into the writings of the great British authors of the early seventeenth century, in Christopher Marlowe's *Doctor Faustus*, various of William Shakespeare's works including *King Lear*, *Hamlet*, *Macbeth*, and *Midsummer Night's Dream*, Thomas Middleton's *The Witch*, John Milton's *Comus: A Masque* and the writings of Edmund Spenser.

The witchcraft connection persisted, with Walter Scott in his *Letters on Demonology and Witchcraft* (1830) describing the head of a Scottish covine of witches practising necromancy as a Hekate. The nineteenth century also saw an asteroid named in Hekate's honour, the one hundredth one to be discovered, on July 11th 1868 by J.C. Watson, taking the connection between her name and one hundred (*Hekaton* in Greek).

The early twentieth century would see a return to the perception of malevolent witch goddess, largely through the works of Aleister Crowley (in his poem *Orpheus* and novel *Moonchild*) and Dion Fortune. Whilst seeming neutral in her fiction (in *The Sea Priestess*), Dion Fortune expressed a more negative view than Crowley in her *Psychic Self-Defence*, linking Hekate to the unbalanced Qliphothic forces on the Qabalistic Tree of Life. However in spite of the negative press from these two major occultists, Hekate's worship grew rapidly in the latter half of the twentieth century, expanding to levels probably not seen since the ancient world. She has become a popular figure amongst practitioners of numerous traditions and spiritual persuasions including, Angelic Magic, Ceremonial Magic, Dianic Witchcraft, Druidry, Goddess Spirituality, Grimoire Tradition, Initiatory Wicca (BTW), Luciferianism, Paganism, Reconstructionism, Root Magic, Thelema, Traditional Witchcraft, and many others.

In the Luciferian current she is seen as the mother of Lucifer: thus Hekate the female light-bearer (*Phosphoros* in the Greek) gives birth to the male light-bearer (*Lucifer* in the Latin) a role which echoes the connection in the *Aradia* of Charles Leland (1899). Leland recorded the tale told to him by an Italian witch of how Diana loved her brother Lucifer, the god of the Sun and Moon, who had been driven from Paradise for pride in his beauty. They produced a messianic daughter called Aradia who was sent to earth to teach the witches. Significantly Diana is described as the creatrix and her worship once a month with cakes described in a clear echo of the Hekate Suppers of ancient Greece. Considering their conflation in ancient Rome it is easy to see how Diana and Hekate could be interchanged in this tale. Of course we should also remember that Diana had the title Lucifera in ancient Rome. Ancient precedents of the idea of Hekate giving birth to Lucifer can be seen in Bendis (who was conflated with Hekate) giving birth to Sabazius (who was conflated with Dionysos and particularly associated with Hermes). Considering the attributes of Dionysos, especially as the liberator, it is very easy and plausible to see parallels between him and Lucifer.

Hekate has also appeared widely in modern popular culture, in comics, books and on television. Popular series like *Buffy the Vampire Slayer*, *Charmed* and *The Twilight Zone* have all referred to her. Her name has also been used for characters in Manga comics, as a super-villain from the future in Marvel comics and as herself in the cult *Sandman* series by Neil Gaiman. Other examples of her presence in the modern age include her depiction with Dionysos on a Romanian stamp in 1976, and a life-sized fresco which includes Hekate Triformis in a modern setting painted by the well-known artist Benjamin Long in a shopping centre in the city of Statesville, itself set on the intersection of two major freeways in North Carolina, USA.

Hekate is an exceptional goddess who has endured through the centuries in the hearts of her devotees, her many manifestations expressed through such forms as amulets, architecture, art, literature, numismatics, pottery and sculpture.

The following timeline displays many examples of these manifestations, showing the passion and dedication she has inspired over the millennia. It represents a cross-section of views held over the centuries, giving glimpses and insights into the complex nature of her mysteries.

Where my timeline ends, the path leads onwards to the numerous contributions by her devotees from around the world, expressing their visions and experience of this illuminating goddess in the modern age through their essays, prose and artwork as part of this project. For each one of the contributors, there are hundreds, maybe thousands, more who honour and pay homage to the Goddess of the Crossroads, whose torches continue to illuminate the Mysteries today and, undoubtably into the future.

TIMELINE: VISIONS OF HEKATE

Date	
6000 BCE	Neolithic Period begins
(6000-5500 BCE)	*A voluptuous woman enthroned with lionesses on either side, may be a an earlier form of the Mother Goddess Kybele.* [Katalhoyuk Goddess, Katalhoyuk]
2900 BCE	Early Bronze Age begins
2000 BCE	Minoan culture begins
1700 BCE	Rise of the Hittite empire
1600 BCE	Foundation of temple at Eleusis Mycenaean culture begins
1500 BCE	*Two female figures holding snakes, one also girdled with snake.* [Minoan Snake Goddesses, Minos, Crete]
1400 BCE	Minoan culture ends
1180 BCE	Fall of the Hittite empire Rise of the Syro-Hittite states
1100 BCE	Mycenaean culture ends The Greek Dark Age begins
1000 BCE	
800 BCE	Foundation of the Delphic Oracle
750 BCE	Dark Greek Age ends Archaic period begins

700 BCE	**Syro-Hittite states end**
(C8th-C7th BCE)	"And she conceived and bare Hekate whom Zeus the son of Kronos honoured above all. He gave her splendid gifts, to have a share of the earth and the unfruitful sea. She received honour also in starry heaven, and is honoured exceedingly by the deathless gods." *[Theogony, Hesiod]*
(C8th-C6th BCE)	"I know that Hesiod in the 'Catalogue of Women' represented that Iphimede [Iphigenia] was not killed but, by the will of Artemis, became Hekate." *[Catalogue of Women, attributed to Hesiod, quoted in Pausanias]*
(C7th BCE)	"Some say there are many kinds of Nymphai, [eg Alkman]: Naides and Lampades and Thyiades . . . Lampades those who carry torches and lights with Hekate." *[F63, Fragments, Alkman]*
(C7th BCE)	"Only tender-hearted Hekate, bright-coiffed, the daughter of Perseaeus, heard the girl from her cave" *[Homeric Hymn to Demeter]*
600 BCE	Hekate enthroned and in a pose more often associated with the Great Mother Goddess Kybele. This is the earliest known example of a statue depicting the Goddess Hekate. *[Terracotta statue, Athens]*
(C6th BCE)	Hekate as "Protectress of Entrances", Earliest known inscription on altar naming the Goddess Hekate. *[Temple of Apollo Delphinius at Miletus]*
(550 BCE)	**The Temple of Artemis of Ephesus is Built.** **This temple is one of the Seven Wonders of the Ancient World.**
500 BCE	**Archaic period ends,** **Classical period begins** **Roman Republic begins**
(C5th BCE)	The famous sculptor Alkamenes creates what is believed to be the first of the tri-formed statues of the Goddess Hekate. Subsequent triformis statues would be based on his design, which unfortunately did not survive. *[Description of Greece, Pausanias]*

(C5th-C4th BCE)	*Hekate wearing a peplos (long dress) and wielding twin torches.* [St Petersburg State Museum]
(C5th-C4th BCE)	*Hekate in profile with raised torches, on her right is Kybele in a lion-drawn chariot and to her left Hermes, with eight-rayed star above his head.* [Gold disc, Stathatos collection]
(early C5th BCE)	*"We pray; and that Artemis-Hekate watch over the childbed of their women."* [Suppliants, Aeschylus]
(early C5th BCE)	*"Lady (Despoina) Hekate, before the portal of the royal halls."* [F216, Fragments, Aeschylus]
(early C5th BCE)	*"But either thou art frightened of a spectre beheld in sleep and hast joined the revel-rout of nether Hekate."* [F249, Fragments, Aeschylus]
(480-440 BCE)	*A wooden statue of single bodied Hekate made by the sculptor Myron in Aigina.* [Description of Greece, Pausanias]
(470 BCE)	 *Hekate with her feet becoming a twin bodied dog, whose upper head holds a man in its mouth, and with three female figures, possibly the Erinyes.* [Athenian Lekythos]
(462 BCE)	*"and the red-footed maiden, gracious Hekate, announced the saying that will come to pass."* [Pythian Odes 4, Pindar]

(mid C5th BCE)

"O Lord Helios and Sacred Fire
The spear of Hekate of the Crossroads
Which she bears as she travels Olympus
And dwells in the triple ways of the holy land
She who is crowned with oak-leaves
And the coils of wild serpents."
[The Root Cutters, Sophocles]

(440 BCE)

Hekate with her twin torches leading
Persephone back from the underworld.
[Attic bell-krater (bowl)]

(431 BCE)

"For, by Queen Hekate, whom above all divinities I venerate, my
chosen accomplice, to whom my central hearth is dedicated"
[Medea, Euripides]

(420 BCE)

"that each citizen would have himself a little tribunal constructed in
his porch similar to the altars of Hekate"
[The Wasps, Aristophanes]

(412 BCE)

"Menelaus: O Hekate, giver of light,
send thy visions favourably!
Helen: In me thou beholdest no spectre of the night,
attendant on the queen of phantoms."
[Helen, Euripides]

(late C5th BCE)

"The Ephesian vengeance was sent down.
Firstly Hekate harms the belongings of Megara in all things, and
then Persephone reports to the gods."
[Mycenaean inscription]

(410-390 BCE)

Hekate immolating the giant Klytos with her two torches in the
Giant Wars.
[Attic vase and Attic amphora]

(late C5th – C4th BCE)

"If the patient is attended by fears, terrors,
and madnesses in the night,
jumps up out of his bed and flees outside,
they call these the attacks of Hekate
or the onslaughts of ghosts."
[On the Sacred Disease, Hippocrates]

400 BCE	
(Early C4th BCE)	*Hekate in profile with raised torches, on her right is Kybele in a lion-drawn chariot and to her left Hermes. Above Hekate is a small wreath-bearing Nike and a star surmounted by a crescent.* [Silver disc, Olynthus]
(C4th BCE)	*Hekate with twin torches riding a horse.* [Greek coins from Thessaly]
(C4th BCE)	 *Hekate bearing a torch and placing a wreath on a mare's head, accompanied by a dog.* [Marble frieze, Crannon, Thessaly now in the British Museum]
(late C5th or early C4th BCE)	 *Seated Cybele, with a lion next to her. On the left pillar Hermes, and on the right Hekate.* [Marble relief in Museo Archeologico, Syracuse]
336 BCE	Classical period ends Hellenistic period begins

300 BCE	
(early C3rd BCE)	Great Library of Alexandria founded
(C3rd BCE)
Hekate Triformis with four torches, a patera and pitcher.
[Temple relief, Aegina] |
| **(C3rd BCE)** | *"and had called seven times on Brimo, nurse of youth, night-wandering Brimo, of the underworld, queen among the dead, in the gloom of night, clad in dusky garments."*
[Argonautica, Apollonius Rhodius] |
| **(C3rd BCE)** | *"the maiden daughter of Perseus, Triform Brimo, shall make thee her attendant, terrifying with thy baying in the night all mortals who worship not with torches the images of the Zerynthian queen of Strymon, appeasing the goddess of Pherae with sacrifice."*
[Alexandria, Lycophron] |
| **(C3rd BCE)** | *Hekate Triformis around a central pillar with the three Charities dancing.*
[Attic Hekataion]
|

(C3rd-C2nd BCE)	*"I call, Melinoe,* *saffron-veiled, terrene,* *who from Persephone dread venerable queen,* *mixt with Zeus Kronion,* *arose"* Orphic Hymn to Melinoe (Dark Mind)]
(C3rd-C2nd BCE)	 *Hekate with torch carrying a baby, recalling her role as Kourotrophos.She has a dog by her feet. This also hints very strongly at her later conflation with the Egyptian Mother Goddess Isis.* [Believed to be in the Varna Museum of Archeology]
(270 BCE)	*"I will chant softly to you, Goddess, and to infernal Hekate – before whom the dogs shiver when she wanders over the graves of the dead where the dark blood lies. Hail to thee, dreadful Hekate, and stay with me to the end;"* [Idylls 2, Theocritus]
200 BCE	 *Hekate with three heads and six arms wielding spear, sword, shield and torches battling giants.* [Pergamon Frieze – photograph Mary Davis]

Hekate in side profile with twin torches and a small winged Nike bearing a wreath above her head, standing next to Kybele enthroned with Hermes on other side of her.
[Bronze matrix, Smyrna]

Hekate Triformis made from wood, with hints of the Artemis, the huntress, indicated by a quiver and baldric.
[Wooden Hekataion, Alexandria]

Zeus standing holding a staff in his left hand, and Hekate Triformis bearing two torches in his right hand.
[Greek coin]

(160 BCE)	*Small Hekate Triformis standing next to a giant Apollo with lyre.* *[Greek coin]*
(150-140 BCE)	*Hekate as three heads facing three ways atop a pillar around which the three Charities dance.* *[Hekataion, Basel museum]*
146 BCE	**Hellenistic period ends** **Roman rule of Greece begins**
100 BCE	
(C1st BCE – C3rd CE)	*Hekate in triple form with two torches, pillar behind her surmounted by a crescent containing the sun. Underneath are the figures of the husband and wife whose grave this would have marked.* *[Funerary Stelae, Soa, Turkey]*
(42 BCE)	*Hekate as the Torchbearer holding two torches and wearing a long dress. On the reverse of this coin is Apollo, the twin brother of the Goddess Artemis, with his lyre.* *[Silver Denarius]*
(19 BCE)	*"Then, earth began to bellow, trees to dance* *And howling dogs in glimmering light advance* *Ere Hekate came."* *[The Aeneid, Virgil]*
0 CE	
(C1st CE)	*Hekate's head surmounted by a lunar crescent, and Hekate riding a lion.* *[Carian Coin]*

(C1st CE)	*Hekate Triformis with torches in her upper hands, whips in the middle hands, and serpents in her lower hands.* *[Defixio, Athens Agora]*
(8 CE)	*"Oh grant the power, great goddess of the triple form, that I may fail not to accomplish this great deed!"* *[Metamorphoses, Ovid]*
(8 CE)	*"You see Hekate's faces turned in three directions, To guard the crossroads branching several ways"* *[Fasti, Ovid]*
30 CE	**Roman Republic ends** **Roman Empire begins**
(Mid C1st CE)	*"Now, summoned by my sacred rites, do thou, orb of the night, put on thy most evil face and come, threatening in all thy forms."* *[Medea, Seneca the Younger]*
(60 CE)	*"Persephone, who dost detest heaven and thy mother, and who art the lowest form of our Hekate ...And you, Hekate, wasted and pale of aspect, who are wont to make up your face before you visit the gods above, I shall show you to them as you are and prevent you from putting off the hue of Hell."* *[Pharsalia, Lucan]*
(Late C1st CE)	*"When it [the dog] is sent to crossroads as a supper for the earth-goddess Hekate, it has its due portion among sacrifices that avert and expiate evil."* *[Roman Questions, Plutarch]*
(C1st-C2nd CE)	*Hekate Triformis, wearing peplos, with torches in all her hands, around a pillar, with smaller figures of the three Charities dancing around her.* *[Roman hekataion, now in the Metropolitan Museum of Art]*

(C1st-C3rd CE)	*"Saffron-cloaked Goddess of the Heavens,* *the underworld and the Sea ...* *Unconquerable Queen, Beast-roarer,* *Dishevelled One of compelling countenance ...* *Keyholding Mistress of the whole world ..."* [Orphic Hymn to Hekate]
100 CE	
(C2nd CE)	*Hekate Triformis, missing left side, but three right arms holding bow* *and arrow, whip and torch, with a crescent moon above. A stag is* *to her lower right and a dog to her left.* [Damaged plaque, Athenian Agora]
(C2nd CE)	*"of the gods, the Aiginetans honour Hekate the most and they* *celebrate her mystery every year, saying Orpheus of Thrace* *established it for them. Inside the enclosure is a temple with a* *wooden statue by Myron having one face and body."* [Description of Greece, Pausanias]
(C2nd CE)	*"I heard a voice like a thunderclap, and saw a terrible woman* *approaching, not much less than three hundred feet high. She* *carried a torch in her left hand, and a sword in her right; the sword* *might be thirty feet long. Her lower extremities were those of a* *dragon; but the upper half was like Medusa--as to the eyes, I mean;* *they were quite awful in their expression. Instead of hair, she had* *clusters of snakes writhing about her neck, and curling over her* *shoulders."* [Philopseudes, Lucian]
(C2nd CE)	*Hekate Triformis, with four torches, two of which are inverted in her* *lower hands, and a dagger and serpent. The central forward face* *has a large lunar crescent surmounting it, and she has a dog on* *either side of her.* [Relief, Bucharest]
(C2nd CE)	*"the phantoms of Hekate, or any other demon or demons"* [The True Word, Celsus]
(C2nd CE)	*"I come, a virgin of varied forms, wandering through the heavens,* *bull-faced, three-headed, ruthless, with golden arrows; chaste* *Phoebe bringing light to mortals, Eileithyia; bearing the three* *synthemata [sacred signs] of a triple nature. In the Aether I appear* *in fiery forms and in the air I sit in a silver chariot"* [Chaldean Oracles]

(C2nd CE)	*"Rhea truly is the font and stream of the blessed noetic (substances). For she is the first of all in power and having received into her marvellous womb. She pours forth a whirling generation upon All"* [Chaldean Oracles]
(C2nd CE)	*"For I have come, a goddess in full armour and with weapons."* [Chaldean Oracles]
(C2nd CE)	*Hekate in a long chiton (robe) bearing two torches, with hounds at her side.* [Relief, Thasos]
(C2nd CE)	*"Isis was called Hekate in Caria"* [Papyrus Oxyrynchus 1380]
(late C2nd CE)	*"the Phrygians, first born of men, call me Mother of the Gods ... the trilingual Sicilians call me Ortygian Proserpine ... some call me Hekate,"* [Metamorphoses, Apuleius]
(C2nd-C3rd CE)	*"Ortho [Artemis], Baubo [Hekate], ... Ereschigal, ... sovereign gods and angels, bind with your spell all those herein written."* [Curse Tablet, Asia Minor]
(C2nd-C4th CE)	*Hekate Triformis with seven rays coming from one head (central ray is broken off).* [Hekate Chiaramonti, Vatican]

(C2nd-C5th CE)	*"The third order is called Triple-faced Hekatē,* *and there are under her authority seven-and-twenty [arch]demons,* *and it is they which enter into men and seduce them to perjuries* *and lies* *and to covet that which doth not belong to them.* *The souls then which Hekatē beareth hence in ravishment,* *she handeth over to her demons which stand under her,* *in order that they may torment them through her dark smoke and* *her wicked fire,* *they being exceedingly afflicted through the demons."* *(The Gnostics demonized Hekate, making her the ruler of one of the* *five archons i.e. rulers.)* [Pistis Sophia]
(193-222 CE)	*Hekate Triformis,* *Hekate on a lion-drawn chariot,* *Hekate with a crescent and kalathos (wine-holder) on her head,* *bearing a torch and patera and with a dog at her feet* [Roman coins]
200 CE	
(200-250 CE)	*Three figures of Hekate each bearing different items, including* *torches, serpent, dagger and whip* [Triangular bronze ritual platform, Pergamon]
(250 CE)	*Hekate bearing two torches and standing on a globe* [Phracian coin]
(C3rd CE)	*"Infernal and earthly and heavenly Bombo, come. Goddess of* *waysides, of cross-roads, lightbearer, nightwalker, Hater of the* *light, lover and companion of the night, Who rejoicest in the baying* *of hounds and in purple blood; Who dost stalk among corpses and* *the tombs of the dead Thirsty for blood, who bringest fear to mortals* *Gorgo and Mormo and Mene and many-formed one. Come thou* *propitious to our libations."* [The Refutation of All Heresies, Hippolytus]
(C3rd CE)	*Hekate triformis with torches, whips and serpents, & Nemesis, with* *both goddesses trampling a man underfoot* [Dacian gem, Danube]
(C3rd CE)	*"But Hekate, when invoked by the names of a bull, a dog, and a* *lioness, is more propitious."* [On Abstinence, Porphyry]

(C3rd CE)	*"Wherefore her power appears in three forms, having as symbol of the new moon the figure in the white robe and golden sandals, and torches lighted: the basket, which she bears when she has mounted high, is the symbol of the cultivation of the crops, which she makes to grow up according to the increase of her light: and again the symbol of the full moon is the goddess of the brazen sandals."* [On Images, Porphyry]
(C3rd-C4th CE)	*Hekate bearing two torches and standing on a globe with lunar crescent on her head.* [Engraved Roman gem]
300 CE	
(Early C4th CE)	*"The symbols of Hekate are wax of three colours, white and black and red combined, having a figure of Hekate bearing a scourge, and torch, and sword, with a serpent to be coiled round her"* [Praeparatio Evangelica, Eusebius]
(325 CE)	First Council of Nicaea establishes the Nicene Creed and parameters of early Christian worship
(330) CE	Byzantine Empire begins
(C4th CE)	*"Star-coursing, heavenly, torch-bearer, fire-breather, woman four-faced, four-named, four-roads' mistress."* [PGM IV.2559-60]
(C4th CE)	*"Darkness, Brimo, Immortal, heedful, Persian, pastoral, Alkyone, gold-crowned, the elder goddess, shining, sea-goddess, ghostly, beautiful, the one who shows ... wearing headband, vigorous leader of hosts ... saviour, world-wide, dog-shaped, spinner of Fate"* [PGM IV.2270-80]
(C4th CE)	*"Hekate with three heads and six hands, holding torches in her hands, on the right side of her face having the head of a cow; and on the left side the head of a dog; and in the middle the head of a maiden, with sandals bound on her feet." (Drawn on a flax leaf)* [PGM IV.2118-2124]
(C4th CE)	*"Take a lodestone and on it have carved a three-faced Hekate. And let the middle face be that of a maiden wearing horns, and the left face that of a dog, and the one on the right that of a goat."* [PGM IV.2880-2885]

(C4th CE)	*"Janus, who, they say, being sprung from Coelus and Hekate"* *[Against the Heathens, Arnobius]*
(C4th CE)	*"ceremonies performed just as much in the name of Seth, that is, Typhon, as the one for Tithrambos [a title of Dionysos] the indigenized Hekate"* *[De Fides, Epiphanus]*
(380 CE)	Christianity made Roman state religion by Emperor Theodosius I
(391 CE)	The Destruction of the Great Library of Alexandria
(392-396 CE)	Closure of the Temple of Eleusis
(395 CE)	Closure of the Delphic Oracle (after centuries of decline)
400 CE	
(401 CE)	The destruction of the Temple of Artemis at Ephesus by a Christian Mob
(C5th CE)	*"Hail, many-named Mother of the Gods, whose children are fair Hail, mighty Hekate of the Threshold"* *[Hymn to Hekate & Janus, Proclus]*
(C5th CE)	*"O Selene (Moon), driver of the silver car! If thou art Hekate of many names, if in the night thou doest shake thy mystic torch in brandcarrying hand, come nightwanderer"* *[Dionysiaca, Nonnus]*
(C5th CE)	*"Others again hold the view that she [Bona Dea] is Hekate of the netherworld"* *[Saturnalia, Macrobius]*
492 CE	The Fall of the Roman Empire
500 CE	
(C6th CE)	*"From whence they hand down the mystical doctrines concerning the four elements and four-headed Hekate. For the fire-breathing head of a horse is clearly raised towards the sphere of fire, and the head of a bull, which snorts like some bellowing spirit, is raised towards the sphere of air; and the head of a hydra as being of a sharp and unstable nature is raised towards the sphere of water, and that of a dog as having a punishing and avenging nature is raised towards the sphere of earth."* *[Liber de Mensibus, John Lydus]*

(C6th CE)	*"The Great Hekate emits a life-generating whir."* *"The life-generating Goddess … possesses the separated and manifest whirring-forth of the life-generating light."* [Difficulties and Solutions of First Principles, Damascius]
(C10th CE)	*"Some [say that she is] Artemis, others the moon, appearing in strange manifestations for those invoking curses. Her manifestations [are] humans with the heads of dragons, and of immense size, so that the sight stupefies those who see it."* [Epsilon 364, Suda]
1000 CE	
(C11th CE)	*"So the Oracle teaches that it is the motion of the strophalos which works the ritual, on account of its ineffable power. It is called 'of Hekate' as consecrated to Hekate."* [Commentary on the Chaldean Oracles, Michael Psellus]
(C14th CE)	*Female figure between two male Riders, Which has been identified as possibly being Hekate-Artemis-Bendis-Cybele.* [Tombstones, Bosnia and Herzegovina]
1453 CE	Byzantine empire falls
(1484 CE)	Pope Innocent VIII issues Papal Bull against Witchcraft
(C16th CE)	*A depiction of Hekate with the Four Seasons.* [Neo-Attic base, Rome]
(1575)	*Hekate with single body and pig, dog and horse heads.* [Le Imagini Degli Dei Degli Antichi, Vicenzo Cartari]

(1582 CE)	*"I name you the one whom we call Hekate, Latona, Diana, Phæbe, Lucina, Trivia, Tergemina, and the threefold Goddess"* [Incantations of Circe, Giordano Bruno]
(1585 CE)	*"On ane thre headit hekate in haist þair they cryit:"* *(On a three-headed Hekate in haste there they cried)* [The Flyting of Montgomery and Polwart]
(1586)	*"Saw Hecat new canonized the Sourantisse of hell, And Pluto bad it holliday for all which there did dwell ... The Elves, and Fairies, taking fists, did hop a merrie Round:"* [Albion's England, William Warner]
(1595 CE)	*"Affecting the glory of such great majesty the demon, in the year 1121, appeared with three heads to a certain Premonstratentian canon and tried to persuade him that he was that threefold Deity (whereas in truth he was the Triform Hekate) in the contemplation of whom the canon so fixedly occupied his mind"* [Demonolatry, Nicholas Remy]
(1596 CE)	*"And many of them afterwards obtain'd Great power of Jove, and high authority: As Hekate, in whose almighty hand He plac't all rule and principality, To be by her disposed diversely to gods and men, as she them list divide"* [Two Cantos of Mutability, Edmund Spenser]
1600 CE	
(1600 CE)	*"Now it is the time of night That the graves all gaping wide, Every one lets forth his sprite, In the church-way paths to glide: And we fairies, that do run By the triple Hekate's team, From the presence of the sun, Following darkness like a dream, Now are frolic"* [A Midsummer Night's Dream, William Shakespeare]
(1604 CE)	*"Pluto's blue fire, and Hecat's tree, With magick spells so compass thee"* [Doctor Faustus, Christopher Marlowe]
(1606 CE)	*"And I, the mistress of your charms, The close contriver of all harms, Was never call'd to bear my part, Or show the glory of our art?"* *Hekate's chastising speech in Macbeth, commonly believed to have been added by Thomas Middleton.* [Macbeth, William Shakespeare]

(1634 CE)	*"He and his monstrous rout are heard to howl* *Like stabl'd wolves, or tigers at their prey,* *Doing abhorred rites to Hekate* *In their obscured haunts of inmost bow'rs."* [Comus: A Masque, John Milton]
1700 CE	
(1725 CE)	*"dread Hecat comes; the screech-owl's voice pierced shrill my ear;* *the silent bat has flown across our cavern; and the drowsy hum of* *swarming beetles trumpets her approach"* [Orestes, A Dramatic Opera, Theobald Lewis]
(1786 CE)	*"Hekate was certainly a Chaldean deity under the name of Achad,* *by which they signified the Moon,* *as Millius has well explained"* [Collectanea de rebus hibernicus vol 4, Charles Vallencey]
(1795 CE)	*"By the mysteries of the deep, by the flames of Banal, by the power* *of the east, and the silence of the night, by the holy rites of Hekate,* *I conjure and exorcise thee, thou distressed spirit"* [A New and Complete Illustration of the Occult Sciences, Ebenezer Sibly]
1800 CE	
(1824 CE)	*"To aid me Hecat comes,* *at whose approach* *The Moon goes out,* *and the stars hide their heads."* [Il Pastore Incantato, a student of the temple (Charles Leslie)]
(1842 CE)	*"Hekate goddess of midnight,* *discoverer of the future which yet sleeps in the bosom of chaos,* *mysterious Hekate! Appear."* [Immortalita, Gunderode]
(1846 CE)	*"There! there!* *like Hekate on her broom,* *or Scott on Satan's back-* *or meteor through the midnight gloom- or* *arrow on its track,"* [Steam Carriage Excursion in The Mountain Minstrel, Evan M'Coll]
(1881 CE)	*"Lo! while we spake the earth did turn* *away, Her visage from the God, and* *Hekate's boat; Rose silver-laden, till the* *jealous day Blew all its torches out:"* [The Garden of Eros, in Collected Poems, Oscar Wilde]
(1890)	*Beautiful colour image of Hekate with two torches in the style of the time. Top left is written "Hekate" and the name of the card is "Goddess of Darkness"* [Gasoline card] GODDESS OF DARKNESS

1900 CE	
(1907 CE)	"O triple form of darkness! Sombre splendour! Thou moon unseen of men! Thou huntress dread! Thou crowned demon of the crownless dead! O breasts of blood, too bitter and too tender!" [Orpheus, in Collected Works Vol 3, Aleister Crowley]
(1908 CE)	"Originally an ancient Thracian divinity, she by degrees assumed the attributes of many, Atis, Cybele, Isis, and others ... Gradually she grew into the spectral originator of all those horrors with which darkness affects the imagination" [The Book of Witches, Oliver Madox Hueffer]
(1929 CE)	"and thirdly, she is Hekate, a thing altogether of Hell, barren, hideous and malicious, the queen of death and evil witchcraft ... Hekate is the crone, the woman past all hope of motherhood, her soul black with envy and hatred of happier mortals;" [Moonchild, Aleister Crowley]
(1930 CE)	"Hence it is that when the unstable soul advances by the path of Saturn that bridges the Astral and enters the Sphere of Luna, he touches her Hekate aspect and finds himself en rapport with the Gamaliel, the Obscene Ones [Qliphoth]" [Psychic Self-Defence, Dion Fortune]
(1938 CE)	"Astarte, Aphrodite, Ashtoreth – Giver of life and bringer of death; Hera in Heaven, on earth, Persephone; Levanah of the tides, and Hekate – All these am I, and they are seen in me" "Mine is the kingdom of Persephone, The inner earth, where lead the pathways three. Who drinks the waters of that hidden well Shall see the things whereof he dare not tell– Shall tread the shadowy path that leads to me - Diana of the Ways and Hekate, Selene of the Moon, Persephone." [The Sea Priestess, Dion Fortune]
2000 CE	"Hekate is a Goddess like no other..." "Loved, feared, hated and worshipped by people throughout history, the Witch Goddess of the Crossroads, facing three-ways, with her three faces, remains an image of power and awe in the modern world today, amongst those who understand and respect her power..." (Sorita d'Este, Hekate Keys to the Crossroads, Avalonia, 2006)

BIBLIOGRAPHY

Alexander, Christine. *A Wooden Hekataion of the Helenistic Period.* In *The Metropolitan Museum of Art Bulletin,* Vol. 34.12 (December 1939), 272-274

Apuleius & John Gwyn Griffiths (trans). *The Isis-book.* Leiden, Brill, 1975

A Student of the Temple. *Il Pastore Incantato.* London, Hurst Robinson & Co, 1824

Bernabe, Alberto. *Imago Inferorum Orphica.* In *Mystic Cults in Magna Grecia,* Austin, University of Texas, 2009

Clarysse W., & A. Schoors & H. Willems (eds). *Egyptian Religion: The Last Thousand Years - Studies Dedicated to the Memory of Jan Quaegebeur.* Holland, Peeters, 1998

Cormack, J.M.R. *A Tabella Defixionis in the Museum of the University of Reading.* In *HTR* (1951) 44:25-34

Crowley, Aleister. *Collected Works Vol 3.* London, SPRT, 1907

Crowley, Aleister. *Moonchild.* London, Sphere Books Ltd, 1979

D'Este, Sorita & David Rankine. *Hekate Liminal Rites.* London, Avalonia, 2009

D'Este, Sorita (ed). *Hekate Keys to the Crossroads.* London, Avalonia, 2006

D'Este, Sorita. *Artemis Virgin Goddess of the Sun and Moon.* London, Avalonia, 2006.

Edwards, Charles M. *The Running Maiden from Eleusis and the Early Classical Image of Hekate.* In *American Journal of Archaeology,* Vol. 90.3 (July 1986), 307-318

Farnell, Lewis Richard. *Cults of the Greek States vol 2.* Oxford, Clarendon Press, 1896

Fortune, Dion. *Psychic Self Defence.* London, Rider & Co, 1930

Fortune, Dion. *The Sea Priestess.* London, Star, 1976

Gager, John G. *Curse Tablets and Binding Spells from the Ancient World.* Oxford, OUP, 1992

Gates, Charles. *Ancient Cities: the Archaeology of urban life in the ancient Near East and Egypt, Greece and Rome.* Routledge, London, 2003

Graham, A.J. *Abdera and Teos.* In *The Journal of Hellenic Studies,* Vol. 112 (1992), 44-73

Gunderode. *Immortalita.* Boston, E.P. Peabody, 1842

Holl, J. (ed) *Epiphanius 3.* Berlin, Akadamie Verlag, 1933

Hollmann, Alexander. *A Curse Tablet from the Circus at Antioch.* In *Zeitschrift für Papyrologie und Epigraphik,* Bd. 145 (2003), 67-82

Hueffer, Oliver Madox. *The Book of Witches.* London, Eveleigh Nash, 1908

Hunter, Richard L. (ed). *The Hesiodic Catalogue of Women: Constructions and Reconstructions.* Cambridge, Cambridge University Press, 2005

Johnston, Sarah Iles. *Hekate Soteira.* Georgia, Scholars Press, 1990

Karouzou, Semni. *An Underworld Scene on a Black-Figured Lekythos.* In *The Journal of Hellenic Studies,* Vol. 92 (1972), 64-73

Leeming, David. *Jealous Gods, Chosen People. The Mythology of the Middle East.* Oxford, Oxford University Press, 2004

Lesser, Rachel. *The Nature of Artemis Ephesia.* In *Hirundo: The McGill Journal of Classical Studies,* Volume IV (2005-06), 43-54

Lewis, Theobald. *Orestes, a dramatic opera.* London, John Watts, 1725

Mair, A.W. & G.R. (trans). *Callimachus Hymns and Epigrams. Lycophron. Aratus.* London, William Heinemann, 1921

Marinatos, Nanno. *The Goddess and the Warrior: The Naked Goddess and Mistress of Animals in Early Greek Religion.* London, Routledge, 2000

Marquardt, Patricia A. *A Portrait of Hekate.* In *The American Journal of Philology,* Vol. 102.3 (Autumn, 1981), 243-260

M'Coll, Evan. *The Mountain Minstrel.* London, Simpkin Marshall & Co, 1846

Mead, G.R.S. (trans). *Pistis Sophia.* London, J.M. Watkins, 1921

Milton, John & Jessie M. King. *Comus: A Masque.* Nabu Press, 2009.

Mladenova, Yanka. *The Image of Hekate in the Bulgarian Lands.* In *Archaeology,* 1964

Parisinou, Eva. *The Light of the Gods.* London, Gerald Duckworth & Co, 2000

Parker, Robert. *Miasma: Pollution and Purification in Early Greek Religion.* Oxford, Clarendon Press, 1996

Reeder, Ellen D. *The Mother of the Gods and a Hellenistic Bronze Matrix.* In *American Journal of Archaeology,* Vol. 91.3 (July 1987), 423-440

Remy, Nicholas & Montague Summers. *Demonolatry.* Kessinger Publishing, 2003

Roller, Lynn E. *The Great Mother at Gordion: The Hellenization of an Anatolian Cult.* In *The Journal of Hellenic Studies,* Vol. 111 (1991), 128-143

Ronan, Stephen (ed). *The Goddess Hekate.* Hastings, Chthonios Books, 1992

Shakespeare, William. *A Midsommer Nights Dreame.* Classic Books, 2007

Shakespeare, William. *Shakespeare's Tragedy of Macbeth.* Bibliolife, 2008

Spenser, Edmund. *The Works of Edmund Spenser, Vol 7, The Fairie Queene.* London, F.C. & J. Rivington, 1805

Stevenson, George (ed). *Poems of Alexander Montgomorie.* Edinburgh, William Blackwood & Sons, 1910

Tudor, Dumitru. *Corpus Monumentorum Religionis Equitum Danuvinorum: The Analysis and Interpretation of the Monuments.* Leiden, Brill, 1997

Vallencey, Charles. *Collectanea de rebus hibernicus vol 4.* Dublin, Luke White, 1725

Van de Velde, Carl. *A Roman Sketchbook of Frans Floris.* In *Master Drawings,* Vol. 7.3 (Autumn, 1969), 255-326

Wenzel, Marian. *A Mediaeval Mystery Cult in Bosnia and Herzegovina.* In *Journal of the Warburg and Courtauld Institutes,* Vol. 24.1/2 (January-June 1961), 89-107

Wilde, Oscar. *The Collected Poems of Oscar Wilde.* London, Wordsworth, 1994

Internet:

http://www.vroma.org/, the VRoma Project, accessed 31 March 2010

http://www.benlongfrescotrail.org/statesville.htm, accessed 17 April 2010

VISIONS OF THE GODDESS

HERE ARE GATHERED THE ESSAYS, PROSE, ARTWORK AND PHOTOGRAPHY OF 50 INDIVIDUALS FROM ALL OVER THE WORLD WHO SHARE THEIR ENCOUNTERS WITH THE GODDESS HEKATE IN THE 21ST CENTURY. THESE CONTRIBUTIONS ARE EXPRESSIONS OF HOW THE GODDESS HEKATE IS VIEWED TODAY IN DIFFERENT SPIRITUAL AND CULTURAL TRADITIONS, SHOWING CLEARLY HOW MULTIFUNCTIONAL SHE CONTINUES TO BE.

Figure 10 - Hekate with Dionysos, believed in Thracian Orphism to be a unity of Sabazeus and Zagreus
by Georgi Mishev

THRESKEIA

THE WORSHIP OF THE GODDESS IS ALIVE IN THE ANCIENT LANDS OF THRESKEIA!

BY GEORGI MISHEV

My name is Georgi Mishev, I am 27 years old and I am from Bulgaria. It is quite complicated to describe the connection and interrelation between oneself and a deity especially when it comes to the Great Goddess. I have always admired the many romantic stories told by people about how they have found Goddess.

My story is a little bit different and started back in 1989 when I was seven years old. At that time my parents worked in Libya and I lived with them for two years. In 1989 we visited the ancient city of Cyrene located in Eastern Libya. After coming back to Bulgaria, in the same year I started suffering a strange illness in November. Every night, at midnight, I ran a high temperature and as a result of it I hallucinated – mice, snakes and other frightful creatures and there was always that woman standing outside the window. She was taller than the usual height of a human; she was dressed in black and was making a gesture with her hand as if to hush me. The strangest thing was that there was nothing wrong with me during the day – I ran a temperature always at midnight. I've always been a believer, but in my own personal way.

The Christian tradition in Bulgaria, especially its folklore reflection, is strongly affected by the pagan past. The traditions and rituals preserved and practiced by old people are purely pagan in their essence and quite different from their ecclesiastical image. However, to a large extent they are accepted or rather tolerated by the church. As I was raised by my grandmother, I was also brought up in the spirit of folklore traditions. I have always perceived the Christian concept of Virgin Mary and Jesus in a different way from how it was taught. I used to worship Her first, and then Him as Her Son – for me this was the right order. I have always believed that the Full Moon symbolizes the Virgin Mary's halo and that is why even when I was a child I used to pray to the Full Moon.

During the years that followed I developed a keen interest in ancient mythology and in the process of study, my attention became focuses on the image of the Triple Goddess called Hekate by the ancient Hellenes. The moment I saw Her single images I knew it was the woman I saw as a child and the one whom I addressed under the Full Moon. At that time I was twelve or thirteen years old, and it was at the same time that I started developing an interest in magic, healing rituals and other similar practices. It is worth noting that these practices as well as their consequences are still very much an everyday occasion in Bulgaria today.

In the summer of 1996 when I was 14 I went to Libya again to visit my mother who worked as a doctor there. An acquaintance of hers there taught me how to read the cards and I soon indulged myself in it. Since many of the things I had foretold came true, a lot of my friends, as well as friends of theirs, starting to come to me asking me to do readings for them about their future, this was another crucial time for me as because of it my knowledge of cards improved significantly.

Upon my return to Bulgaria a relative of mine told me that my grandma on my mother's side of the family, used to be one of most famous herbalists and healers in our town, but that only a few of her rituals had survived – against evil eye, against fear, for breaking a magic, and some magical practices. They were all handed down to me to be kept within the family. I continued to seek and gather information on magical rites, healing rituals and herbs from old people who were willing to share their wisdom and knowledge on these subjects with me.

During my study, which of course has not finished yet as the sea of knowledge is endless, I found some quite astonishing things which explained my accidental interest and spiritual commitment, so to speak, to this exact hypostasis of the Great Goddess – namely, Hekate. I was born in the morning on May 20th, 1982. That year the New Moon was on May 23rd, so I was born in the days of the Dark Moon and in ancient times these were days considered to be sacred to the Goddess. I was born at dawn and this is what Hesiod says about Hekate:

> "... And the son of Cronos made her a nurse of the young who after that day saw with their eyes the light of all-seeing Dawn..."

Figure 11 - Georgi Mishev as a child with his mother in Cyrene
Behind them the ruins of the Hekate Temple, the large columns are from a temple to Apollo.

At my birth the umbilical cord was three times wrapped around my neck and according to some traditional beliefs, this is a sign that the person being born would live a life devoted to magic. Even my conviction that everything started after my visitation to Cyrene was not a coincidence. There used to be a temple of Goddess Hekate there and even now Her statue is on display in the museum in Cyrene. There was also an explanation for my nightmares, high temperature and fever I had suffered after visiting the place as a child – according to the ancients this was a form of katabasis of the soul (descent to the hypo-chthonic, underworld reality). Visions of fearful images and passing through such an ordeal, is a form of initiation.

As time passed my studies, in the sphere of mythology, grew into a scientific interest and well-established knowledge, thus the initial difference in inner belief found expression in many ritual practices which followed the ancient tradition. Since it is a natural instinct to seek kindred souls, I also started looking for people who thought in a similar way and believed in similar things. I was lucky enough to find them and together we started gathering, organizing and preserving the ancient beliefs which had been ruined for so long.

Bulgaria is a country which has a long way to go in some ways before it will reach the standards of the West, but when it comes to cultural and historical heritage it has an enormous profusion. Thanks to its location and due to a number of significant historical events which have taken place in our lands, common traditional beliefs have always remained in favour over that of the written Christian tradition. The conservatism of the beliefs professed and the strict observance of rites inherited from our ancestors has always had an advantage over that of the meagre Christian written tradition. In many cases the people have made Christian priests take into consideration the inherited traditional rites. The worship of Virgin Mary by the people, as well as of many other saints, carries the genuine features of the belief in Great Goddess. The multitude of ancient cult sites as well as the so called living relics in Bulgarian culture such as fire-dancing rituals and mummery, festal rite cycles around St. George's Day and St. Marina's Day, worshipping of a great number of areas, springs and caves from ancient times till today show a continuity between faith and ritualism. In this connection our group has set a goal not to preach since the ancient belief cannot be preached but to provide opportunity and alternative to those who seek them.

What unites us is the common concept and belief in the Goddess as an all-embracing force. We consider Her to be the source and beginning of everything, the universal womb wherein the flame of the Creation has flickered. We believe that the Goddess is the One who shelters all and everything at their end before the new beginning. The name of Hekate is used by us because it has been historically certified as a name of the Triple Hypostasis of the Great Mother in our lands.

We consider the Goddess to be the initial and eternal force which is self-creating and comprises everything in Herself. We see the Goddess as a unity of Her comprehensiveness and all-manifestation in the three dimensions of time and the three worlds which according to our ideological doctrine are respectively land, sky and sea. We assume and believe that the Goddess self conceives and gives birth to Her divine son, who is symbolized by the Sun in the daytime and by fire at night and He is

Figure 12 - Threskeia for the Summer solstice rite at the entrance of the orphic
underground temple in Starosel, Bulgaria

Figure 13 - Georgi and Ekaterina - priest and priestess of Threskeia
In front of the sacred womb cave in Nochevo, Bulgaria

called Sabazius during the day and respectively Zagreus during the night. The united image of the God is called Dionysos.

We also honour and celebrate other deities belonging or connected with the society and history (deities worshipped in ancient times in our lands). We consider all other goddesses to be another manifestation and another name of the Goddess, respectively all other gods are considered to be another manifestation and another name of the God. We honour and celebrate Nature's cycles including the cycles of birth, death and rebirth.

We believe in the existence of a spiritual reality bound up with the physical one which can be explored and modified using the respective knowledge.

The reason for writing this story as a part of a book containing people's experiences who still believe and worship the Great Goddess was an opportunity for me to show that the Goddess is still alive in the lands of the ancient Thracians.

The Goddess reveals herself even nowadays as it was in the ancient times and awakens our belief and therefore we seek a way to preserve the worship to Her in the present as well as in the future.

Figure 14 - Honouring the Gods by Threskeia

Figure 15 - Ceremonial Procession, Ekaterina Ilieva

THE RED VEIL

IT IS BETTER THE GODDESS CHOOSES YOU

BY EKATERINA ILIEVA

It has always been quite hard for me to explain why and how I found that Hekate is the Goddess that I should honour. Some see Her, some hear Her, I just had a persistent thought about Her.

My name is Ekaterina, I am 24 years old and my homeland is Bulgaria. I am a priestess in *Threskeia* – a tradition based on the ritual beliefs of our ancestors the Thracians. I honour the Great Goddess, who we call Hekate and the God, who for us is Dionysos – epithets of the Gods used in our land since antiquity. As a priestess I am working hard on my studies of divination, magic and most of all herbs and healing rituals. Like most women do, I had an interest in magic and the occult since I was a little girl. I actually started reading such books at the age of 15 and also by that time started following the path of Wicca.

For some years it suited me just fine, because it had what I needed – a respect for nature and a Goddess, alongside the God. But, as I assume you all know, people change and during the years I've learned, explored and seen a lot of things that changed my spiritual needs and my actual life. No longer was I happy to call the Great Goddess by all Her epithets, no longer did I have the will to worship Her in every form and have no particular name to call Her when I stood up at the altar.

By that time I knew almost nothing of Hekate. I believed her to be what is most commonly spread about Her – a triple Goddess or a dark magic Goddess that wanders with her hounds at the crossroads. If I am honest I was kind of scared of that image of Hekate, but somehow it was in my mind that this was the goddess I should honour. It took me about two years of searching, reading, hesitating, asking myself why of all the other goddesses exactly that particular one was constantly in my head. And when I embraced that idea and followed my inner feelings I almost coincidentally met a person – Georgi Mishev, who showed me that Hekate is not only a dark witch. By that time I was 21 years old and the opportunity of meeting Georgi was like a door to another world opening to me. I found that Hekate was honoured in our lands and I understood Her nurturing and bright side. Over the years our work has become greater and now we have a full organization working on revealing the old ways, not to everyone, but only to those who seek knowledge in Her ways and the traditions of our land.

And that was the secret of all my hesitation – my heart had known the truth all the time, only I had to go through some difficulties to reveal it. Maybe it is true what they say - you can choose a deity, but its better that the deity chooses you.

Figure 16 - Hekate from Cartari, 1571

HEKATE'S ANGELS

BY THOMAS STARR

Angels are the powers which keep the universe running. That is the view I was trained with in the magical group which nurtured me and initiated me into the mysteries. And like any teenage student, I rebelled and ran away when I felt my liberty was too constrained by rules and ideas which seemed nonsensical. However the power and appeal of angels was something which deeply appealed to my nature, recalling a childhood of adoring angels, faeries, birds, bats and anything else which I saw as flying.

Wynn Westcott's edition of *The Chaldean Oracles* introduced me to the Iynges (*Wrynecks*), Synochesis (*Connectors*) and Teletarchai (*Rulers of Initiation*), the three orders of angels who were servants of the goddess Hekate. At this point in my life I was deep in the pages of old grimoires, studying reams of paper gleaned from the British Library, translating old dusty French manuscripts and finding more coherence than I expected.

A particular line in *The Chaldean Oracles* fuelled my imagination, and set me off on a different tangent, albeit rooted in my Solomonic work. The line declared *"Let fiery hope nourish you upon the Angelic plane."* Somehow this phrase summed up both Hekate and the angels, and drove me to look for more connections.

I did not agree with Westcott's attribution of the three orders of angels to what would be the Ethical Triad on the Qabalistic Tree of Life, and looked for a set of attributions which suited me. I instinctively concluded that each order of angels should rather belong to a triad in itself, and be embodied by one of the types of angel in that triad. Each triad comprises three of the Sephiroth (*'emanations'*) of the Tree of Life. There are three such triads with the tenth Sephira, Malkuth, being elemental and not in a triad. Due to their whirling motion, the Iynges were an obvious equation to the Auphanim (*Wheels*), the order of angles attributed to Chokmah (2), the Sephira of Wisdom. The Synochesis due to their harmonious and unifying essence I equated to the Seraphim (*Fiery Serpents*) of Geburah (5), the Sephira of Strength. Both the fire and serpents were also obvious Hekate symbols and this also seemed satisfactory. The Teletarchai I struggled with, but in the end I decided to try equating them to the Cherubim (*Strong Ones*) of Yesod (9), Sephira of the Foundation and the Moon.

Rather than trying to simply graft these angels onto the Solomonic format, I wondered if there was any existing material I could use. And I was in luck, for in the 'Lunar Spell of Claudianus' in *The Greek Magical Papyri* (PGM VII.862-918), I discovered that angels were requested from Hekate-Selene. Not only that, but the goddess is requested to *"give a whirring sound, and give a sacred angel"*. To me this clearly indicated the summoning of one of the Iynges, for they are the angels who whirl and spin.

The actual spell had to be modified, as it is essentially a love spell to attract somebody against their will. Nevertheless it formed an excellent foundation around which I could create an evocation to try and communicate with Hekate's angels, and see what I could learn from them. Drawing on the writings of the Byzantine historian Michael Psellus, I created a strophalos to use in the rite, making a spinning top which used a bronze cage around a lapis lazuli globe. I applied gold leaf to the strophalos when it was finished, in line with Psellus' description, but felt bronze was both easier and cheaper to work, and also was particularly appropriate to Hekate as one of her sacred substances, she of the brazen sandal.

Whilst I felt I could apply the standard purification process prior to the ceremony, abstaining from meat, alcohol, tobacco and sex for a week, it seemed inappropriate to use Hebrew divine names on the magic circle, and I decided I needed something more appropriate written in Greek. Fortunately the answer to this dilemma was close at hand, and I decided to simply use the string of goddess and barbarous names in the *Lunar Spell of Claudianus* as the divine names written between the rings of the magic circle. Thus the words *Orthō Baubō Noēre Kodēre Soire Ereschigal Sankistē Dōdekakiste Akrourobore Kodēre Sampsei* graced my magic circle.

As I could find virtually no information about the Iynges as an angelic order, I decided to keep my conjuration simple and concentrate on using the strophalos to bring the angels down, as was said of them in the ancient world. As I had equated the Iynges to the Ophanim, the image of the latter as eye-encrusted wheels was to provide the initial mental formulation to help provide a medium for them to descend through. My plan was to visualise this image onto my crystal ball on the triangle outside my circle. I placed the triangle in the east as the place of the rising sun, which seemed most appropriate. I also replaced the name of the archangel Michael in the triangle with that of Hekate as being more appropriate. As a lunar ointment is talked about in the spell in the PGM, I decided to use a simple lunar scent, and burned camphor, which I have always found sharpens my mental faculties considerably.

After several minutes of spinning the strophalos like a bull-roarer I found the noise was bringing forth all manner of bizarre visions from my unconscious mind. I paused and performed a centring exercise, and then continued whirling my strophalos. The images did not reappear and I found the sound helped me shift into a more receptive state, blocking out all stimuli and shifting my consciousness into that centred state where I feel the connections to everything around me.

At this point the Iynx manifested in the crystal. Despite my use of the wheel like image to provide a point of reference for the Iynx, in fact it largely resembled a classical angel. It had two pairs of wings, one facing up and one down, reminding me of the wryneck's toes, two forwards and two backwards. The wings beat like those of an insect, rapidly, and producing a subtle sound which resembled a buzz or hum, and the references to a whirring noise suddenly made sense.

It wore a blue tunic (I was expecting white, but that it just my prejudices speaking) which reminded me of the colour of the lapis lazuli globe in my strophalos. Flashes of gold randomly appeared around it in the crystal (the use of lapis lazuli in the strophalos also now made sense!) as I gazed at it and began my communion and started working through my list of questions. For some reason I have never had the same success when trying to contact the other orders of angels, it seems like whatever I try, the Iynges are the ones who turn up. Not that I am complaining, for truly Hekate is the great queen who no aerial or infernal daimon can ignore, and through her angels she has taught me a great deal. Of course I could ask her, but I prefer to call on her when there is great need, or when I perform devotional rites, whereas her angels are ideal for all those other occasions when assistance may be required. After all isn't that what they are there for?

BIBLIOGRAPHY

Betz, Hans Dieter (ed). *The Greek Magical Papyri in Translation.* Chicago, University of Chicago Press, 1986.
Rankine, David. *Climbing the Tree of Life.* London, Avalonia, 2005
Rankine, David, & Sorita d'Este. *Practical Qabalah Magick.* London, Avalonia, 2009.
Westcott, W. Wynn (ed). *The Chaldean Oracles of Zoroaster.* Wellingborough, Aquarian Press, 1983.

I am indebted to David Rankine and Sorita d'Este for making available to me some of their personal research, and to the work being done by David Rankine, Stephen Skinner and Paul Harry Barron towards making available previously unpublished material from obscure grimoires in an accessible format, thus allowing us all to move forward with our Work.

Figure 17 - From Cartari, 1571

Figure 18 - Vikki Bramshaw

SWAYING WITH THE SERPENT

A STUDY OF THE SERPENT GIRDLED HEKATE

BY VIKKI BRAMSHAW

> '...I speak indeed of the fire-filled source, the She-Serpent, and Snake-Girdled, girt in Serpent coils ...*
>
> The Chaldean Oracles

With its venomous bite and constricting coils, the snake has remained an awesome symbol of instinct, death and regeneration for thousands of years. As both a theurgic priestess and snake enthusiast, I have been working with the Serpent Girdled and Helicoidal Hekate for several years now; and my understanding of her has grown through both experiential work and historical study. To me, the snake symbolises an innate freedom and liberation; an untamed, primordial connection to our past which defines the fundamental necessities of our very existence such as the need to live, to feed, to procreate and ultimately, to die. Throughout the ages the significance of the serpent has remained within a counterbalance between its opposing roles as both life giver and life destroyer, creating an intriguing antithesis within religion and literature; which was similarly reflected in the mythology and worship of Hekate. In truth, there is only so much you can learn about this aspect of Hekate from books alone, and so I have written this essay to reflect what I have learnt from my own experiences and my subsequent research.

Frequently the serpent was considered as a creature of the chthonic underworld realms, a harbinger of death; and the Greek name for snake or serpent, *erpeto* (ερπετὸ) meant to *'crawl'* (ἐρπομαι) along or below the ground, equating the snake with the infernal depths of the earth. The ancient Greeks also considered the snake as a symbol of the afterlife, and it was generally believed that the dead would appear in the form of a serpent: the spinal cord of the deceased person was said to transform into a snake and come to life. It is within this context that we meet the first aspect of our Serpent Girdled Hekate: the subterranean underworld Goddess who guides the souls of the dead through Tartaros. However, the early functions of chthonian deities were not simply limited to the processes of death; neither did the definition of the word chthonic entirely mean as such. For the earth was also considered as a place of hidden potential and power, and so the chthonic role was also one of regeneration, enlivening potentiality, and growth. The snake also became associated with the powers of fire and the sun, fertility and prosperity, altered states of consciousness, and even the ecstatic journey of the soul; all notions which recall the ancient origins of Hekate and which will be discussed in further detail during this study. In keeping with its universal associations of vital life force and regeneration, the snake even featured in many creation myths and became a universal symbol of whirling fire, orgiastic energy, and of the sun; Hekate's role as Mistress of Life.

The *Chaldean Oracles*, a collection of ritual trance-prophesies dating from around the second century CE (well after Hekate's Greco-Roman lunar identity had already been formed) also portray Hekate as a solar or fire deity; the origin of the cosmic soul and a Goddess of vital life force, portrayed as (or identified with) spiralling and serpent-like fire or energy. With a closer examination of Hekate's heritage we find that this type of symbolism is in many ways more in keeping with her original character, and just some of Hekate's Helicoidal roots can be found in such deities as Hekate of Lagina in south-west Turkey, who was accompanied by serpents and worshipped as a deity of fertility and dance; the Syrian Goddess Atargatis, who was originally revered as a serpent-girdled tutelary deity; and the chthonic aspects of the fertility Goddess Mater Magna of Anatolia.

In this essay I will also be making reference to several male deities who were companion to, or indeed identified with, Hekate. Whilst in many ways the snake is a masculine symbol (often used as a phallic representation of fertility) it seems from my practical experience and subsequent research that the force of this life-generating solar serpent is awoken by the power of a chthonic-fertility deity, such as Hekate. These serpents are often depicted wrapped around the body of Goddess or as flanking companions ready to carry out her bidding. This can perhaps be seen reflected in the symbology of the *cista mystica*: a basket used during the mysteries which was often depicted either wrapped with snakes, or with snakes emerging from inside it – perhaps, symbolic of the revelation of the mysteries themselves.

Indeed, several initiation friezes (now in the *Museo Nazionale delle Terme*, Rome) show snakes coiling out of the *cista mystica* and into the lap of the fertility deity Demeter and even *The Chaldean Oracles* refer to Hekate carrying the *'source of the life generating primordial soul'* about her hips; recalling the serpent wrapped Goddesses of art and statuary. Early Greek coins minted at Pergamon (Turkey) also show the snakes crawling from the *cista mystica*. The coiling and undulating movement of the snake was both beautiful and entrancing to watch, and it is likely that the serpent would have been considered as possessing hypnotic qualities which aided altered states of consciousness. A black-glaze jug from around 300 BCE readily recalls this aspect of her nature, as Hekate dances up to a blazing altar with an hypnotic gaze in her eyes, and snaking ringlets flowing about her shoulders. This is particularly interesting when we consider the trance-like effect that snake venom was perceived to have on the human mind and body: the word '*venom*' itself coming from the Latin *venenum*, which originally meant potion, or magical charm. Hekate's skill with poisonous herbs and entheogens may be purely circumstantial, but it is a tempting thought nonetheless. The *Greek Magical Papyri* (PGM IV.2801-2815) described her with:

> '...*fearful serpents on your brow ... whose womb is decked out with the scales of creeping things, with pois'nous rows of serpents down the back ... to you, wherefore they call you Hekate ...'*

The art of snake handling and charming, a practice which celebrated the regenerative and chthonic qualities of the snake, became an important part of several ancient mystery cults and their ordeal rites. It also found its way to Rome, where *La*

Festa Dei Serpari remains today as an important annual event of snake charming, divination and dance. Nowadays it is celebrated in honour of the Christian Saint Domenico, but it is generally accepted that the festival finds its Pagan origins in the worship of the Goddess of snakes and toxins, Bona Dea (or the earlier Angizia, from the Latin *angius* – serpent) who was almost certainly a later syncretisation of Hekate. Like Hekate, Bona Dea was also involved in funerary rites and the afterlife. A Roman funerary inscription (given in Burkert's *Ancient Mystery Cults*, p25) for a young boy from 300/400 CE describes him as a priest of:

> *'... first, Bona Dea, then of the Mother of the Gods, and of Dionysos Kathegemon...'*

The mention of the name Dionysos together with this conflated serpent-aspect of Hekate is very interesting, as the worship of Dionysos was fused with that of Meter's chthonic and regenerative aspects from a very early date. The cult on the Greek island of Samothrace celebrated the mysteries of the Theoi Megaloi (*'the Great Gods'*) with a major focus on Meter, the fertile Great Mother. Certainly, *The Chaldean Oracles* also refer to Hekate as a fertile Goddess of creation, and her life-giving womb is described as being the *'origin of the whole world'*. Whilst the names of specific deities were not usually given to non-initiates, it is generally accepted that the cult embraced a wide variety of practices surrounding the different facets of Meter; which certainly included the chthonic mysteries of Hekate-Brimo (or Brimo-Trimorphos) together with her consort Sabazios (Dionysos). Cult rites of Dionysos often involved snake handling and wearing snakes as decoration upon the body; as well as a rather cruel custom which involved tearing poisonous snakes to pieces as an offering. However, other sources (such as the *Greek Magical Papyri* LXX.4-10) show that ivy wreaths, which were considered as having kinship with the snake, were destroyed instead.

> *'...Virgin, Bitch, Serpent, Wreath, Key...'*

I have worked closely with the mysteries of Dionysos over the years, whose rites usually involve spontaneous acts, trance work and intuitive offerings. Initially, I was quite surprised to find that Hekate was so keen to work with Dionysos, and visa versa; an enigma which became clear with just a little more research into Hekate's serpentine-helicoidal nature, and her function as unifier of opposing principles.

Another similarity shared by Dionysos and Hekate was their role in aiding mortals to achieve a ritual state of consciousness; a role they both offered to the process of Theurgy. More examples of the serpent-girdled Hekate's role in aiding trance states will be discussed below; however in terms of the bacchic-frenzy both deities were involved in the processes of ecstatic ceremony as a way of facilitating passage between the physical world and the spiritual world. The fifth century poet Nonnus (*Dionysiaca 3. 61 ff*) paints a colourful picture of the Pelasgian choral song and bacchic rites at Samothrace, which honoured Hekate:

> *'Korybantes were beating on their shields ... leaping with rhythmic steps ... while the double pipe made music, and quickened the dancers ... bears joined the dance, skipping and wheeling ... lions with a roar from emulous throats mimicked the triumphant cry of the priests of the Kabeiroi, sane in their madness; the revelling pipes rang out a tune in honour of Hecate'.*

The Samothracian cult also followed the mysteries of Hermes, referred to as Kadmylos. Sharing the epithet Chthonia, Hermes was considered a companion or equivalent to Hekate and *'escort of souls'*, sometimes pictured holding his staff the Caduceus which was entwined with twin serpents. Just one example can be seen in a *Charm for Acquiring Business* from the *Greek Magical Papyri* (PGM IV.2373-2440), which also makes reference to the syncretic Goddess Isis-Hekate. The Caduceus was a potent symbol of vital life force and was intrinsically linked with the energy of the body, symbolising both a balance and neutrality between polarities. The Caduceus has also been linked to the conflated Syrian serpent girdled Goddess Atargatis.

In ancient Greece the serpent came to be considered as a personification of zoë (life) and the connection between Hekate and zoë has been described as both close and logical, based on the belief that Hekate's cosmic soul was both the origin and animator of all life. The symbolism of the snake as an icon of indestructible life was also reflected in the rites of Dionysos and chthonic-fertility aspects of Meter, as well as the mythology of Æsculapius the Greek God of medicine, who learnt the innate power of the snake to heal the sick and resurrect the dead. Æsculapius also shared the epithet *'Paeëon'* with Apollo and was considered as being descended from him. Apollo was often worshipped alongside Hekate and was one of the Gods most commonly called upon together with Hekate in the *Greek Magical Papyri*, although sometimes in the guise of Helios. Hekate's heritage as a solar deity of regeneration may provide a link to her role as feminine equivalent to the solar Gods Apollo and Helios; a companionship which persisted even after her lunar identity was formed. Hekate and Apollo even shared the epithet Hekatos, which meant far-darting, and Hekate was frequently considered as the feminine equivalent to Apollo. Whilst purely speculation on my part, the epithet *'far-darting'* certainly seems to conjure up the movement of a snake as it strikes toward its prey; and from my experience the motion of Hekate's rites and magic.

Snakes are decisive, and strike with intent and precision; and so it is perhaps fitting that the Greek poet Hesiod described Hekate as the wilful goddess: *'the one by whose will prayers are fulfilled and success granted.'* This important statement reflects Hekate's role as arbitrator between the astral and the material, and her ultimate decision in granting or denying a request. I once petitioned helicoidal Hekate for certain improvements in my own life, and within three days all of my requests had been fulfilled - with three options for each thing I had asked for.

Yet on other occasions, I have been firmly disciplined for not thinking the petition though further before asking! Hekate either grants or denies, and makes her decision quickly and precisely. In *The Chaldean Oracles* it is said that *'the sources around (Hekate's) girdle ensure the fulfilment of things'* and it becomes clear why Hekate was called upon for so many magical operations which could be described as *'spells of passion'*.

This girdle of fulfilment is particularly interesting when we revisit the possible connection between Hekate's life generating girdle and the symbology of the serpent.

Snakes spend much of their time conserving energy, however within the snake lies an impulsive and instinctual source of power which can quickly be used for evading predators and hunting prey. Within the human body, a similar force has been described as the kundalini: a coiled serpent fire or inner serpent which dwelt at the base of the body and could be awakened and risen up the spine by using certain techniques. My brief training in kundalini was probably also my first contact with helicoidal Hekate; although it would take me several years to identify it as such. Whilst kundalini is an eastern concept, the idea of a fiery serpent within the body was common in many cultures. Art is abundant with images of Hekate (and other associated deities) flanked or girdled with coiling snakes and, like the *cista mystica*, the iconography of the snake wrapped round the body of the deity may indicate certain female deities as the bearer of the mysteries. *The Chaldean Oracles* also described Hekate's fires as winding or enwrapping, and the Gnostics embraced the concept of a fire snake as the embodiment of Sophia (or wisdom) which rose up the spine and enabled the practitioner to cross the threshold and ascend to spirit. This whole concept becomes particularly interesting when we reconsider the ancient Greek belief mentioned earlier: that the spinal cord transformed into a snake after death. Yet another symbol of indestructible life, and a crucial intermediary or vehicle for the soul.

The Chaldean Oracles describe how Hekate, standing on the threshold between the material and the spiritual planes of existence, aids mortals in achieving trance-like states in which they could receive prophesies and instruct daemons and spirits and utilise celestial spheres. It is likely that Hekate's consecrated ritual tool, the Strophalos may have also been used to reach these ritual states of consciousness. *The Oracles* suggest that the Strophalos represented the Iynx, a fiery being which moved between the worlds as an intermediary or a messenger. In my opinion, the role of the wheel was probably to act as a vehicle to alter the consciousness and assist the practitioner to communicate with otherworldly beings. The strophalos was sometimes described as a spinning top, which was also sacred to Dionysos. Decorated with labyrinthine serpents and spirals, the Strophalos was spun in the air to create hypnotic whirring or hissing sounds, described as both persuasive and enchanting. The hissing may have been accompanied by bacchic primal noises, inarticulate words, cries and beast-like sounds made by the priests and priestesses during the ceremony. It is also interesting to note that 'hissing' is also one of the sacred sounds used during the rites of *Prayer to Selene* in the *Greek Magical Papyri*, another practice which I have found aids the practitioner in their transition to a trance-like state. As a final and tempting consideration; comparisons have been made between the Iynx bird (the wryneck) and the serpent, due to the birds' ability to extend its neck and appear like a snake to its predators.

I find working with trance one of the most powerful ways of getting in touch with this particular aspect of Hekate. I particularly like trancing with Hekate in the late hours of the evening just before I go to bed, in order to influence my dreams. Incidentally, Hekate was considered as bestowing the gifts of prophecy through sleep, and *The Chaldean Oracles* describe her as being both the 'substance and origin' of symbols and dreams. At the Sanctuary of Æsculapius at Epidavros snakes were released into the sleeping quarters during a time of incubation, when the snakes were believed to send oracles through the medium of dreams. Not all the dreams I have received whilst working with Hekate have been pleasant; but that is the nature of Hekate and her serpents, after all. Yet, every dream carries an important message and if, like Hekate, the snake really is instrumental in the uncoiling of the mysteries, then these gifts are certainly shown through sleeping states of consciousness and Hekate's role as mistress of oneiromancy, that is dream divination. It is also interesting to note that *The Chaldean Oracles* specify that it is Hekate's life generating girdle which symbolises and provides dreams; the same girdle which has been suggested as being akin to the snake.

Hekate is often depicted in the company of snakes, either girdled or flanked by them, and sometimes she is shown with her three-headed dog Kerberos who is similarly depicted as part-snake or wrapped with snakes. Other chthonic deities who were associated with Hekate were also sometimes depicted with the snake; such as the Greek underworld God Hades, and the Hellenistic-Egyptian Serapis who is sometimes called upon with Hekate together with Kerberos in the *Greek Magical Papyri*. Artemis is also connected with both the serpent and Hekate, in particular Artemis Iolcos who in the narrative of Diodorus Siculus is described as *'riding upon serpents'* - a mode of travel which scholars (such as Farnell) have described as *'suitable only for Hekate'*. Some images of Athena were also reminiscent of the Serpent Girdled Hekate, and early statuary of Athena depicts her as a corporeal and expressive Goddess, heavily wreathed with snakes which coiled around her head and fringed her shawl. She also held a shield decorated with serpent-skinned Gorgons. Lucian of Samosata described her in *Philopseudes* as:

> *'Her lower extremities were those of a dragon; but the upper half was like Medusa ... At the sight of her, I stood stock still ... whereupon Hecate smote upon the ground with her dragon's foot, and caused a vast chasm to open, wide as the mouth of Hell.'*

Like Brimo and Baubo, the name Gorgon or Gorgo (meaning *'dreadful'*) was used to describe either spirits sent by Hekate (Apotropaioi) or to describe functions of Hekate herself. In legend, the Gorgons were three snake-like sisters named Stheno, Euryale and Medusa: who served as guardians at the entrances of buildings for protection in a similar fashion to Hekate's tutelary statues and shrines, and decorated the temple of Artemis at Ephesus. The Gorgons were reminiscent of the Erinyes, three chthonian Goddesses of vengeance who were similarly depicted with serpents for hair and wrapped around their bodies. It is also interesting that the Apotropaioi were often recorded as being more active during the daytime than during the night, which may suggest a link back to Hekate's original solar form. The Erinyes are also mentioned alongside Hekate in her guise of the moon Goddess Selene in the *Greek Magical Papyri* as well as another incantation from the same book of spells which petitions Hekate to summon the Erinyes (PGM IV.1416-18) to rouse underworld souls:

> *'... Lady (Hekate) ... send the Erinys, Orgogorgoniotrian (Gorgon) ...'*

Besides her associations of whirling and life generating fire, Hekate was also historically associated with the infernal fires of the netherworld. She carried blazing torches with which she guided souls through the underworld, and her followers regularly made offerings to her into fiery pits in the earth. However it is interesting to note that during the Greek Eleusinian rites of Thesmophoria. which honoured the Greek Kore's journey to the underworld to become the dark Queen Persephone, this theme became coupled with the presence of snakes. Vase art from the period (such as a fifth century BCE Lekythos vase painting now in the *National Museum of Athens)* shows us that sacrifices of live pigs were made by the light of Hekate's three torches which were set at the edge of a deep pit called the Megara; which rather than being filled with fire, was filled with writhing snakes.

Certainly, Hekate was associated with the Demeter-Kore-Persephone myth on a much deeper level than just being their underworld guide and companion. All three shared the epithet, Brimo and Persephone herself was identified with Hekate (PGM IV.1402-3): '...*Three headed Goddess ... key holding Persephassa (Persephone) ... With fiery serpents...*'

The descent of Demeter's daughter Kore-Persephone is also reminiscent of the descent of the Sumerian Goddess Inanna, who is often depicted holding a caduceus of entwined serpents in her hand. Like Kore, Inanna descends to the underworld where she meets her dark sister and Queen of the Underworld, Ereshkigal. The word Ereschigal (sic) also features as one of the voces magicae in the *Greek Magical Papyri*, within rituals which call upon Hekate. In turn, Ereshkigal is often identified with the Sumerian Lilitu (or the later Hebrew Lilith) who is similarly depicted girdled by a serpent. Whilst it is generally accepted that Ereshkigal is the character most associated with Hekate in this myth, another character from the story named Ninshubur also bears an uncanny resemblance to Hekate as guide and companion to Inanna; and also like Hekate, she is the one to raise the alarm with the other Gods when she realises that Inanna is missing. The Orphites also followed a descent myth; the journey of a mythical character Orpheus who travels to the underworld to ask Hades to give back his wife, who had died after receiving a lethal snake bite. This story may perhaps recall the earlier Pelasgian tales of Ophion thrown into Tartaros.

BIBLIOGRAPHY

Betz, Hans Dieter (ed). *The Greek Magical Papyri in Translation.* Chicago, University of Chicago Press, 1986
Bonnefoy, Yves (ed) & Wendy Doniger (trans). *Greek and Egyptian Mythologies.* Chicago, University of Chicago Press, 1992
Burkert, Walter. *Ancient Mystery Cults.* Harvard, Harvard University Press, 1989
Burkert, Walter. *Greek Religion.* Cambridge, Cambridge University Press, 1985
Clay, Jenny Strauss. *Hesiod's Cosmos.* Cambridge University ~Press, Cambridge, 2009
Cole, Susan G. *Theoi Megaloi: the Cult of the Great Gods at Samothrace.* Leiden, Brill, 1984
D'Este, Sorita & David Rankine. *Hekate Liminal Rites.* London, Avalonia, 2009
Farnell, L.R. *The Cults of the Greek States.* 5 vols. Oxford, Oxford University Press, 1896-1909.
Fideler, David R. *Alexandria: The Journal of Western Cosmological Traditions.* Michigan, Phanes Press, 1995
Fontenros, Joseph Eddy. *Python: A Study of Delphic Myth and its Origins.* Connecticut, Biblo-Moser, 1959
Fowler, H.W. & F.G. (trans). *The Works of Lucian of Samosata.* The Clarendon Press, Oxford, 1905
Johnson, Buffie. *Lady of the Beasts: The Goddess and Her Sacred Animals.* Vermont, Inner Traditions, 1994
Johnston, Sarah Iles. *Hekate Soteira.* Georgia, Scholars Press, 1990
Kerenyi, Carl. *Dionysos: Archetypal Image of Indestructible Life.* Princeton, Princeton University Press, 1996
Kramer, Samuel Noah & Diane Wolkstein. *Inanna, Queen of Heaven and Earth.* London, Rider, 1983
Morgan, Diane. *Snakes in Myth, Magic and History: The Story of a Human Obsession.* New York, Praeger, 2008
Nagy, Gregory. *Greek Mythology and Poetics.* New York, Cornell University Press, 1992
Phene, John Samuel. *On Prehistoric Traditions & Customs in Connection with Sun & Serpent.* Kessinger, 2010
Ronan, Stephen (ed). *The Goddess Hekate.* Hastings, Chthonios Books, 1992
Rouse, W.H.D. *Nonnus Dionysiaca Books 1-48.* Cambridge, Harvard University Press, 1960
Smith, William. *Dictionary of Greek and Roman Antiquities.* London, John Murray, 1874
Thompson, William Irwin. *The Time Falling Bodies Take To Light: Mythology, Sexuality & the Origins of Culture.* New York, St Martins, 1996

Figure 19 - The Seer by Emily Carding

GODDESS OF SUPREME CONSCIOUSNESS

BY JADE SOL LUNA

In Dark Goddess mysticism, Hecate is the first of the Great Astronomical Powers, because in a certain way she is the one who "*spins the wheel of the universal time.*"

On the other hand, at the end of the manifested world, she devours all the universes and the three planes of creation: the physical, the astral and the causal universes.

The "*Great Astronomical Power*" Hecate finally devours the time itself and this is the very reason why Hecate is viewed as the primordial cause of creation and destruction of the universe.

Hecate is the everything, representing both the being (the existence) and the infinite consciousness in manifestation.

According to the Chaldean belief, the whole manifested world springs from the Infinite Consciousness of the illumined union between light (inactive state) and Hecate (the active state).

The knowledge of creation bears the name Hecate. The universe thus created has to be maintained in the manifestation, function performed by Hecate.

Nonetheless, both the creation and the preserving aspects imply a molecular "*death*" or "*destruction*" of each form of the universe, function performed by Hecate.

Her darkness dissolves everything

The simultaneous existence of these three processes within the creation clearly expresses the statements included in ancient Greek writings, that the creation of the universe did not occur once, in the past, nor will the universe be destroyed once in the future, and that rather in every instant these aspects manifest as rays creating the illusion of continuity and reality.

Although the human body and mind are permanently assailed by innumerable sensorial perceptions, the state of divine ecstasy implies the disappearance of all mental functions and of the physical awareness into the Supreme consciousness of Sol Caelum, that which is beyond all duality.

From a different perspective, Hecate is also the creator of universes, as they come to life from the ashes of the "*Divine Consciousness*" and the purifying fire of this Black Goddess. Consequently, Hecate's action is deeply evolutionary, as she impels the human beings towards evolution, sometimes in a challenging manner.

Nonetheless, Hecate performs her actions in divine light and harmony, knowing that this is the best thing to do. Those who manage to pass all the tests and go through all the stages are in truth spiritual warriors, and they will be rewarded with Hecate's spiritual grace.

Hecate is the time beyond time

Hecate has been associated and often equated with Nyx (night), the first of the Great Astronomical Powers.

Hecate is also named Nyctipolus, in her quality of energy and terrible Cosmic Power who impels humankind towards action and the universe towards manifestation.

Hecate's representation reveals her holding a torch. This is not a trivial manner of representing a fire, but instead this fact stands for the transcendence of all limitations, the holder of light.

Her action in the manifested world implies the destroying and in the same time purifying action of time.

However, as the mystic is more and more concerned with spiritual aspects, and firmly oriented towards obtaining spiritual freedom at all costs, he or she will be blessed with Hecate's overwhelming grace.

She destroys the ego

One of the most important hypostasis in which one can worship Hecate, is the one who defeated the Giant Clytius. This Giant represents the forces of ignorance in Greek spirituality.

For the worshiper of God in the aspect of the Divine Mother, Hecate is the only hypostasis that destroys the evil of the world in its numerous aspects.

Thus, Greek mythology describes how the goddess has vanquished the Giant Clytius, saving the gods from captivity and who set up the divine order in the universe.

Hecate grants her support and help to those who ask for it and worship her, so that the spiritual forces develop and gain supremacy over the negative influences of the psychic and mental.

Hecate is thus the "*Divine Light*" who destroys and burns in the terrible fire of her pure consciousness, any malefic force and leftover ignorance.

Her force awakens Hydra (Kundalini)

The spiritual practice recommended for the worship of the Great Hecate implies the effort of purifying and activating the Chakras, so that the fundamental energy Hydra ascends from Saturnus Caelum to Sol Caelum.

The ascension of Hydra represents one of the most important aspects of this Great Astronomical Goddess.

The mysterious influence of Hecate is so complex and hidden that only few pure souls may see through her actions their real significance. Hence she is Trivia, the Great Mystery.

We meet a frequent representation of Hecate as the Cosmic Mother, surrounded by a great number of different gods and goddesses. Lacking any dimensions or spatial-temporal limits, she takes on different forms and names in order to meet her worshipper's most secret desires.

In certain situations, Hecate embarks into action to destroy that which is weak, or useless. Thus, we may see her representation as having six arms, in which she holds different objects that are helpful in restoring or preserving the divine order of the universe.

In her most elevated aspect, Hecate Soteira is the Divine Bliss itself, that which is beyond ordinary human perception, and the nature of conscious Light.

Consequently, there are two ways of worshiping her: as the great Goddess bestowing her grace and blessings upon all those who deserve it, and as holy energy who grants spiritual freedom (Sol Caelum).

The purifying fire that burns the ego to ashes

Hecate is black, the source of all colours. This also indicates the fact that she is associated with the depths of God's mystery.

However, this terrible and scaring aspect is backed up by a smiling attitude of the goddess, looking upon the being of the universe with kindness and affection, sustaining their life and nourishing them with her three heads.

Her ironic laughter is for all those who, due to ignorance, imagine that they can elude spiritual evolution. The Great Goddess has three all-seeing heads, *"supervising"* the universes from the past, present and future. No one can escape her glance!

As Hecate Sol, she holds a skull on the left and a whip on the right, whose significance is double: on one hand it is the receiver of the universal mysterious teaching (whip representing task), and on the other hand it is a reminder of what endures after the dissolution of the body (bones).

Through her infinite grace, all universe dissolves in her

Hecate holds an athame, whose role is to cut all worldly connections and attachments, so that the worshiper is prepared for the ultimate spiritual freedom.

It is also interesting to mention that her hair is long and dishevelled, representing the power of Hecate's all-pervading grace.

Her benevolence and compassion are underlined by two of her hands, one holding a torch, representing casting away fear and the other hand holding a key, offering spiritual gifts and powers to those that open hidden doors.

Around her neck there is a necklace made of male testicles belonging to various malefic entities, symbolizing her complete victory over the senses.

In the Greek iconography, Hecate appears under a number of other forms, with minor differences as regards the number of the arms, face, of symbolic objects she holds.

Thus, Lucifera, Inferna, Trivia, Triceps, Sol, Enodia represent just as many aspects of the Goddess, worshiped in different areas of the Mediterranean.

Among these forms, remarkable is the form of Hecate Soteira, described as a master power, ready to devour any illusory aspect of the universe.

This is an extract from the book

~ Hecate II: The Awakening of Hydra by Jade Sol Luna

Figure 20 - Thracian Hekate by Georgi Mishev

FROM HEAVEN TO EARTH

BY JOHN CANARD

Hekate has been my guiding light for many years. Several years ago I contributed an essay to *Hekate Keys to the Crossroads* on my use of aconite to make a flying ointment for use at Hekate Suppers, and the results I achieved. When I was asked if I would contribute to another anthology, I did not have to think long, as I had felt after my last essay that there was another topic which I didn't cover and perhaps should have. That topic is meteor showers, the stones that give us fire in the sky and remind us of Hekate's mother Asteria, the Star Goddess.

There are numerous meteor showers through the year, most of which are not easily visible. However one of the most visible is the Perseids, which may be seen from mid July to late August, and which peak around the 12th-13th August. Considering that Perses (Perseus as derivative) is Hekate's father and meteor showers are also associated with Asteria, this shower is the one that must be included in the August celebrations for Hekate. On a clear night, you can see at least one shooting star a minute when the shower is peaking in mid-August, making it an incredibly magical backdrop to celebrations in Hekate's honour.

The Quantock Hills in Somerset are on my proverbial doorstep, and a fantastic place to perform midnight ceremonies under an unpolluted sky. This is where I go to see the shooting stars of the meteor showers. I have found the flash of fire in the sky has several beneficial uses for ceremonies.

My favourite is to lie on my back after I have made all my offerings, and gaze at the starry sky. As I look I utter the words of a charm, drawing out the last word so it hangs in the air building up the pressure, until I see a shooting star, and in that moment cutting off the sound and clapping simultaneously, sending the spell on its way with sound and light to speed it on, like the lightning and thunder of her storms. If I am lucky I catch sight of two shooting stars at the same time, and then I see these as her torches and know that my endeavour has been particularly blessed.

I dare say to most people I would look a sight, lying on my back in the middle of nowhere clapping my hands at irregular intervals! But then that is why I pick my spots carefully. No point in being disturbed mid-cantrip by an inquisitive dog-walker or teenage pot-heads! Another way I work with the meteor showers is to hymn them. Once I am lying comfortably, I vibrate the first of the Greek vowels as soon as I see a shooting star, alpha. I carry on with this until the next one is seen, and move on to the next vowel, eta. I do this through the cycle of the seven vowels and then start again. This technique shifts your consciousness quite quickly, and can send you spinning off into the stars or even projecting out of your body. For this reason it can be a good one to do with company, as a second person seems to act as an anchor and both enter a trance state without leaving the body. My anchor, or perhaps I would be more accurate in saying I am her anchor, is Sorita d'Este, my fellow student under the dame Hilda Starling. As we both have family commitments we do not meet up as often as we did in the past, but it is always worthwhile when we do. Indeed it was Sorita who came up with the hymning of the meteorites some years back. Although this is not a part of my tradition, I am always happy to try things that work, and use them when they are relevant or useful. And as Hekate can be connected to the use of the vowels I find it a very beneficial inclusion.

As meteors are effectively lumps of earth (stone or metal I know, but the element of earth) in the upper atmosphere (air) catching fire from the heat (fire), all that is missing is water to complete the elemental cycle. One way to combine these is to draw down the power of the three elements whilst you are in water, either standing in a stream or the sea, or immersing more of yourself. As I discussed in an earlier essay (*Quenching the Thirst, Drinking the Spirit*, in *From A Drop Of Water*, 2009), immersion prayer is a powerful technique used in root magick, and by combining it with meteoric power as well, you can make yourself a supercharged elemental receptacle, and put a huge amount of energy into achieving a result you desire.

There is a belief that each shooting star is a soul being released, and if that is the case, it seems obvious to me that they are returning to Hekate. Shakespeare drew on a version of this with his quote in *Richard II* that *"meteors fright the fixed star of heaven"* as being indicative of the death or fall of a king, with all the chaos that would bring. Interestingly this is reminiscent of the Persian belief that meteors were antithetical to the planets, and represented negative influences which combated the positive ones of the planets.

Another old belief is that a shooting star represents a birth. Either way it is a liminal moment, and that is the driving force behind getting out to see them. As you gaze at the sky, you cannot help but be transported and leave the mundane behind. If you are on top of a hill, closer to the sky, or on a beach next to the sea, this feeling is intensified even more. Some country folk still subscribe to the idea that the more meteorites you see, the worse the winter will be, and pray for cloudy night skies to hide the shooting fire and encourage a mild winter!

I like the image of meteors as dragons or fiery serpents found in the Middle and Far East, as it reminds me of the dragon-borne chariot ridden by Medea, and I find it very easy to see Hekate bearing her twin torches in a chariot, with a triple-headed dragon pulling it through the night sky. Perhaps not entirely a classical image, but one which she has presented to me on many occasions.

The obvious tool to use during these times is a piece of meteorite. The magical connection between them is obvious, a manifestation of the principle of *'As above, so below'*. A piece of meteorite makes an excellent conduit for drawing energy down from the heavens, particularly if you time it to coincide with seeing the flash of a flaming meteorite (shooting star). Meteorites, or Baetylic stones, have been connected with a number of deities, including Hekate, who was said to possess a black meteorite which could hold spirits, be a place for deities to dwell, and prophesy. Obviously it makes a very powerful receptacle and transmitter of stellar energy, and an excellent item to have on Hekate's altar.

If for some reason I can't make it for August 13th, I always make sure I celebrate Hekate at some of the other showers which I feel are particularly relevant to her. These I have chosen by the simple factor of their names being animals which are linked to Hekate, i.e. dragons, bulls, lions and unicorns. Of course there are others one could use, but this harsher time of the year works better for me. Sometimes I will try and do all of them, but it is a rare year when that is possible. For me the other showers I like are the Draconids, peaking around October 8th-9th, the Taurids, peaking around the 5th and 12th November, the Leonids peaking around November 17th and the Monocerotids peaking around November 21st. Of course research is called for, as showers vary in brightness from year to year, and can move from spectacular to uneventful very easily. Likewise a clear sky is a must to really enjoy her fires in the sky.

In closing my contribution, I would like to leave you with a wonderful quote from a poem by the nineteenth century Romanian poet Alecsandri, which reminds us of the transitional and liminal nature of not just meteorites but love and life itself:

Pleasures of love, charming pleasures!

Feelings! Great dreams of a wonderful future!

You disappeared suddenly just like the travelling stars

Which leave a deeper darkness after them.

Steluta (Little Star), Vasile Alecsandri (1821-1890)

BIBLIOGRAPHY

Alecsandri V. *Vasile Alecsandri – Poems*. Eminescu Publishing House, 1970.
Canard, John. *Quenching the Thirst, Drinking the Spirit*. In *From A Drop Of Water*, London, Avalonia, 2009.
D'Este, Sorita (ed). *Hekate: Keys to the Crossroads*. London, Avalonia, 2006.

Figure 21 - Offerings by Emily Carding

PAEAN TO HEKATE

BY SHANI OATES

TO HEKATE AND JANUS

Hail, many-named Mother of the Gods, whose children are fair
Hail, mighty Hekate of the Threshold
And hail to you also Forefather Janus, Imperishable Zeus
Hail to you Zeus most high.
Shape the course of my life with luminous Light
And make it laden with good things,
Drive sickness and evil from my limbs.
And when my soul rages about worldly things,
Deliver me purified by your soul-stirring rituals.
Yes, give me your hand I pray
And reveal to me the pathways of divine guidance that I long for,
Then shall I gaze upon that precious Light
Whence I can flee the evil of our dark origin.
Yes, give me your hand I pray,
And when I am weary bring me to the haven of piety with your winds.
Hail, many-named mother of the Gods, whose children are fair
Hail, mighty Hekate of the Threshold
And hail to you also Forefather Janus, Imperishable Zeus,
Hail to you Zeus most high.

(HYMN VI, PROCLUS)

Though one of the simplest Procline Hymns, revealed herein are three fundamental deific attributes germane to hearthstone and threshold boundaries, including secular and Temple constructions.

In the first and perhaps finest examples of these, *Hekate Propolos,* and *Hekate Phosphoros,* as sentinel and vain glorious psychopomp, she takes us through the gate and beyond. Twinned enigmatically with Janus as guardians of all such thresholds, portals, gateways and liminalities, *Hekate Propylaia* is presented in perhaps one of her least celebrated yet most important magical roles. In fact, throughout antiquity, Hekate is benignly valorised, particularly by Hesiod, Homer and within the *Chaldean Oracles,* denoting her public devotions contra to the creative literary motif of poets and playwrights. Many dwellings would have housed a personal shrine dedicated to Her where special offerings on the morning of the New Moon (the 13th day) secured protection from baneful witchcraft and the *'mal occhia.'* These supplemented the more spectacular suppers held at public altars upon crossways and pathways.

Secondly, she features extensively within the complex theologies of Sethian Gnosticism and *The Chaldean Oracles* as *Hekate Soteira,* the Saviour and World Soul, receiving little attention beyond those traditions. So, it is her third role, that of *Hekate Chthonia,* wherein she accrues extensive testimony. This serpentine mother is the matrix of life and death – she is both midwife and reaper, leading us in, out and beyond all worlds. We may easily construe these three primary functions of the Divine Hekate, or *Deva Primal* as cognate with the *Muses, Charites* and the *Moirae* respectively.

When comparing the functional and mystical qualities of the *'Supreme Triad'* within transcriptions drawn from the Sethian Gnosticism of the *Nag Hammadi* texts and those of the *Chaldean Oracles*, it is immediately apparent that we may consider the Sophianic principle as synonymous with them, especially with regard to Wisdom, Providence and Her role as Redeemer. In order to fulfil these roles, she has been awarded Titanic status, having dominion over the celestial, tidal and geo-magnetic spheres of influence upon and within the geo-centric Universe of the former disciplines.

These particular qualities of Hekate are those with which I am most familiar, and my emphasis and engagement of Her as mystical psychopomp rather than *'witch queen'* per se is also the role she holds within the Clan, so the distinction is for me imperative; for others, perhaps less so. We celebrate *'The Feast of Hekate'* as a reconstruction based upon her dominion as Mother of the Seven Divine Hypostases coterminous with her role as the Supreme Queen of the seven *wind gods* enabling us to embrace and *move through* the Fate she carries. This dedicated Rite is performed on an ancient track-way that is also a bridge over a river, uniting the land, air and sea within the geophysical landscape.

What I hope to share here rather, is a private derivative of this rite, a congress of unsurpassable profundity, experienced several years ago, during a committed and protracted Observance across three consecutive months. This required intense and disciplined study in addition to work and prayer to properly *prepare* the body as a Temple, a Merkabah, the Inner Palace and Treasure of the Beloved. Harmony occurs where all contradictions are dissolved as Truth. Realisation is the experience founded within knowledge. Gnosis is the understanding gained in pursuit of this idiom. The veil blinds us, and so we seek to lift it to peer into the Holy of Holies, the Tabernacle of the Arc, the Grail – even the Seat Perilous, such are Her Mysteries. She is the First Cause and each epiphany brings us closer to Her.

Within the heart, lies the mystery of the *'Golden Mean and the Golden Spiral'* - the perfection of Her Creation, underpinning the visual and creative aesthetics of Sacred Geometry that formulate all principles of harmony within a dynamic triadic unity. It represents the point of inspiration between the *self* and the divine within, the Source we open to in our aspirational search for the Mysteries.

Gorgon-like, it is often said that to look into Her eyes is to invite the *death-stare* of the Basilisk. But the Gorgon Medusa was once an archaic and beautiful Wisdom goddess, whose eyes penetrated even the darkest heart, to burn away illusion, offering instead the vision of Truth. This *death* of the ego has become garbled through misogynist literary tradition as a physical death by a vengeful killer deranged by spite. For it is said that only those who doubt seek to stare face-to-face into the eyes of God, that is to trust and believe only that which the physical eye sees rather than what the heart perceives. Devoid of gnosis, the person stares only into death, which is again not a literal death, but of the eternal return.

Her vital role then is clear, to guard, guide, test and qualify all true seekers into, by and through her dark light. She is the Trimorphis par excellence!

THE TRI-PARTITE RITE:

On the Eve of the New Moon within each of the three months a specific place was chosen to represent each of the three spheres of Her dominion: a cave, by the sea and upon wild upland moor, open to the winds and the stars. For each location, votive *keys* were created, chosen by divination appropriate to metaphysical element. As Mistress of Fate, She made Her choices known to me. Each *votive'* is offered as a *sacrifice* (i.e. that aspect of ourselves) to Fate through its opposite element for our evolution and eventual supremacy over it. For example, as the *serpent tool* or votive is of Earth (Providence - Fate), it must be thrown up into the air and allowed to decay naturally, exposed to Air. Both *torch* and *dagger* symbolise Fire (Gnosis - Nemesis), so must be placed into water representing the Sea/Abzu. The *flail* and *rope* are of Air (Redemption - Grace) and must be buried within the Earth. All her three domains are thus included and transposed into a unique form of the Alchemical Marriage. At each host location for this tripartite rite a closing offering of a raw egg, broken into a shallow dish formed of earth, should left for Her *Genii Locii*.

In the Hekate Rite as given, HER presence is invoked as the Source, First cause and Primal Genetrix. Irrespective of the order in which these three invocatory rites occur, Grace correctly asserts itself as the equilibrating force between Fate and Nemesis - the fulcrum between two extreme forces of activity. The Graces represent action through *passivity*; Fate is interaction and Nemesis is reaction. The *central pillar* and our return to it, is thus always Grace.

These then, are the abridged notes from my diary covering this period:

THE FIRST MOON

Hekatê of the triune Path, I invoke Thee, beautiful Lady of the eternal road,
Chthonian, Oceanic and Celestial One, our Lady of the Saffron Robe.
Sepulchral One, celebrating the ecstatic Mysteries among the Souls of the Dead,
Daughter of Eternal Night, and Mother of Eternal Light, Beloved of Solitude, rejoicing in
the sacred beasts of creation.
Nocturnal One, Lady of Hounds and the Hunt, Invincible Queen.
She whose primal cry peals across the starry heavens,
Ungirt One, having irresistible Form.
Sovereign mistress, Keeper of the Keys of All the Universe,
Torchbearer, Beloved, Lover, Revealer of Truth, Eternal Wanderer.
I pray Thee, Glorious Maid, be present at these Hallowed Rites in thy honour,
Bestowing always Thy graciousness upon the elect.
(adapted from Orphic Hymn 1 to Hekate)

How does one begin to speak of a passion that burns even the stars? Where to mark the journey yet begun in antiquity? How to end a pilgrimage where each step brought me closer to YOU...Many Moons and Suns have risen and set o'er the course of my fragile existence, must I even consider such things?...perusing these thoughts yet having no answers I descend still further into the welcome dark. The inky, fetid odour assails my senses as my feet slip cautiously upon uneven ground. In my hand, the key is warm, it begins to tingle. My thoughts race ahead of purpose....Providence, providence guided me through illusive miasma towards my anticipated Destiny – Your Light has seared my soul; Your Lamp now guides me back to You!

Time is relative and only shadows remain. Pre-empting nothing, I prepare myself in Truth, a declaration of my innermost being. Surrender is the highest cause – the highest love. Inner turbulence electrifies my limbs as I move awkwardly, arching and flexing against the slow rhythm, beaten out by my staff upon the ground. I begin to pace the seven circuits of the labyrinth, seven initiatory steps to Your Void, three clockwise and four in reverse reflecting the retrograde motion of Mercury/Hermes, whose solar and lunar eyes radiate complementary kalas – the psychopompic torches that guide all visitors to the Netherworld regions of Your realms, each turn, is a shift in Fate, a re-working of the thread that binds all Wyrd.

Adrenalin gushes, pounding my heart against my ribs as a low bark echoes through the dank chamber; I think of Anubis, and other canine companions in your subterranean region. ...encouraged thus, my paean peals out to You. Gravid visceral primality surges, piercing all distraction. Time and space are breached as I spin faster now; euphoric, I snatch my breath hurriedly between lines of Invocation...my private ballet unfurls in the Stygian darkness....seeking, seeking in mantic rhapsody, the litany declares my intent. Silence deafens me. Engulfed in Shadow I become entranced within Your sublime aromas - sweet vetivert, honey and pungent Myrrh alight my senses, then with heart pounding, I collapse exhausted into Your embrace - my body is spent, offered up, a willing sacrifice to You ... I am lost, intoxicated within a single moment of forever... the Ouroboric serpent consumes even itself, the purging transit of the Soul through Wisdom, from the bonds of ignorance into the Liberty of Light. The outgrown self must be discarded, a true offering to You.

Liquid star-fire burns sears my throat, the libation is taken...passion is the Shekinah, the Shakti, the Prima Devi Herself – primal fire of all flesh...

Retrieving the key a short time later, I return somewhat shakily to the valley beyond the Cavern's Maw, breathing in the fresh cool air, delighting in its unfamiliar sweetness. Looking skyward, I raise my arms, waiting for the wind to take my small token - the first key to Her Kingdom.

THE SECOND MOON:

Hekate,
Beloved Mistress, Three-faced Gorgon...
Hear my sacred call, chanted upon the seven winds.
Your arms wield the dreaded lamps,
Fearful serpents coil upon Your brow
The roar of bulls sing out from Your lips.
Fierce dogs are dear companions to You,
Hekate,
She of many names and forms.
O ancient one of the Triple Ways, who embraces
Untiring, the Triple Flame of Illumination.
Gracious Maid, protect the traveller upon their quest.
Exalted above all others, Mother of Gods, men and all Nature,
For you frequent the broad and boundless Chasm.
You traverse all Beginnings, and all ways lead to You.
You alone rule all.
For all things are from You, and in you do
All things, Eternal one, find their end.
Hail, bright and dark queen, attend Your epithets,
I burn for You this incense.
Hekate,
Fleeting one of the starry skies, heavenly mover and guardian of seas,
Of mountains, and the many pathways and crossroads to and from all realms,
O nether and nocturnal one.
Infernal frightful one who dines amidst decay,
Amidst the charnel mounds and the bone-yards of the fallen.
You bring torment, Justice, destruction and Illumination.
O serpent-girded Devourer of the untimely dead, strike not madness here,
But hearken to these pilgrim's keys, each to pass thy many gates
Divine and Holy Creatrix, bringer and destroyer of worlds and of life,
Shining guide, accept these offerings,
And bestow benediction upon us.
Iao Hekate, Iao Hekate
(inspired and adapted from an anonymous source)

How soft the light upon the shore. Mist guises the horizon beyond, blurring already my perception of boundaries. Sky melts into Sea, a suffused amber glow, rippling hypnotically, lulling me gently into trance. Water laves my form, cool against the warm sand. Sea spray dampens my skin, layered now in the atomised vaporous Abzu. Prostrate, I expect nothing, but hope for everything.

This time, my paean is a siren-song, each note lost within the bubbling sea-foam, as it dissipates into rocky niches along the promontory. This time, no frenzied dancing, just stillness as the sea's own tide breaks down my consciousness in harmony with the descent of the sun into a fan of topaz, magenta, violet and cerise. Seduced by such unbearable beauty not ethereal, but stark reality, shimmering before me in pearlescent twilight - a poignant reminder perhaps of our mortality? Images are fleeting as I ponder upon the smallest atom of my being... suddenly, I'm filled with an astonishing vision – in a blinding flash I see the event horizon, absolute zero, the primal No-Thing, eternal and infinite space of Ur-Khaos and sentient eye of the Serpent/Dragon Queen - within a fraction of a second this has become the point of force, then the line of form, followed by the triangle of manifestation, the Yoni, hidden eye and Aegis of Hekate, then the square of involution - the Mother, Divine Adoratress, the pentagram of the twin sons/serpents, and finally, the hexagram of the Father.

Rapidly my Mind perceives these seven geometric symbols as emanations from the One, then adding the numbers, they total 21, which becomes 3 added together or divided by the seven. Profound cosmology in explicit simplicity! On some level I am able to acknowledge the Gnostic creative principle of Hekate Soteira, her seven archons and her divine triplicity. Stunned by the experience of this revelation of mankind's origins through sacred geometry, from exploding nuclei to the cube of matter itself, I sit in cogitation - of the cube as a three dimensional representation of Her: Height = Her Starry realm above; Width= the breadth and extent of the earth itself and Depth =the Abzu, Great Sea – Marah, Mary Lucifera, the mournful light over the waters... Hers truly is the Power of the Holy Malachi (the seven shadows of God), the Kingdom (the Throne/Seat) and the Glory (of the Celestial Heavens), the Aleph, Mem and Shin – Triple Flame of Truth... an aeon passes.

Saluting the Sun in its death throes, my pain-wracked body arcs and twists, yet re-vitalised in true Manna. My Oblations made and second key presented, I turn reluctantly homewards. Reflection draws intense humility and paradoxically, strength of purpose, an acute brevity and joy – indescribable heady confusion. Attachment falls away as life attracts new meaning – how am I to make sense of these dichotomies? The veil of illusion has been breached and alarming clarity sears my senses. Seeking answers I immerse myself in theology, in cerebral activity – the words say little, but impressions convey that wisdom is food for the soul yet torture to the spirit.

Without symbols the Mind is blind. Without Love, the Heart is dead. The inner eye, or pearl of Shiva perceives Truth; the inner heart or pentamychos perceives Love and Beauty. Experience is gleaned not in learned practise, but in active knowledge. Without such experience, our perception of reality is merely an illusion. My Mind ruminates relentlessly. Only when we see ourselves reflected through the 'eyes of god' do we truly know ourselves. She annihilates us to engender this evolution. Which is the eidolon, which is the daimon?

Days move on and I sink into morose introspection. Silence is intimate, where chatter maintains separation. It is the Aeon of Set/Anubis. Awareness grows in the wonder of Truth. Visions maintain the tension, creating the dynamic to pursue the pilgrimage to its conclusion. The serene still point generates communion, my petition taken in the exquisite peace, the cessation of all distraction. My Solitude is marked by the Stag, otherworld guardian of boundaries and thresholds, my protective and visionary companion along the inner pathways of exploration.

THE THIRD MOON:

Sleep eludes me, so apprehensively I rise to journey out beyond the sounds of mundanity, into the raw edges of exposed and chilling landscapes, stark and un-welcoming. Bitterly cold, the winds rage in frenzy unbidden across the undulating desolate moorland, swirling gusts tease and pull me hither – undaunted, I march on, struggling to keep afoot upon treacherous terrain. A nightjar screeches eerily ahead of me, and I shiver involuntarily. I resist fear, the negative form of desire, both of which are rooted in the past. Musing further, it occurs to me that desire is but the fallout of a fleeting memory of some pleasurable experience we seek to repeat; fear, conversely is the haunting memory of a pain we seek to avoid. Both, if allowed, become projections of the future, effectively blocking the experience of the present. Brushing aside such distractions, I cautiously continue on my final pilgrimage determined in my mission. My breath keeps pace with step and I am conscious of the final key within my pocket, it is of air and will need grounding upon completion, burying in the rich vibrant earth.

An infinite Lapiz sky blazes overhead, a pure Celestial arc. Adamantine light sparkles from a myriad nimbus points, dazzling my vision. Draco, archaic symbol of Tiamat, Titanic birther of Gods and Mother of all Creation, guardian and protector of the Abzu Void, and the eternal Abyss, winds about the North star above me, as if in embrace. Momentarily mesmerised, the enormity of this concluding Rite yawns before me, and the true awe of it brings me to my knees. Stumbling around, I pause, briefly to gaze ahead – the vista is breathtaking, cogent fire flashes above me, then another in a spectacular display.

"You're showing off now," I mutter...

Biting stinging gusts blow against me, hindering every step, hours seem to pass before I reach my destination, when reason tells me it is but two miles. Disorientated but determined, I cast aside my heavy woollen cloak, desiring ease of movement. Poised at last I focus, lowering my eyes to the eye within - 'the nub of the storm.' Raising my arms for the final time, I open my heart, singing out my supplication, slowly at first, increasing the tempo until glossolalia ensues... my Novena, mystic rosary of renewal is complete, all now is grist to the Mill of the Winds, whirling, raging, lashing about me now. Captured within its dense vortex I am oblivious to all else, rent...head pounding, heart racing, I fall, fall, fall into a symphony of pure bliss... ... ... overwhelmed, I sink... ... ... the Noetic Saffron flame of Sophia unfurls, pulsing, coursing through every cell... I am on fire!

Each level a flaming stem upon the blazing trident of Shin, the spiral antakharana bridge combining Sophia (Mind) and Shekinah (Passion) within Barbelo, the Xvarenah of Grace, the Pleromic World Soul. Moth to Her Eternal Fire, it is too fierce, and so, fazed and shivering, the Herald of Dawn transforms my Paean into a Glorious Magnificat...

Mother,
Naked I stand before You.
My arms raise in supplication to you,
Even as the arc of Your Celestial Canopy,
Engulfs me beneath its comforting radiance.
Hail O Bounteous and Beautiful One,
She of the Bright Hair of shining Serpents.
Hissing Queen, I am dazzled by Your Light!
Your Terrible Form compels me to You.
"Dance with me" You say,
And so I dance.
Enrap't, entranced, I am lost in You.
Thus entwined we syncopate the Universe.
Your lips part, uttering the Seven Wisdom Kalas,
The Arcane Winds – The Holy Malachi.
Each, pare at my being, layer by layer.
The Rhythm of my heart, is the rhythm of my soul,
Offered, beating to you, I am alive, only in You.
In Eternity, You hold the flame of my destruction.
Truth is Veiled – I change, but cannot Die,
Except in You!
You are my Guide, my Refuge and Salvation.
Shadow, breathe steady.
Spirit flies free to fuse with the light
"Dance with me" You say,
Swaying, faster, I desire only to sink into Your Great Sea,
To perch upon Your Holy Mountain,
To burrow into Your Cavernous Abyss.
Lift me then as a wave, a leaf, a cloud,
My Will is Thine!
A maelstrom of madness,
I dance into the dark,
Into the Glorious Matrix that is You.
I taste the rainbow, riding its arc to You!
O Lamp of Wisdom feed the flame of the Beloved.
Sentinel of Light, bind the Sepulchre!
Your reflection reveals our shadows.
O Magnificent darkness,

O divine effulgent light,
O re-birther of souls,
Hearken to my entreaty!
Mother of phantoms, stars and all vision,
Illuminate me that I might see Your True Form.
Open me from within.
Pierce me with your Glittering Eye
Lend me Your Veil of Sleep.
Death is Your gift.
Silence is Your Holy Word.
Mother,
I can dance no more.
Mother,
Naked I stand before You,
Quivering in Your wake!

BIBLIOGRAPHY

Turner, John D. *The Figure of Hecate and Dynamic Emanationism in the Chaldean Oracles, Sethian Gnosticism and Neoplatonism.* University of Nebraska, in Lincoln the Second Century Journal 7:4 (1991), 221-232.
Vogt, E (ed). *Procli Hymni.* Weisbaden, 1957

Figure 22 - Animal Headed Hekate, Photograph by Emily Carding

Figure 23 - Valkyrie by Emily Carding

THE HEKATINE STRAIN

HEKATE AND TRADITIONAL WITCHCRAFT

BY TRYSTN M. BRANWYNN

In Traditional Witchcraft, we are seen as paying a lot of attention to our work within the Luciferian Stream. Indeed, many writers from the outside have tried to call us *"god centred"* and *"male oriented"*. Our lore is rife with tales of the Fall of Spirit into flesh and the promethean gift of divine awareness – that we call the Fire in the Head. We deal with the story of the Fallen Ones, how they became bound into the Earth, and how their divine natures as the Bene Elohim thus became bound into the forms of humanity.

Striding through all of this, through mythology and history, with his hammer in hand we meet the larger-than-human figure of Cain. We see him as the Man or Prisoner in the Moon (as described by Robert Cochrane, in the *Robert Cochrane Letters*, p164); disparaged first murderer; Master of the Four Winds, and the Omega of *"Alpha and Omega"*.

But in our homage, if you look, you will find another, more shadowy, figure. Less understood, even more complex, and more mysterious, we call her *"The Queen of the Castle of Roses"*. We find her every bit as mighty as our Cain/Woden. While he gallops across the sky and through the pages and words of myth and history upon his black horse, with the four white feet (Scottish Flotsam, Traditional Horsemen's Toast); she walks among the tombs and weeps silvery, moonlit tears over the grave of the First Slain. He flexes a powerful arm, wielding his mastery of Wind and Fire; she, like Lilith, births, lovingly slays, and rebirths those who are able to become his successors. These are his sons and daughters – the Witches – today's Nephilim.

Her hidden name varies from strain to strain. Indeed, I was once cautioned by Shani Oates, Maid of the *Clan of Tubal Cain*, that to become too focused on one spirit-name can be foolish, even dangerous as it can lead one into a maze of illusions. But one of the names, whispered upon the breeze and just short of hearing, as well as carried within our lore, is: *Hekate*.

Hekate carries a long association with sorcery, and indeed with Traditional Craft. Her influence extends far beyond her Mediterranean home regions and into Europe and Britain and Ireland, and thence the Americas. Many attempts have been made to pin her down and to neatly pigeonhole her. All of these fail, due to their proponents' oversimplification and to the incredible complexity of the Queen of the Crossroads.

Two cosmological symbols, house the complex of associations and understandings that we draw upon in our work. These serve us as the bones to which, the muscles of myth and rite attach. This is a very common analogy for us, and the tie-in to the human body is very appropriate as we view everything in our cosmos as connected to, and mirrored in, the human form. Thus, when we speak of the Rose, and her Castle, we refer not only to symbols found at the stellar and land levels, but very much to the Rose in every woman. The names we give to these symbols are: The Crossroads and the Castle of Roses and they are, like everything else in our cosmology, inextricably linked. To describe one is to describe the other.

The Crossroads is the symbol-form we will concentrate upon, and I will try to take you on a journey through its labyrinthine associations. On the surface, it seems a simple symbol. We see merely a place where two roads meet at right angles. They join, and then each continues on in its own direction.

This figure already carries a host of occult associations. Traitors were hanged and buried, and thieves gibbeted, in crossroads. The mandrake – sacred to Hekate - was thought to spring from the voided semen of these individuals. This gives the plant a complex, multi-layering of symbolism not unlike that of the Goddess, herself. These run from the toxic and saturnine, to the fertile and venusian, to the psychopompic and mercurial. As Hekate carries keys of all of these natures, it should not surprise us that a root prominent in her lore should do so as well.

Hekate carries with her the association of Saturn, as his Lady, Fate. In Greek Mythology, we can see her as the handmaid of Persephone, the Queen of Hades, whose name translates most easily as 'Screaming'. We can tie this to several interesting items, one being the Castle of Weeping, which can seen for our purposes here, as the north tower in the Castle of Roses, and another being a quality of the ritual practice known as the "Witches' Cry," (referred to by Robert Cochrane) although this ritual act has additional content and associations of its own. One can understand the eerie, keening sound of the Cry as an invocation to Hekate/Persephone.

In the associations with Saturn, we can find some very important keys. Saturn, of course, rules time, and therefore both life and death, or creation and destruction, and all of the processes of change that take place between. Operating as Fate, Hekate therefore decrees the orderly passage of these processes via cause and effect. Thus, she is both the Great Mother and the Cruel Mother of our Lore. As the Luciferian mythology deals with the overthrow of Fate by the divine awareness – first freeing itself from and then combining with the unconscious and instinctual – we see in this role that Hekate works as the Cruel Mother, who harshly tests her aspirants while admitting us to the Mystery Experience that allows us to cast off the chains that bind those who are ruled by the instinctual and who offers her children up to the sacrificial rites of magical death and rebirth.

She operates here as Great Adversary, Great Temptress, Great Oracle, and Great Ally, all in the same sequences of experiences. We can also see these roles mirrored by figures in other myths. We can see a part of this pictured in the Tarot Trump: Judgment, which often depicts figures rising from the tomb, and understand this to mean the survival of the magical ego-death by the Soul, rather than the "resurrection of the body," or the "rapture," invented by the wishful thinking of Christian literalists. Another part of this symbolism can be seen in two of Hekate's totemic animals: The Serpent and the Hound.

The Serpent has long been a symbol of Wisdom. *Genesis 3:1* says *"The serpent was more crafty than any of the wild animals ..."* and goes on to have it offer Eve the fruit of Knowledge. Her acceptance is, of course, badly misunderstood as *"original sin"* when it should be seen as *"the end of sin."* *Sin* is properly understood as the doings of nature. We understand it as a distraction from higher purpose by fear or illusion. It is therefore a behaviour that stems from unconscious, instinctive reactions. The Serpent by contrast, offers awareness, and understanding of conditions of which, the biblical primordial couple had been kept in ignorance, previously, by the machinations of the Elohim. Many occultists understand this as a manifestation of the Seraphim (*Fiery Serpent*) Samael, Archangel of Mars. The Sumerian Lilith mates with a Serpent – again Samael – and is thus united with him. The serpent acts, of course, as an agent of change, but what interests me here is his mating with Lilith. This, for me, creates a hermaphroditic image, consistent with the nature of Hermes (or Mercury), who is also associated, sometimes as son, sometimes as lover, with Hekate, who also shares his psycho-pomp traits. In this image, we see Samael, as the representative of Force and Spirit, mated to Lilith's human form and flesh.

When we take these ideas to Hekate, who wears serpents as her girdle, we find that she acts in much the same manner as both of these figures. As Mistress of the Crossroads, she clearly stands at the point where Force meets and mates with Form. She presides over the processes of change, creation and destruction that this interaction precipitates. She certainly acts as a sorceress and Goddess of Lust, witness how many such spells invoke her power. She also acts in much the same way as Samael, granting her initiates magical, and some would say, divine awareness along with access to knowledge that is written upon the winds or hidden in plain sight, just as is the simple, even silly, fact of Adam and Eve's nudity.

In Traditional Witchcraft, we can also draw a second symbolism from the fact that Hekate's girdle comprises twin serpents. This references the Caduceus of Hermes, also seen arising from the crotch of Levi's Goat of Mendes figure. For us, this represents the force of the Serpent who lies coiled about the roots of the word tree. Hindu mythology refers to this symbol and its attendant force as Kundalini and experience of it begins with a heated stirring at the base of the spine, coupled with intense arousal, and then a sensation of fire shooting up the spine – much as the caduceus arises from the groin of the Baphometis – to explode when it strikes the base of the skull. In this hyper-aware state, one can have a variety of magical experiences ranging from seeing visions to uttering oracles. Again, working with Hekate is certainly known for conferring these sorts of experiences.

The Hound, we find operating in a number of different ways, but for the Traditional Witch, the Hound remains a particular bi-united symbol. Anyone familiar with the rites ascribed to Hekate from Classical times knows that dogs were sacrificed to her. We can see a more modern echo of this in the 18th and 19th Century sorcery used to produce The Churchyard Grim. Whether Hekate was directly invoked in this operation is a matter for question, but the symbols of the dog, the sacrifice, and the resting places of the dead remain unmistakable. This was very much a working in her realm, whether a Christian doing or not.

For the Traditional Witch, the dog symbolizes the animal and the instinctual on two levels. First we see the domestic dog, man's best friend, who has served as companion, hunting partner, herder, and guard for millennia. The second is that of the dog's direct, species ancestor – the wolf - who has been likewise maligned for millennia. All one needs do to see this latter is browse the repertoire of common knowledge. Tales such as *Little Red Riding Hood,* featuring the *"Big Bad Wolf"* leap out at us. The epithet *"wolfshead,"* meaning *"outlaw"* comes hot on their heels, as does the more familiar *"wolf in sheep's clothing,"* along with the biblical comment from *Matthew 10:16, "I am sending you as sheep among wolves."*

In Traditional Witchcraft, one comes to understand that man's best friend and the big bad wolf are, in fact, one and the same. Both are *Canis lupis.* However, one symbolizes the fearsome, running wild and unbridled in the dark places of the wilderness and in our imaginations, whilst the other remains, we hope, leashed and kennelled. Nevertheless, we all experience fear when approaching a doorway guarded by a barking dog. Indeed, atavistically, we see the old churchyard as a haunted threshold into the Underworld, guarded by its snarling Grim. This, of course, reminds us of the story of Orpheus, who must pass through the threshold of Hades' domain – also the demesne of Hekate. To do so, he must confront, and overcome, Cerberus – a three headed dog and clearly, right on the face, a symbol for Hekate.

Thus the dog becomes a symbol for fear. This is one of our deepest and most primal emotional reactions. It comes from our primitive, reptilian brain, and operates as our self-preservation mechanism, provoking one of two responses: Fight or Flight. In modern times, we can see the fight response in nearly any violent or self-defensive behaviour. We can also see fear expressed as anger when either of these mechanisms is thwarted by circumstance. We feel cornered and we respond harshly and angrily. In occult terms, this understanding covers the gamut of instinctual, emotional response, while the higher emotions – love, trust, loyalty – we understand as products of our divine awareness.

In the Initiation sequences of ritual, we induce fear to provoke a confrontation between these two forces – the higher emotions of love and trust, or the *"serpent's gifts"* – and the instinctual self-preservation of that layer of the psyche we term The Beast. In the figure of Hekate Soteira, we see these two symbols combined into a single form. This is to say: The Archangel (or Freud's Superego) symbolized by the serpent head and the Beast (the Id) symbolized by the dog head, united. I find it worthwhile to note that the Soteira depiction does not display a human head. For the Traditional Witch, this indicates that the middle layer of the psyche, the Man (Freud's Ego, which we now understand as a social construct rather than a *"self"*) has been removed. It has died. We can find references to this death of the ego self, and the three-stage process that works it, in many sources of Lore. Two of the most accessible are the *Gospel According to Matthew 4:1-10,* where the Christos – after forty days of fasting – confronts his beast and overcomes it in what some call the Temptation Game; and the Fourth Branch of the Welsh *Mabinogi,* where Lleu Llaw Gyffes must overcome the three curses sworn upon him by his mother, Arianrhod.

In the first example, the Christos confronts the body's (Beast's) fear of death, brought on by extreme privation, when he is tempted, and refuses, to turn stones in loaves of bread. The message here practically shouts: *"Give in to the fear, worship the Beast. The body is gratified and the soul withers and dies."* Frank Herbert was more than right (in his novel *Dune*) when he said *"Fear is the mind killer."* Fear is the soul killer. I find it worthwhile to note that Fundamentalists within the established religion of Christianity operate in a manner exactly contrary to this principle. Their leading demagogues do everything in their power to terrorize their own followers into towing the party line. The same can be said for nearly any established form of religious dogmatism. The objective, clearly, has nothing to do with redemption and freedom, as promised in its Holy Writ, but clearly everything to do with fearful servitude and control. Sadly, many Pagan and Occult organizations seem to be headed down the same slippery slope.

In the second example Gwydion, helping Lleu, reverses the fear key and directs it back upon Aranrhod. He deceives her into a panic with a mirage of an invading Viking (Lochlann) fleet. Aranrhod has sworn that Lleu will never gain the arms of adulthood – never mature past the childish and instinctual – until she arms him, this is to say, until she admits him into the world of mature awareness. In a desperate bid for self-preservation, she does so. I think it interesting to point out that Arianrhod translates, not as the popular *Silver Wheel*, but rather as *Round Hill*. This can be seen as denoting a burial mound. So again we find references to Fate – as the fate of all living things is to die – and to the Underworld realm of Hekate via the tomb.

But Hekate Soteira is not a bi-form but rather a tri-form figure, and we have yet to account for the horse head in our examination. For the Traditional Witch, the horse has several associations and all of these will serve us well. First, we can examine the well known Sovereignty Key. We find this consistent with our earlier description of Hekate as Queen of the Crossroads, this is to say, Queen of the Four Cardinal Directions. In Traditional Witchcraft, we understand this as Queen of the World, or World Mind. This view is also consistent with the Neo-Platonist understanding of Hekate. We can also understand her as thus the Anima Mundi and Queen of the Axis Mundi, as her consort is King. I will go further and suggest that the Axis and its Royal Couple are one and the same. She is the altar of sacrifice, while he is the sacrifice upon it.

In Traditional Witchcraft, we symbolize this concept in our use of the Stang, a forked pole set upright in the north of our working area. Robert Cochrane, in a letter to Qabalist William G. Gray, references this understanding in a line of rhyme: *"... the staff that's owned by the maid ..."* Many popular writers have attempted to equate this symbol with the Horned God of Wicca, but this is a matter of simple misunderstanding. The easiest and most intimate way to understand it accurately is to visualize the Maid or Magistra, standing upright in the centre of the working space – the Crossroads – with her arms raised to the night sky. The Maid and her stang are one and the same.

To bring this discussion back to our examination of Hekate's horse head, we must look back to the Northern Traditions that partly spawned Traditional Witchcraft. In Norse Mythology, the name of the World Tree, or Axis Mundi, is Yggdrasil or the Horse of Odin, and indeed he spends nine days and nights hanging upon Yggdrasil in order to gain the insight to create the runes or the written language of the North. This clearly shows the sacrificial nature of the Horse, and when we take into account the other associations we've examined, we can see that the female Axis Mundi – Hekate – serves as the vehicle for this initiatory sacrifice. The other Horse of Odin – Sleipnir – is described as eight-legged, for us this signifies the eight directions or Quarters and

Cross Quarters of the Compass Rose, a figure found in the marginal information of many old maps. We can also see in this the Horsemen's reference to Cain's *"Black horse with the four white feet"*.

This brings us back, once again, to the Crossroads – although it is now an eight directional figure – signifying the centre of the world and all directions that meet there. Coupling this with what we know of the associations of the World Tree and the Stang, we find that this works as a symbol for Hekate, and connects to her horse head as well. The image conveys her role as sovereignty bearer for the manifest world, as well as indicating the vehicle, which one may use in navigating her otherworld.

BIBLIOGRAPHY:

Cochrane, Robert; & John Evan Jones, ed. M. Howard. *The Robert Cochrane Letters*, Somerset, Capall Bann, 2002

Cochrane, Robert. *Witches Esbat*, in *New Dimensions Magazine* Vol. 2.10, November 1964

D'Este, Sorita (ed). *Both Sides of Heaven*, London, Avalonia, 2009

D'Este, Sorita & David Rankine. *Hekate: Liminal Rites*, London, Avalonia, 2009

Herbert, Frank. *Dune.*(Fiction) London, Ace Trade, 2005

Jackson, Nigel, & Michael Howard. *The Pillars of Tubal Cain.* Somerset, Capall Bann, 2000

Jones, Evan John; Robert Cochrane, ed. M, Howard. *The Roebuck In The Thicket.* Somerset, Capall Bann, 2001

Levi, Eliphas. *Transcendental Magic.* Maine, Weiser Books, 1972

Parker, Will. *Four Branches of the Mabinogi.* California, Bardic Press, 2007.

Schodde, Rev. George F. *The Book of Enoch.* Ohio, Capital University, 1882

The Holy Bible, New International Version, Authentic Media, 2008.

The Lutheran Hymnal. St Louis, Concordia Publishing House, 1941

Online Resources

Scottish Flotsam on Scottish Radiance: A Journal on Scotland 2008
http://www.scottishradiance.com/flotsam/flotsam602.htm

Trubshaw, Bob, Black Dogs: Guardians of the Corpse Ways, At The Edge Magazine, Heart of Albion Press, 1996
http://www.indigogroup.co.uk/edge/bdogs.htm

Heiner, Heidi Anne, Sur La Lune Fairytales, 1998, Little Red Riding Hood, from Charles Perrault 1697
http://www.surlalunefairytales.com/ridinghood/index.html

Olive Bray trans. The Elder or Poetic Edda, commonly known as Sæmund's Edda, part I: The Mythological Poems, London, pp. 61-111.
http://www.pitt.edu/~dash/havamal.html#runes

Figure 24 – Shrine of Hekate

Figure 25 - Dark Mother Shrine by Paul Harry Barron

Figure 26 - Thracian Hekate with her Animal Emanations by Georgi Mishev

PERSONALIZING THE MYSTERY

DEVELOPING A BOND WITH THE LADY OF THE CROSSROADS

BY RAVEN DIGITALIS

Lady Hekate has been featured in everything from Shakespeare's *Macbeth* to the wonderfully Witchy film *Practical Magic*. This ancient goddess's reign, due in part to her association as a Queen of Witches (whether you go by an ancient or modern definition of the '*W-word*'), is likely to perpetuate in human consciousness and the magickal arts for as long as humankind exists. This is the nature of archetypes, of deities, of those worshipped and praised – even if it appears that a god has become forgotten or obsolete, we see it resurfacing in one form or another. This is human necessity; for every energy, emotion, action, mood, or intention that exists, a parallel can be drawn with a deity, a sephira, a colour, and just about anything else; the world is full of associations and archetypes.

Even if a magician believes that all gods have been created by the minds of man, it doesn't negate the fact that every deity exists in his or her or xyr own right. It's equally limiting to believe that the *"I"* identity—this ego attached to our own minds—is solid. One of the beautiful (yet sometimes perplexing) truths of reality is Divine Paradox: everything *is*, but everything simultaneously *is not*. We all exist individually, but are simultaneously one in the same. There is separation, but there is simultaneous unity. We can apply these laws to gods and spirits just as easily as we can to ourselves – or anything else in existence!

To understand a god or goddess, we must understand both the archetypes they embody, and the cultural context from which they originate. Magick, I believe, requires a balance of academia and experience; of the mental and the emotional. Lady Hekate can (and probably should!) be approached in numerous ways.

As deities are worked with, their *egregore*—or astral energy pool—gathers in strength. It's for this reason that *"current"* gods, including Yahweh, Allah, and Christ, have become such powerful entities. Lady Hekate, however, has fallen out of the spiritual limelight (like virtually all Pagan gods have, save perhaps Hinduism) in terms of mass-familiarity. This renders Hekate's energy hidden and preserved from the congregation of monotheists across the globe – just as she would have it, I'd imagine!

I tend to view Hekate as the embodiment of mystery. Even the most advanced scholar of ancient Greece can only theorize her origins. Few deities can claim similar elusiveness!

Hesiod's *Theogony* attributes the powers of *every* god to Hekate – wow! Hesiod also mentions that (regardless of her hidden history), Hekate is the deity most honoured by Zeus himself. There is something special and beckoning about our Lady.

Something very palpable, but something we can't completely grasp no matter how hard we try.

When forming your relationship to our Lady—or with any esoteric force, for that matter—you must really consider which aspects you wish to work with. Deities have many Tarot cards up their sleeves, and your work is a matter of how you wish to tap into these forces on a personal level. Hekate's associations as the Initiatrix and Guide are two of her most powerful attributes, and it's this guiding light that can illuminate your personal connection to her incredible power. Just as the moon is the night-time eye in the sky, Lady Hekate offers up a most powerful light of clarity and spiritual quickening. For those who are just beginning to work with her, perhaps these initiatory aspects are key, at least *"initially"* – yes, pun intended.

Hekate is much more than just some hag-crone goddess; such a view is both incomplete and is (in my eyes) demeaning to her full essence. As most gods do, she carries a multitude of deep associations – and was even viewed as a virginal figure in antiquity! (The information in this tome, as well as in Sorita d'Este's other Hekate books, will help *"new"* Hekate-workers learn some of these attributes.)

If you are comfortable working with the darker, more hidden aspect of your psyche, you are likely to feel comfortable working with Hekate. Since you are reading this anthology, odds are that you've already heard the calling.

She is dark, yes, but there's more to her than the common chthonic associations. Darkness takes many forms, both positive and negative, and Hekate embodies many of these energies. As with virtually all deities, archetypes, and spiritual forces, there are always numerous sides to the esoteric coin.

Regardless of the lunar associations, which most neo-pagan disciplines associate strictly with Goddess energy, Hekate is accessible to both men and women. Mythology backs this up: In the *Argonautica*, Jason himself performed rituals in honour of Hekate, as prescribed by Medea; herself a Priestess of Hekate.

Reasons for which you may choose to summon, honour, and work with Hekate include the following: protection of entrances (the house and home), illumination of one's Will or spiritual destiny, invoking wisdom and clarity in any given situation, necromantic work (including summoning or leaving offerings for a deceased loved one), divination, death and dying, wealth and abundance, shamanic shapeshifting work, occult study, academia, intellectualism, dream prophecy, balancing the menstrual cycle or menopause, sexuality, ageing, canine health/protection, working with earthbound disincarnates or ghosts, fertility of the soil, fishing and farming luck, seeing through façades or illusion, psychic work, past-life regression, bringing justice to a situation, animal breeding, victory in contests, cursing a violator, the protection of children, and the process of childbirth. Hekate is a *"fringe"* goddess, and she is second to none at assisting people who are in unique situations or feel as if they exist on the edge of society or are in some way marginalized—in this sense, Hekate is a master shaman.

I have successfully worked with Hekate for a series of intensely potent magickal workings focused on healing trauma and emotional wounds. Because of Luna's associations with the deep mind, the psyche, and the unconscious, it felt only right to call forth the aid of our goddess. This sort of work is directly linked to Hekate's associations as a master Initiatrix: a force that helps a person cross the threshold into the next level of ability, awareness, or social standing.

Because so much of the anthology you hold in your hands is focused on Hekate's role as *'Initiatrix and Guide,'* you may wish to observe the accompanying articles and come to your own conclusions about the aspects of your life Lady Hekate can assist in illuminating. As Luna is the cosmic light in the dead night sky, so Hekate embodies the sacred flame of clarity and wisdom within us all. If a person works regularly with Hekate's initiatory aspects, they should expect the clarity she offers to permeate all aspects of one's life—especially those things one avoids or doesn't want to face!

Reasons for which a person would choose to work with the Lady should not be taken as strict or limited guidelines. While it may be a contrary ideal to some of the more strict systems of esoteric or ceremonial work, I am fully of the camp who believes that a deity does not necessarily demand rigidly-structured, Masonic-based rituals all the time—these most certainly have their place, but a balance of the *scientific/operative* realm and the *intuitive/theurgic* realm are key for a more actualized connection to a spiritual force of any type. Because of Hekate's alignment to mystery and the unknown, an extreme potential for personalization exists and can easily be expounded on.

Hekate can assist with a number of magickal and personal issues. If you sense resistance while working with the Lady, simply flow with the vibrations at hand by changing your intentions. Allow me use an example: say you are in the midst of petitioning Hekate for the purpose of gaining a new occupation, but feel an overwhelming sense of disapproval from the goddess. At that point you may wish to bring to mind some of Hekate's primary associations and alter your intentions in the moment to something more appropriate, such as gaining the ability to see the *direction you are meant to take* in terms of employment. Even if you subscribe to the idea that all deities were once created by human minds, remember that deities are very much of their own essence; an individual consciousness with responses and characteristics all its own. Deific petitioning isn't merely a way to deceive or trick a deity (though I wouldn't say the ancient Greeks took issue with such a thing!), but is a way to more acutely actualize and personalize your connection.

If proper respect is given to this powerful goddess, one can petition her help for a wide variety of reasons. For those who have worked with her for an extended period of time, a direct link and relationship is honed; this opens the door to a multitude of additional purposes for which the goddess can be summoned, not least of which may be therapeutic communion, or simply the desire to be in the comforting presence of the potent and divine mother herself. Indeed, our Lady can help us sleep and give us visions in the dreaming.

You can choose to work with Lady Hekate for reasons of destruction: destroying a person you don't like, causing unwarranted harm, cursing someone into a state of fear... but I wouldn't recommend it. Spirituality and ethics, for some people, is something divorced from the magickal arts. This unfortunate view is often founded in reasons of inferiority complexes or insecurities (a person feels the need to compensate with destructive, controlling, self-asserting power). Like any neutral force, magick can be used in any way. Hekate certainly has aspects of darkness and destruction, of chthonic power and death—but still, without exercising proper spiritual ethics, the magick performed with the goddess will be for naught. As an aside, it should be known that some of the darker, more destructive attributes of Hekate weren't formed until *well after* some of her more positive and life-protecting associations were formed. I feel it's particularly more potent to access this deity's magick in its more ancient form.

You can choose to supplicate yourself before the Lady, to worship at her feet, to beg her for mercy and magickal prowess; or you can command her, demanding that she do your bidding... but once again, I wouldn't recommend it. Fear is a strong vibration, and is something that's been used to control the masses throughout all of time. Demeaning yourself before this goddess—or any deity—puts you in a position of *"lesser than thou."* Is this empowering? Is it even aligned to a person's true personality type? Is it really a sign of respect, and is it even really genuine? While it would be silly to think that humans and gods are one in the same, I believe it was Uncle Al Crowley who expertly summed it up by saying that humans are little gods and gods are mighty humans. I tend to think that treating deities as we treat good friends is a step in the right direction. (If you're asking a good friend for a ride in their vehicle, a small loan, or advice on a situation, do you supplicate yourself at their feet? I hope not—albeit in jest!)

Hekate is not a mere force to be reckoned with; such a perception can easily divorce a person from the true levels of communion possible with our Lady. Instead, she is a force to be communed with, appreciated, respected, and loved.

It's essential to pay your proper respects to a deity when choosing to work with them. Ideal offerings for Hekate include the following: snakeskin, dog hair (ideally black), deer fur or bones, wolf claws/fur/bones, a lit white candle, honey, ice, crow's feathers, apples, an antiquated key, black poplar, oak leaves, cannabis/marijuana/hemp, yew, willow, cypress, hazel, myrrh, mugwort, and poppy/opium. Some researchers have linked the herbal family of *Solanaceæ* to Lady Hekate. This family includes a wide variety of plants and herbs including tomato, potato, eggplant, and petunia. The dark side of the Solanaceæ family is its group of toxic plants often called the *nightshades*. These include belladonna, henbane, datura, mandrake, and tobacco. Because of their poisonous, maligned properties, these dark herbs became known as *Witches' Herbs* in the Middle Ages for obvious reasons: Witches are evil-doers!

Another unique idea for a Hekate offering is something of your own creation. Because Hekate is associated partially with inspiration and art, you may wish to craft your own art in her honour. You may also wish to dedicate dog food (preferably a meaty bone or wet organic dog food) in her name, and feed it lovingly to one of her canine children.

As far as ceremonial timing, Hekate is a lunar goddess: both the full moon and the new moon are ideal times of the month (with blue moons, black moons, and lunar eclipses being particularly powerful).

The best location for a person to work with Hekate is at the crossroads in either a cemetery or dog park (yes, a park where people walk and play with their dogs—hey, there is much residual canine energy *'afoot'* in such a location!). I have had much success communing with Hekate at graveyard crossroads, have worked with her numerous times in my own Temple/altar space, and have even extended my magick with her to including meditative Gnosis in an ancient hotsprings (the lunar/wombic energies are just too perfect). I urge the reader to not only be intelligent and traditional when working with Hekate, but also to experiment, modify, and otherwise personalize your levels and methods of communion.

So: what types of initiation are you seeing in your life? An elevation into a higher awareness? Realizing your spiritual Will? Stepping into your ability as a healer, diviner, magician, parent, or something else? What aspects of your life, of which you are in the process of progressing, could possibly be considered 'of Hekate,' if you will? These are the things most suitable for your magickal work with this ancient goddess. Remember that you have, on one level or another, *chosen* to progress to the next step in something. The very choice to walk one particular path over another is the very essence of the crossroads.

As you deepen your work with our Lady, you will discover the ways in which you connect with her energy the best. Let intuition be your guide, and back it with heavy research and respect. Look for Hekate's influence in your life as you work on forming a bond with her. Open yourself to newness as you merge with the essence of our dark-yet-illuminating Lady Hekate.

Figure 27 - The Sun (card) from the Tarot of the Black Mountain by Emily Carding

SUFFER TO LEARN

BY PAUL HARRY BARRON

"Hekate, Hekate, Hekate, Dark Mother,
you walk with me like no other, Dark Mother!"

This was the chant I was muttering under my breath, as I, along with another dozen or so members from my training Circle, was setting my feet upon the path towards the Priesthood of the Wise, miserably trudging over rain saturated Wiltshire hillsides, towards Hekate's Oracle waiting for us at Wayland Smithy, that ancient and sacred monument overlooked by that other famous and equally ancient landmark, the White Horse of Uffington, a symbol that is pertinent to me on account of my Chinese leanings. This was the day of our group's Dedication into the Craft and the axiom, *"Art thou willing to suffer to learn?"* rang aptly in our heads, as clearly, the dank, dark and torrential rain of the British summer was determined to deter and dampen our enthusiasm.

More than a few of our little band were quite prepared to give up and head back to the cars waiting for us in the car park, as this was almost far too great an endurance test for us. But had it not been for the authority and strong-headedness of our High Priestess leading us on our gruelling quest, maybe some might indeed have yielded to the temptation of promised warmth and comfort of the cars' interiors. I, too, was tempted, so tempted, but the chanting blocked out the misery and focusing on the goal, I trundled on.

Maybe the weather was not so much punishing us, as defying us, as in truth, the Patron Goddess of our training circle, Hekate, can demand not just allegiance, but also personal sacrifice and believe me, that afternoon of deprivation of comfort, warmth and dry clothes was a great sacrifice for all. As we arrived at Wayland Smithy, the weather decided that we had been challenged enough and as if by *'Magick'*, the rain stopped and the clouds parted, allowing some bright sunshine to finally filter through and warm our sodden clothes. *"There is no point complaining,"* our HPS declared, *"as I did warn you to wear appropriate clothing!"* Naturally, most of our band were city-dwellers, who had no idea what horrors the countryside could inflict upon them; jeans, trainers and tracksuit-tops were definitely not appropriate apparel for a country ramble in a heavy downpour. I dare not boast too much, but having been brought up in the country, I at least had the perspicacity of predicting the unpredictable and brought waterproofs and decent footwear with me. But even so, if I was miserable, how much more miserable would the others have been, who did not enjoy my modicum of protection from the elements?

On a mundane level, it could be said, that maybe we had just been unlucky with the weather for the day of our Craft Dedication Rite, but there was definitely another mystical element at work. Hekate was and still is a real and powerful entity to me and I have no choice but to concede that She was more than likely to have been in control of the weather in order to test our worthiness before we faced Her Oracle in that dark (but dry!) cavern. She is a Goddess, to whom lip-service is just not good enough. Those whom She calls, must indeed be worthy and be prepared to demonstrate their commitment to Her. And this insufferable trek that we had just undertaken should have been demonstrative enough to separate us, from those who are just following Her to be *"cool"*. The change of weather at the climax of the hike did not go unnoticed by us and we were indeed in awe of what was transpiring and considering the most difficult and unenviable trek we had endured and survived, we truly did feel worthy.

PREJUDICES, OPPOSITION AND DREAMS AND PORTENTS

After Dedication, and while I was progressing on my path towards Priesthood anticipating my First Degree Rite into the Craft, I found it very difficult to initially connect with the Goddess Hekate. Conditioned and influenced by my former Judeo-Christian life and prejudices, I just could not give myself to Her, as I still entertained negative ideas and opinions that made me fearful. I found it difficult to even pick up a book in order to learn more about the subject, let alone worship Her Essence. To cut a long story short, as it was required to perform some devotional work dedicated to Hekate for me to be accepted into the Craft, I had no choice, but to bite the bullet and get on with it, gritting my teeth as I did so. But things would not actually progress until I had recorded my dreams for a month, as we were also required to do. At the end of the month, when I looked through my dream diary in order to analyse the dreams, it was clear that there was a theme running through them: dogs, snakes, death, fires and more. A little concerned and definitely confused, I just scratched my head in puzzlement as to why all these themes had been cropping up every other night – I hesitated to call them nightmares, as despite their dark and gloomy themes, they in no way felt threatening. And so I was eventually compelled by some unknown force (ok, I admit, it was not so much due to esoteric forces, as it was due to the demands from my High Priestess and High Priest nagging me to get on with it) to pick up a book and actually do some research about Our Mysterious Lady. And as I read more and more about Her, it struck me: many of the symbols I had been seeing in my night-time visions were symbols and imagery associated with Hekate, who was clearly trying to communicate with me. You have to understand that I had no prior knowledge of Hekate and so it could not have been my subconscious at work, picking up clues about what I had already read. Till that date, I had barely picked up works on Classical Greek Mythology, and since most of those were aimed at children, they were nice stories with no mention of the Gods' emblems and symbols. She assuredly came to me in my dreams; maybe not nightly, but certainly repeatedly, constantly and persistently. She clearly wanted me and was not going to give up. But as I have already written about my initial experiences with Hekate in *Hekate Keys to the Crossroads* (Avalonia, 2006) I will invite you to read that part of my story there.

REFLECTIONS ON THE UNFATHOMABLE MYSTERIES

After working actively as an initiate in the Craft for almost a decade now (although, I had been sitting on the side-lines for 10 years prior to this, waiting for suitable teachers to appear), today, I can look back and reflect at why I might have been reluctant to work with Hekate in the first place. I have mentioned my prejudice, based on ignorant, religious dogma, but there was something else. Becoming a Priest in the Craft involves growth – spiritual growth. Things change within and without; sometimes they are easy changes and sometimes they are difficult, but they are all necessary for us to grow spiritually. Nobody wants painful changes to happen – we would rather they all changed in a nice and pleasant manner and slowly, please. But when Hekate comes into your life, you need to start cutting away the rotten and the negative from your life, immediately and these changes can be quite dramatic, often traumatic and definitely painful. It is pointless railing against a Goddess that seems to enjoy inflicting pain on us. She doesn't but most of these afflictions have more than likely been caused by our inattention to the way we have been living and we have more than likely attracted these woes upon our own pitiful selves, either by default or through carelessness. Hekate is just a catalyst for stripping your life of things that should have been dealt with a long time ago. If the negative aspects of your life are glued onto you fast, then there is no easy way to rip them off without inflicting some kind of discomfort! And of course, realising this, and wanting a nice quiet life, my nervousness of working with Hekate grew as I had not just a skeleton or two in my closet that needed to be dealt with, but a whole cemetery!

DESCENT INTO HELL AND BACK

There is no denying that there is something dark about Hekate, as She is Goddess of Mystery, Magick, and Witches after all, and let's not forget, Mistress of the Underworld, being the One, who cuts the cord from life to death and then from death to life! The fact that one of Her roles is that of Psychopomp, who leads the way into the Underworld is quite likely one of the reasons for the negative stereotypes that the uninitiated hold. In Christian and Islamic Mythology (not so much Judaic, however), the Underworld (Hades) translates into the Christian version of Hell, a place of eternal Torment and divine retribution.

Originally, the Hebrew term *She'ol* just meant a place of the Dead and was not necessarily a place of torment. It was translated as Hades in the Septuagint, the Greek translation of the Hebrew Bible in the 2nd and 3rd centuries BCE. But the very association of Hekate with Hades/Sheol and especially Hell as a place of punishment was enough to scare anyone away from Her. It is a place associated with evil, Satan and dæmons. Ha-Satan in Hebrew, means The Accuser or The Adversary, an angel under the command of God in Judaism, and in Islam, not necessarily under the influence of Christianity, he becomes a Jinn; but according to the Book of Job in the Hebrew Bible, he did not actually create or cause evil, but instead pointed out the evil that mankind perpetrates on his own accord and without external influence. Despite the fact that the concept of Hell as a place of eternal torment is largely a Christian invention, albeit influenced by Hellenic philosophy, as much of the philosophy of Christianity is, I needed to realise and understand that this, and related doctrine, has no correspondence to the concept of Hades in Classical Greece. And indeed, Hekate would lead those, who had lead exemplary lives into the Elysian Fields, a paradisiacal place, which was more akin to Christian concepts of Heaven.

Before I could shatter those negative millstones from around my neck and move forward, I had to reflect and meditate a little on the World to Come and try to understand why I allowed myself to be influenced by those philosophies/religious doctrine that taught me to fear such a chilling place and try to balance that with common sense, direct experience with the dearly departed (of which I have had many) and modern theological research and thinking.

Many years before I had experienced a near-death experience, whilst I was a student in China. After a protracted bout of food-poisoning, complicated by flu and due to lack of medical attention, pneumonia had set in and I became very dehydrated. At this time my University was on an organised trip to the South of China, so there was no one to watch over me. Until a few of my co-students, who had not gone on the trip looked in on me, as they wondered where I was, and saw me slowing passing into unconsciousness. The alarm was raised and I was rushed to hospital and while floating in and out of my body, I tried to talk to the friends that had accompanied me there to tell them that I was at peace, was pain-free and just wanted to drift off; *"This dying process isn't as bad as I thought"*, I remember thinking to myself. And I felt no threat of doom or judgement and I was happy to go sail up into the Spiritual Realms; although also regretful that I was barely 20 years old and had not yet lived to my full potential and sorry that my friends and family would feel pain and sorrow at my passing. But I was not afraid to die and that is the key! When the antibiotic-laden Intravenous Line was stuck into my arm, there was a sudden jerking sensation as my spirit was hauled unceremoniously back into my body, with a shocking and excruciating bang accompanying the retrieval of my Soul! I gasped at the pain I was suddenly feeling all over my diseased and withered body, angry that I had not been allowed to pass over in peace and go on that Great Journey to the Elysian Fields, but at the same time, still glad to be alive. The British Consulate in Shanghai, where I was living at that time, had already informed my distraught parents back in the UK that they would make arrangements for my body to be repatriated, as they did not expect me to survive the night, according to the doctor's assessment But I had a mission to fulfil and it was not my time to go and survive I did, and I have actively pursued discovery of what my mission is, and having found it I am actively engaged in carrying it out.

This life-changing experience has followed me all my life and it was the catalyst that allowed me to shed the fear of the Grave and of Hekate. From the discussions I have had over the last few years, I get the impression that a number of Priests and Priestesses who have been called to the service of Hekate may also have faced their own mortality and glimpsed into the Mysteries beyond the Veil, either through protracted illness or near-death experiences from accidents. And so, after contemplating the consequences and lessons of my own near-death experience all those years ago, I heaved a great sigh of relief, shed my old way of thinking, like a snake sheds its skin and embraced Hekate Soteira.

PHILOSOPHERS, ETHICS AND VEGETARIANS

It is fair to say that most people who follow one of the Hellenic Traditions believe in some kind of reincarnation. The Classical Philosophers certainly did and this belief directly influenced their dietary choices. A great number of these philosophers, and I mention only Porphyry, Plato and Pythagoras amongst many, were ardent devotees of Hekate and what is significant and maybe surprising on account of the animal sacrifices made in Her honour, is that they were largely staunch and strict vegetarians, teaching their disciples that eating animal flesh is tantamount to cannibalism, since an animal or fish is a living, breathing and feeling creature that is on its own spiritual journey towards becoming human in its next incarnation. While those who indulged in the eating of flesh, would be lowered to the base ranks of animals in their next incarnation. Some of these philosophers also included beans as taboo and forbidden foods. You would correctly assume that much of this is very similar to Hindu teachings on the Transmigration of the Soul, especially those of the Hare Krishna sect. And not all of the teachings of these philosophers were welcomed with open arms, but were sometimes censured and ridiculed.

In modern times, it would be difficult to determine how many followers of Hekate also practice vegetarianism in actuality or even believe in Transmigration of the Soul. But it is safe to say in relation to our diets today that our food products, being easily obtainable from supermarkets, have become denatured and we probably give little thought to where it comes from. In this crazy world, natural foods have become more expensive than processed foods! I used to teach Vegetarianism to schools that had it on their curriculum and I remember once, when asking where ham or beef came from, one of the pupils retorted in all seriousness and without guile, *"From the fridge!"* There was no association at all between the meat on her plate and the slaughter of an animal to produce it. We have become desensitised to the way in which our food is produced. But once under the aegis of Hekate, these and other issues bubble to the surface and need to be dealt with. And this does not always occur in a pleasant way, as I mentioned previously. In my own personal experience, most of the modern-day Hekate followers I have met, although not all, have also been vegetarians of one description or another; many having adopted their diets long before their call to the Service of Hekate. And this is significant in that it is clear to me that there is a historical continuation of dietary practices associated with the worship of Hekate. And what is even more momentous, is that I doubt whether many of those vegetarian followers were aware of their philosophical predecessors from Classical Greece!

Adopting a vegetarian diet was indeed personally important for my own spiritual growth and I had already started along the vegetarian route many years before I became a Priest of the Craft. After initiation, it became even more important for me, as an expression of my ever-developing sense of Ethics. All religious and spiritual/philosophical institutions have a set of Ethical codes to follow, although in Wicca, these are underdeveloped and by no means standard across the different Covens that exist in the world. The Modern Cult of Hekate is no different in this respect, as it is still in its fledgling years. And while we can look back at what the Classical followers preached, we live in the 21st Century and our understanding of the World has changed, as have our circumstances. Therefore any discussion surrounding the Ethics that may be adopted should reflect this. But unlike certain religious institutions that are stuck in the past, we must move forward with the times and scientific enlightenment.

It is certainly clear that modern Ethical discussions generally no longer concern matters such as personal or sexual morality, eating forbidden foods, praying at prescribed times and the role of women, what is blasphemy and so forth; this is something that many of the more fundamentalist Abrahamic religious are still struggling to reconcile in this Modern and increasingly Secular World. Neo-Classical and Neo-Pagan Ethics have almost wholeheartedly jumped onto the *"Eco"* bandwagon, and issues such as The Environment, Deforestation and Desertification, Global Warming, Recycling, Reducing Carbon Emissions; GM vs. Organic crops, Animal Welfare, Child Welfare, Planetary Welfare; Women's Rights, LGBT Rights, Children's Rights; Abolition of Poverty, Slavery and Capital Punishment; Social Justice, Overuse of Medication and the Emergence of New Diseases and indeed Vegetarianism (which addresses and redresses a good many of the above concerns with one fell swoop!) as well as many other concerns are all topics that the New Age (for want of a better word) has engendered, for better or for worse, much to the dismay of Multi-National Corporations and certain evangelical factions in Christendom. And they are certainly topics that the Priesthood of Hekate might be discussing, if they wished to impart a sense of cohesion to the movement.

Even though my life may not revolve around endless ceremonies and rituals to Hekate, my spiritual outlook is definitely directed towards the betterment of myself and ultimately that of the Planet and mankind, including animals! And I like to think that my diet reflects that side of my Spirituality. When I express gratitude, I express it to Hekate; when I wish for a blessing, I petition Hekate and when I eat, I remember Hekate's ancient adherents and through this action, I bring blessing not just to myself, but also to the World.

SACRIFICES

It would be appropriate to mention, at this point, the sacrifices that were carried out in honour of Hekate. There appears to be a dichotomy between the classical vegetarians and those who sacrificed dogs to Her. I am no expert in these matters and I can only give my educated opinion but most World religions have carried out sacrifices at one point or other, although most of them have abandoned them, at least within Western Culture. This may not necessarily be the case in parts of the Middle East, Africa and Latin America, where animal sacrifices are still commonplace. The predominant Culture of the West arguably stems from Judaism and even most Magickal Traditions have a connection with Judaism, including Wicca (oh yes indeed!), through the Kabbalah and its subsequent Grimoire Traditions. Within Judaism, an ancient and prestigious religion, sacrifices were carried out at the Temple in Jerusalem by its priests. These were expiations for sins committed against the Almighty and this theme filtered into Christianity, when Jesus became the sacrificial lamb, whose blood was poured out for the atonement for the sins of mankind. The practice was always controversial in Judaism and in several parts of the Hebrew Bible, it was hinted sacrifices were superfluous and that obedience and prayer, themselves considered a form of sacrifice, were more important. In addition, there is little evidence to support that the Almighty was pleased by these bloody sacrifices and they were sometimes opposed and rallied against by the Prophets. After the destruction of the Temple, prayer substituted sacrifice in the ensuing synagogues of the Diaspora, but Jews today in their Sabbath Liturgy, still pray for the re-establishment of the Temple in Jerusalem in the Messianic Age. Something that causes problems within Orthodox Judaism, as most Jewish authorities would be opposed to the reinstitution of animal sacrifices. So what bearing does this have on the Modern Worship of Hekate for Her Priests? Sacrifices were also criticised by the Classical Philosophers as being an end in itself, rather than a means to an end and as a result, meaningless butchery that gave a corrupt Priesthood access to rich foods. Sacrifices were used to petition the Gods either for their blessings, to avert evil or to appease their anger. I cannot see many of today's Priesthood willing to carry out such acts. If you inspect the Wiccan Liturgy, you can read that the Goddess requires no sacrifice. This section originates from Leland's *Aradia: Gospel of the Witches*, where Aradia is referring to the conditions and consequences of being freed from Slavery to her followers. The vegetarian philosophers, like the Prophets of the Hebrew Bible also rallied against animal sacrifices and I doubt that whether Hekate would also insist on the recommencement of bloody sacrifices. It could be said, that the services, rites and prayers offered up to Her can be viewed as our sacrifices.

WORKING WITH OTHER DEITIES

When you reach maturity as a Priest or Priestess, you finally come into your own power and usually go on to form your own group, circle and/or coven and as I have hinted at previously, many Craft Covens do adopt Hekate as their matron Goddess, as my own Covens have in the past. But once you have experienced working with Her, it becomes difficult to work with other Deities. Very hard. I know; I tried and had limited success. Despite the various Deities being invoked at the appropriate time of the year, such as Brighid at Imbolc, or Cerridwen at Samhain; or maybe because of your location, such as invoking the Welsh Gods when you are in Wales, I could never really establish a two-way connection with them, with the exception of the Genii Loci, who are usually the first to flock to an outdoor celebration, anyway.

My frustrated focus always returned to a delighted Hekate. There was a short-circuit somewhere and maybe it was the Goddess Herself blocking any communication with other Deities, as She might just be demanding exclusivity. But I think that this is unlikely, as She can be a generous Goddess and many others have successfully worked with other Pantheons and I feel it is down to my own limitations. It could be argued, that my work with Hekate has been so successful, that there is no room for other Deities. It should be mentioned, though, that on occasions, I have successfully worked with and received visions and communications from Gods, such as from the Horned God and from Hermes, but rarely from another Goddess (although it has occurred in the distant past!).

Although Hermes is often associated as Hekate's counterpart, She feels complete as an entity in Her own right, without the necessity of the Masculine being present. This makes me wonder whether Hekate might be the anthropomorphic resonance of the Tao, the Indeterminable and Endless One beyond אין סוף אור (Ain Sof Or) or the Monarch of *"Monarchical Polytheism"*. I cannot answer these questions. Not because I am not authoritative enough, but because some of these questions must remained unanswered until I pass beyond the Veil, where my Mistress awaits me and even then I may not receive the answer, and I will enter into Rebirth again to continue my learning, until I one day reach the answers to all our questions. So Mote It Be.

Figure 28 - Kali by Emily Carding

OM HEKATE KRIM

By Hansa

"Sakti is all around us, Sakti is power". This I learned at my mother's knee, with the tales of her many faces, as Kali, Parvati, Lakshmi, Tara, and hundreds of others. In our village there always seemed to be chalk yantras on the ground and flowers on shrines to honour one of the many gods. Of these my favourite was always coal-black Kali, whose face I saw in dreams, grinning with her tongue lolling out as she danced on Shiva's corpse. I spent many hours practising her grin, trying to stretch my tongue so it would hang out further and be more like hers.

The priests noticed how I always hung around the temple whenever I could, having hurried my chores and escaped my mother's watchful eye. Truth to tell I think she was secretly proud and amused that her youngest daughter should show so much interest in Kali Ma. Certainly I was rarely punished, so in my young way I intuited that I had my mother's inferred support for my devotion.

My first step to the realisation that the universal nature of Sakti was not limited to the goddesses of my land came when I was about ten years old. During a Puja for Kali one November I had a vision whilst the conch shell was being blown. She had three heads, and instead of the skull cup and severed head in two of her hands with the sword and trident in the others, she held two torches. I was very bewildered by this and asked the priest about it afterwards. I think he realised the nature of my vision, because rather than laughing or dismissing me, he kindly said he was not aware of an image of Kali in such a form, but that it must mean something for me, and that Kali was giving me a riddle to solve.

I could not get the vision out of my mind, and often wondered about the three heads. Kali usually has one head or ten (Mahakali). I knew Trimurti had three heads or faces, and represented the Lord in his three forms as creator (Brahma), sustainer (Visnu) and destroyer (Siva). So my first assumption was that my vision was emphasising the complete nature of Kali, as creator, sustainer and destroyer.

However the two torches were puzzling to me. Agni the fire god is the lord of the torch, so again the image hinted at masculine symbolism, but this felt wrong. I did not have long to ponder the riddle, as my parents were sending me to England to live with one of my aunts and go to school with them in London.

Aunta Achala was eternally busy running her shop and with four of her own children to look after as well as me. She had an optimistic nature, which was reflected in the happiness and laughter which was always to be found in her household. Her husband, my uncle Jay, often worked very long hours and had a wonderful habit of always being in the right place at the right time, just when he was needed most. I soon also discovered that Kali did not receive the same devotion in England that she had in

India. Instead Ganesa and Laksmi seemed to be most popular. They were the deities of prosperity who have their images in many homes and businesses in London.

Once I was settled in my new home, I resumed my quest to solve Kali's riddle. I now had a powerful friend in the form of the local library. I asked the librarian, whom I had got to know over the months I had been going there, one day if she knew of a Goddess with three heads. She didn't but suggested that I looked in the world religions section. I went in often, spending my afternoons looking for new books to read about the mythology and gods of China, Rome, Egypt, the Incas, and finally Greece. Sometimes the librarian would order books for me from other libraries, this was wonderful as it allowed me to immerse myself fully in my newfound interest. It also helped me to get over my longing to be with my mother and sisters, to be back in India. Book after book I devoured, and still I often wondered about the goddess I had seen in my vision – until one day there was a breakthrough.

After working my way through many books, I found one which gave me the answer. It was *Gods of the Greeks* by Carl Kerenyi. In there I found some references about a goddess with the name Hekate, which said that she had three heads and carried torches. Could this be the Goddess of my vision? I had a name now, so that made it easier to search for more information. Now I had a name it was going to be easier to find out more. Smiling from side to side, I asked the librarian if she could do a search for any books on the Goddess Hekate. She ordered some books for me, amongst them *The Goddess Hekate* by Stephen Ronan.

I had to wait several weeks for the book, as it turned out somebody else already had the book out on loan from its library by the time my request arrived. But I didn't mind, I was on the way to solving my mystical riddle now. When the book finally arrived, I ran all the way back to my aunt's house clutching my bag to my chest like a magic charm of great importance. I spent days reading the book, making notes and looking carefully at all the images in it. I was certain I had found the Goddess who appeared to me, but still had some doubts. After all, why would it be a Greek Goddess appearing to me in a temple in India? It still seemed strange to me.

The way to an answer was provided by my uncle Jay, who is a deeply religious man. He suggested that I set up a shrine to the goddess of my vision and do puja to her, and ask her for another vision. I thanked him for his wisdom, this was the obvious solution, yet I had not thought of it myself. I immediately started planning my puja, which I discovered was known as a Hekate Supper. Ronan's book gave me the information I needed, and I made a number of decisions.

The first was that I would do the puja/supper in the garden of my aunt's home, which was safer than going to a crossroads where I might be disturbed (or worse) by strangers. A young teenage girl out at night by herself in South-east London was not going to be a good idea, and my Aunt would not have allowed it. The dark of the moon was the time for it so that was fine. I did not have a statue to use, so I decided to copy a picture from the book, and adapt it so it resembled my vision and coloured it in bright colours using pencils and markers. As I drew it I chanted Om Hekate Krim, using the Kali mantra but substituting Hekate's name in. It seemed to work as I felt it come alive as I drew.

Next came the food for the puja. I decided to make a cake and put on two candles for the torches I had seen. I thought of using fish, but we are vegetarians and the idea made me feel queasy. Garlic was easy, and for the other cakes I decided the hard candy offered to Kali would be a good replacement. Myrrh joss was my choice for fragrance, in groups of three in honour of her heads. I was uncertain what flowers to use, so I chose picked some wildflowers growing on the banks next to the sports field and a few others from the garden. My structure was simple but sincere. I decided to recite some of the hymns in the book which I had copied by hand between my offerings, and use my mantra as well. I would offer her the cake I made as the final offering, and then ask for a vision.

On the dark moon it was overcast, and I worried it would pour with rain. However the Goddess kept the rain away and I went ahead with my ceremony. Everything went well, apart from the candles going out a few times. When I asked for a vision and sat cross-legged in front of the shrine, I once again saw the image which had started my journey, of the triple-headed torch-bearing Kali. Then she shifted into the form of Hekate like that shown in the book, of a beautiful white woman in a white tunic, with three forms. Then she shifted again into Kali with her four arms and single head. The whole time she was smiling!

I realised that Hekate and Kali were part of the same, they were both Sakti. The message to me was that the ultimate power of Sakti manifests in different ways appropriate to people in different cultures and with different beliefs around the world. The full significance of this did not sink in at the time, and it was only over the years, as my passion for both Hekate and Kali grew hand in hand, that I came to see my two goddesses as reflecting my own personal needs and location. When I am home in Kulgachia India I worship Kali, while I still pay respect to Hekate. When I am in England, or travelling in Europe, I worship Hekate, whilst still recognising and honouring Kali. After all they are ultimately part of the same, like breathing in and out, both form part of the cycle of life.

That was a long time ago. I am now a grown woman, with a daughter who is nearly the age I was back then. We travel between England and India, maintaining household shrines in both our homes. I have taught my daughter about Hekate and she makes regular offerings, as well as reciting her own hymns she has written for the Goddess Hekate at the shrine whenever we are in London. Her connection with Hekate grows and she herself has had dream visions of Hekate as a goddess who nurtures and cares for her daughters and has been named in one of her dreams as a daughter of the torch-wielding one. I am proud of her.

As for Hekate and Kali, they have never merged again in my visions since that time in the temple when I was a child. It was special, but I don't think I would want them too – those two visions set my path in life, a goddess on either side who reflects the other, like two mirrors facing each other repeating to infinity. And for that I will always be grateful.

Om Hekate Krim. Om Kali Krim.

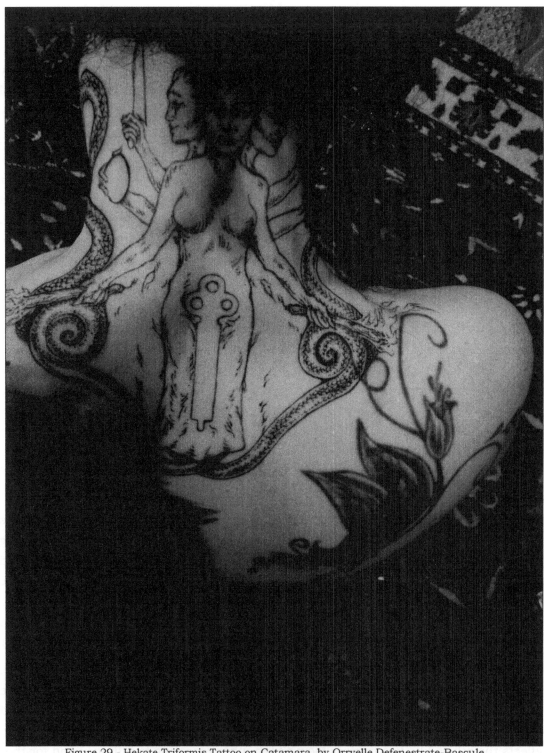

Figure 29 - Hekate Triformis Tattoo on Catamara, by Orryelle Defenestrate-Bascule

Hecate Triformis with serpentine legs, based on a traditional image.
Designed by Orryelle and Catamara, drawn and tattooed on Catamara by Orryelle in September 2009.
Note the hounds of Hecate in the negative space between Her arms and torso.
View more of Orryelle's ritual tattoo work at www.crossroads.wild.net.au/pic.htm

Beyond The Immediate

By Orryelle Defenstrate-Bascule

The incense is thick and sweet, a blend of scents strange yet familiar, both created and burnt in the name of Hecate.

From its fumes entwined with the wyrd sssounds of an improvisational violin voice and electronica session recorded with Emit in SF last year providing ambient atmosphere, and the slow cascading chanting of Her names nine times, emerges a state suitable to receive the dark Goddess's inspiration via evocation.

I am thankful for the ritual ambience Catamara has enticed tonight- too often it is overlooked during the transience of travels, yet it is this very sacred space beyond time and place which renews one to continue the outer journeys.

We are in Vienna, Austria, after spending another day oggling at architextural opulence and astounding art'; the soundscape from my laptop blots out most of the generic disco thudding below the flat; but now we could be anywhere and perhaps anywhen.

A moonth or so ago we were in Mandu, Madyar Pradesh, India, doing a ritual to Hecate in a candlelit cave, with hundreds of small bats shrieking and chittering around us in eerie accompaniment to the same chant.

Another part of that rite was the repetition of a chant to Kali, in homage to the dark Goddess of that land who is akin to Europe's own Hecate. My relationship to each of these dark Goddesses has ever been entwined, and both to varying degrees at different times have at some times showered my life with luscious and fragrant rose-petals of delight, and at others slashed at my soul with sharp and biting blades of bitter steel. But my blood has always flown freely as I learnt to surrender even to their severity. For my Mother/s know best, though it may sometimes seem harsh at the time...

Sacred Words I received along these same lines years ago have helped me live through and even love through the hardest of lessons, given me the courage to keep going and stay (semi)sane even when it seemed the Fates had only great suffering to offer in the short term. But:

'My apparent cruelty
Is but the love of the Mother
Who knows the best for her Children
Beyond the Immediate'

These lines are from *The Book of the Spider* which I received between the crac ks in a dawn trance from the Spider Goddess. They were later incorporated into my rewrite of the Ancient Greek tragedy, *Oedipus Tyrannos*, in which they were spoken by Hecate Moerae to the protaganist.

In my new version of the play (2008) I attempted to turn the fatalistic Classic into a demonstration that Fate and free Will are Not mutually exclusive. With a strong personal belief in Fate and Her powers I did not change the circumstances in the traditional story –for circumstances are often beyond our control- instead I changed the way the characters perceive relate and react to these circumstances. So basically my new version was about making the most of bad or difficult circumstances, and this being ritual theatre (probably the last time I'll venture a Tragedy in this *'genre'*!) the Gods of course tested my own (as writer director performer) capacity to do this to the utmost, rather relentlessly during the 3-moonth period of preparation for the performances. My life situation at the time was dramatically overhauled, causing me to question and doubt some personal values and intrinsic ideals I had maintained strongly throughout my life.

Central to the emotional triggers and painful adjustments in the shattering of my ego at this time was the breakdown of a three-year relationship. One of the bitterest ironies was that the woman in question was going to play the role of Hecate-Moerae (the Moerae are the Greek Three Fates)–representing the very embodiment of Oedipus' (played by myself) tragic Fate in the dramatic reflection. Several times I wanted to throw in the whole production, but there was too much and too many (13 performers) involved already, and this would be giving up on the very integral ideas I was wishing to express with the play- that we can triumph through the most difficult of circumstances. (*'Can you just?'* Countered the Gods, *'Well lets see about that…'*)

She –a priestess of Kali who dallied sometimes too with Hecate- pulled out of the production in the pain and difficulty of our breakup, which made it all both easier and harder. After years as lovers, yet independent artists this would have been our first major creative work together –a potential unfortunately never realized.

By the time her decision was definite it was too late to find someone else to take the part, but she agreed to perform it for the camera earlier. Interactive video projections were already a part of the production so this sufficed.

Several things got me through this period of intense grief and adjustment–of which what I have touched upon only scratches the surface of what I had to deal with during this period: One was intensive energetic and physical practices, energizing my system for more rapid processing- I was doing regular Butoh dance classes and added a Suzuki physical theatre intensive to these for one very intense week during the peak of my crisis. Each day our instructor would push us beyond our supposed energetic limits for three hours. This exacerbated my already tenuous state, and yet allowed me to reassess my capacities on an emotional level also, allowing a rapid transformation by fire.

The other thing which –or rather witch- got me through was Hecate, and Her eastern twin Kali. The two were related in the ritual theatre also, and the reflections therein for me abounded in a way that went far beyond any artifice of *'acting'*.

There is a scene in my *'Oedipus Tyrannos'* in which Hecate-Moerae transforms into Kali-Moerae, the six arms of spinner weaver and cutter uniting into a different form now of the dark Goddess rather than Hecate Triformis. The devouring aspect of inevitable Fate looms over Oedipus, and begins a deadly dance. He cringes in terror and tries to escape, but every time he runs to one edge of the stage he is stopped as if by some invisible net. These etheric cords tighten the more he tries to escape –just like an insect caught in a spider's web, whose every shudder causes the strands to tighten about him. The space he can move within grows ever smaller, his movements become ever more constricted until he is but a trembling taut bound form before Her slowly lowering blade, whimpering in terror.

The first time I 'rehearsed' this scene it felt very real. Afterwards I still felt trapped, confined by awful yet inevitable circumstances and reflectively, physically constrained, my muscles still locked up from my struggle.

Fortunately there is a redeeming scene later in the play: Kali-Moerae again appears, and performs exactly the same dance- video projections were used to make it especially obvious to the audience that it was identical footage. However this time Oedipus –having transformed through his progressive realizations up to that point in the drama- perceives Her dance differently, and reacts so differently that the entire scene unfolds remarkably differently and to the audience also, Kali's dance appears different in such an altered context, though Her actual movements are the same.

Oedipus no longer struggles with his Fate- instead he dances with Her. His dance, rather than fearful or antagonistic, now becomes increasingly more ecstatic. Reflectively, Kali's own extreme and undulating movements now appear more sensual than threatening, and their joyous dance together becomes more akin to love-making than to a struggle.

The dance ends with Oedipus lying down before Her in surrender, and when She brings downs Her blade at the scene's end, he shudders in ecstasy rather than resistance to this little Death.

In rehearsal this felt better, but not always quite as real. It was an exercise in surrender, and this is not always an easy thing. I was ever reminded by this ritual theatre that I needed to surrender, no matter how difficult my situation. And really, what I was going through -though most painful at the time- was really nothing compared to finding out like Oedipus that you have killed your father and married your mother, especially in Ancient Greece's moral climate.

However Fate was relentless in Her severity with me at this time. Each time I surrendered to my circumstances, the Gods would throw another curve ball at me, and just as I was beginning to come to terms with my situation it would get worse again. There were of course many mutual friends within the dissolving partnership, and my relations with some of them also became strained. It seemed the epitome of a progressive breakdown in our clan that had been slowly occurring over the last few years.

Each time some new obstacle or emotional problem arose it became more difficult to surrender, and my faith in the dark Goddess was wavering that my prayers for aid and mercy seemed to come to naught. But I persisted, engaging deeply with the character of Oedipus as a reflective lesson for my own Fate's winding briar-beset path.

The apex of my private ritual activity at the time was on the Autumn EquinoX (March in Australia), also coinciding with my birthday and only about a week before the production's premiere. I had realized the need to take magickal action outside –yet still in relation to- the *'play'* –to implore Hecate for help. The ritual was performed in the large park across the road from where I was living, in a circle of 8 trees which had become a magickal space for me during my tenure there. Some rehearsals for Oedipus had also taken place in that same natural circle in the park.

Basically it was a rite of *'crossing over'*; the EquinoXes are seasonal X-roads of the year, when from that equipoise of light and dark the days become shorter and the nights longer. In this case it was actually a *'double crossing'* though, in that I was soon to also cross over to the other side of the world, where in the northern hemisphere instead the nights would become longer and the days shorter form that same crux-point. And Hecate –as most of the readers of this book are no doubt well aware- is the Goddess of the Crossroads and of crossing over...

Considering what a difficult time I was having with everything and everyone I knew in Australia, I was of course relieved to be going- albeit the fact that I was going again had much to do with some of the problems arising also- and very much felt the need to step into another reality.

The ritual was short and simple, but powerful. With my twisted Gazelle-horn-handled magickal dagger from Egypt, I drew a cross-roads in the dirt between the four quarter-spaced trees of the circle. I cast one side to represent the southern hemisphere and the other the northern. I took the crescent blade and cut- with some difficulty as it was not very sharp- an X on my chest over a section of the web tattooed there, summoning all my pain and grief up into that action so that it flowed out in a flood of release with the blood and tears that dripped onto the earth at the centre of the crossroads. *'Cross my heart, and hope to die, Die to hope anew...'*

I implored Hecate and also Hermes –that other Greek deity of crossroads and crossing over, also God of travel and dear to me- to aid and guide my passage, that I may cross over from pain and dissolution into some new and joyous circumstances, releasing the old to allow the new...

And then I stepped over the line, and felt a sense of relief.

Late the next day I returned to the park to do some yoga, and noticed a bottle-top someone had dropped in the circle. It was right near the central X of the crossroads, and was branded with Hermes' winged caduceus which is used as a glyph by the Mercury (Roman name of Hermes) Cider company! It lay between the two small starling wings –worn on my ears as Hermetic *'earwigs'*- that I had left there as an offering in my ritual...

Of course my ordeals were far form over. My rite had given me hope for change but I was still deep in grief and had quite a while remaining in Australia, where most of my personal relations seemed somehow tainted and even a promising new connection turned out to be a veiled psychopath. I focused my energies on the Oedipus production.

It was only a few nights before the play opened that I reached another crisis point. I felt like I was dealing with my situation far better than I had similar ones in the past, and yet this could not save the relationship. It seemed that the more I surrendered and accepted the blows I was being dealt, the more successive blows were dealt to me, relentlessly. So it got to a point where I questioned the very myth that was so intrinsic to the final scene in the play.

I had long resonated with the story of Shiva lying down before Kali in Her bloodlusting battlefrenzy, and this halting Her rampage. It made sense to me that the same energy that can cause such destruction could be channelled in a more positive manner if not fought as an adversary but instead surrendered to. However now it seemed that the more I surrendered, the more this furious and devastating force continued to tear me apart, even that my surrender seemed to encourage its destructive nature.

So I began to wonder if I should change the ending of the play to reflect this new outlook. It was of course very late timing to make such a major change, but since no other performers were really involved in this final scene and I was also director it was possible, in fact I thought it might be better not to even tell the rest of the cast and crew, leaving them as surprised as the audience. The production was only running for two nights, so I decided to do the first night as scripted while trying to resolve how to change the ending on the second night. I was happy about the idea, as I had felt quite bound to the script with this play. Usually our Metamorphic Ritual Theatre productions had only loose semi-scripts (often collectively devised) or even just basic plots or concepts which performers/invokers semi-improvised around, and there was almost always some spontaneous or unrehearsed ritual element. *Oedipus Tyrannos* was an exception in that it all being written in verse with very specific intentions it was our first fully-scripted play, and such had initially felt less ritualistic because of this. However the overspill in my own life had become so marked that it soon seemed (at least personally) even more magickally charged than looser pieces. The issue then arose, of course, of just Who wrote the script anyway? –it being about Fate and much of it semi-channelled; in fact I'd had a sense of it being my own Fate to rewrite the Oedipus myth for several years before I'd actually dared face the challenge of reworking such a literary classic. So now I had begun to feel bound to the script and its reflective challenges in my personal life, and to alter the ending could be an effective reassertion of my free will.

In my Butoh class the next day, during the climactic group improvisation I found myself in a spontaneous swirling dance with a man of heavier build than myself, who somehow in the flowing momentum of our movement I picked up around the abdomen and held under one arm while I began to spin, dervish-dancing around and around faster and faster. At the apex of this unlikely natural choreography the thin leather cord clad in the spine of a snake around my wrist –which I had consecrated to Kali at one of Her main temples in Kalcutta, India the year before–snapped and serpent vertebrae went flying in every direction across the room even as the centrifugal force also cleaved our collaboration and we fell apart.

The first night of performing *Oedipus Tyrannos* before an audience felt a lot more intense than any rehearsal. It was a new moon and was indeed a ritual, and most of the emotion I expressed was very real, regardless of how practiced the rhyming lines were.

Particularly potent was the final dance with Kali-Moerae. I had released so much in the process of the play and this came now to a sense of completion and transformation. My surrender before Her was much deeper, and afterwards I felt a great relief, almost serenity.

So I began to wonder –if the ending as scripted felt so good, surrendering to the Goddess like this despite all Her apparent severity, why should I change it on the second night after all? And yet what I had felt a few nights prior had been valid also, and perhaps also needed expression.

I remained unsure about just how (or even if) I should alter the ending on the second night until just a few hours before the performance began.

The woman I had recently broken up with turned up to see the play, bringing along her new partner as if to rub salt in the X. She had opted for the stability this connection offered, disenchanted with my polygamous ideals which were now temporarily faltering in the challenge of the situation. What was the good of being able to overcome possessiveness if others could not?

In the final scene, Hecate-Moerae spoke Her lines from the *Book of the Spider* from the webbed screen:

Unless you have found resonance of frequency
With my web's angles askew
Invade not its rays

Unless thou art thus kin
Stick to my spiral
Released only by my venom

But if you choose instead to dance with me
Still you may become my mate
And be devoured yet
But in ecstasy, of ThanatEros' boon
In the Loom of Maya, into the Womb of Gaia

Her three-faced visage morphed, the six arms becoming those of Kali-Moerae. Blue-black thighs dappled with flickering flames, the skull-bedecked Goddess began to dance, and as in the script Oedipus began now not to cringe and struggle but to dance with Her.

But when one leg was lifted high in the stance of Shiva Nataraj, I presented my twisted gazelle-horn-handled knife and with its crescent blade I suddenly sliced at an invisible strand and my leg fell free. I teetered then another arc of the blade freed my wrist from etheric cords of fate. I slashed again and shook my limbs in newfound release, freed from the tale of Oedipus and his torturous destiny, then dropped the knife and turning away from the dark Goddess I began to stride down the long aisle between the pews.

The audience turned their heads to follow my exit, as did the shocked lighting technician and the black-robed Chorus who were waiting on the edge of the stage for their final lines.

But as I reached the door I hesitated, then turned upon my heel and walked back up to the aisle. Taking a vibrant Hibiscus flower (sacred to Kali) from a side-altar, I placed it devotedly upon the platform at the projected Goddess's lotus feet as I knelt before Her. Then I climbed up and lay upon this platform. As Her passionate dance ended, my chest shuddered beneath Her pounding feet. But my head was tipped back with an expression of ecstasy.

This was true surrender. Not surrender because I had to, because I was bound to, but because I chose to.

CODA

There was one more bitter irony in my ritual theatrics with Oedipus: That second night so relieved was I that the production and its entanglements were over that I relaxed a little too soon, and after a few drinks somehow left the video-projector I had hired for the show in the back of a taxi. That fateful mistake cost me the $1000 that was supposed to make my travels to the northern hemisphere that year less shoestring than usual. But I had to laugh when I realized I had not cut myself free from the dark Goddess, merely from a projection of Her!

Several moons later in the UK I met Catamara –a devoted priestess of Hecate and herbalist witch- and the alchemistry between us was wyrdly immediate. Moonths later still in the USA, I ritually tattooed Hecate Triformis on the back of her neck. I found new kindred clan in Seattle and Portland, and new magickal and creative alliances were forged. I saw congenial polyamory lived out, and my faith in humanity was renewed.

Caught as I was in the immediacy of my grief during the reworking of Oedipus, I could not have seen then the pattern of the greater web, or our dark Lady's wider plans.

And even as I type these final lines now almost a year later in Prague, I thread Indian serpent vertebrae onto a red cord, and chant the names of Hecate...

OEDIPUS:

So devour me, Fate, I surrender to your whims!
Even to your apparent caprice
For why struggle with the inevitable
When it can instead be embraced
...And now it is bliss –this release!

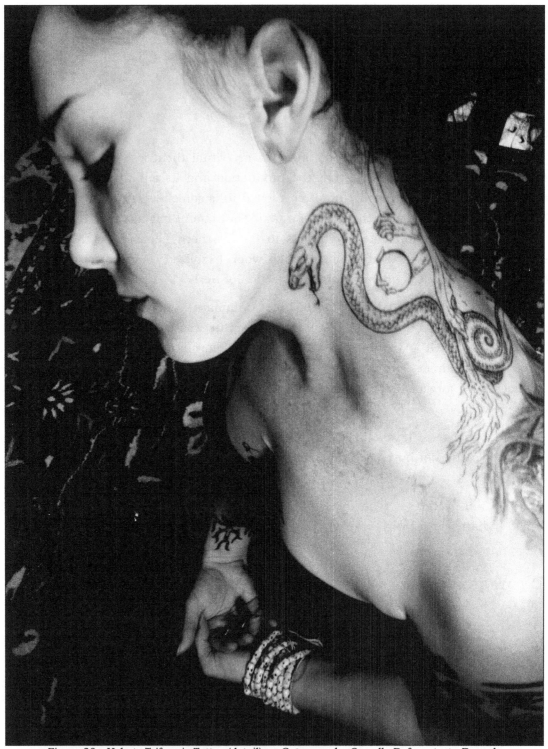

Figure 30 - Hekate Triformis Tattoo (detail) on Catamara by Orryelle Defenestrate-Bascule

THE HEART OF HEKATE

BY CATAMARA ROSARIUM

... The night is stark and cold, thick with the scent of the body of earth, laden with the intoxicating aroma and dew of Aconitum. Neither the sun nor moon illuminates the sky...

Deep in the oneieric realms, I journey.

Cutting through the sweet decay of the night, Her apparition rapidly appeared, alongside it grew an enormous tree. She began to take form gradually scaling to a height insurmountable in comparison~

Standing fiercely in the thick of the night She uttered not a word, yet I felt a deep connection. One which I could not illustrate adequately with words, yet I was filled with an acute sense of understanding. She, a Goddess of import, was much greater than any of this world, the underworld, or the universe for that matter. She is of all worlds...The Great Cosmic Mother.

Her intense smile embraced me as she grabbed the trunk of the tree. With conviction she ripped it from its foundation, out of the ground, roots uprooted from their temple yet still intact. Forcefully she flipped it upside down, the tree now inverted~ Roots tendril into the sky, branches that once grew towards the heavens now thrust deep into the hearth of the earth. Inverted now she stood strong in the heart.

(... An augury of the sacred ritual site to be found two weeks after, when in search of a Xroads in the woods for the purpose of Hekate ritual workings. Our patron tree stands at the XROADS and was to be consecrated on the Sacred Night of Hekate's Crossroads.)

For many moons my Witch Sisters and I had awaited our Witch Mother to reveal Herself to us. We were of course wise in knowing that once She did, the lessons She would teach us and what She would reveal to us would change the very fabric of the universe in which we live. Thus we waited contentedly, steadfast on our path, devoted to our magickal endeavours, awaiting Her embrace.

As the moon waxed and waned, numerous magickal operations were constructed and performed resulting in deep transformation for each of us as well as the egregore of our coven, the *Serpentris Divinum*. Poetic musings and oracles also resulted from these rituals, sometimes cryptic and enigmatic (as they often are), yet with indications that led to deep contemplations both while sleeping and waking.

As the Wheel continued to turn it became more and more apparent, portents leading each of us in our own ways to find our Witch Mother, though we still did not know Her name... I myself kept finding my way through meditation and serpendipitous events hither and thither to various mediums relevant to the goddess

Hekate. So much so it became emphatically clear that Hekate was revealing herself to me as My Witch Mother. Thusly, I was inspired to write a ritual for Hekate's Feast, which would be the first of many I would be inspired to write and present to my coven...

As the fates would have it, by the time of the first working, Hekate was making Herself known to my witch sisters as well, now beyond question or individual synchrony; indeed we realized Hekate is the Witch Mother of the Serpentris Divinum! Hail Hekate!

It's three moonths later since our first ritual devoted to the Goddess Hekate... The night of Hekate's Crossroads.

We converge and begin our journey to the ritual site. It's dusk and the air is dense with fog. Trails to the crossroads now indiscernible, we set forth through the labyrinth of haze using only our intuition and recollection of the area to find our way along the path. After some time we arrive greeting the tree and sacred space. Any large debris that lies about the circumference is removed and large curved branches are used to form a circle around the base of Hekate's tree.

The altar is set at the Eastern base and sections of the branches that were set around the base of the tree are also used to place ritual items. Firstly, three candles are placed, one on each side to mark the extent of the altar, the other set in front of the altar (three points marking the shape of a pyramid). The candles symbolize the torches of Hekate Triformis, as well a microcosm of Hekate's Wheel (the Serpent's power of rebirth to the labyrinth of knowledge and to the flame of life itself). Sausage, egg, onion, garlic, honey, rue, and aconite petals are placed as offerings for Hekate's Feast. A vial of the spirit of Belladonna, Pomegranate cordial and goblets, aconite infused oil, athame, scourge, knotted rope, three more candles, and various other ritual items are placed on the altar to accompany the feast.

Now nightfall, the forest still thick with fog, a light rain falls, the tree's canopy catching most of the droplets. The moon, mostly shrouded by clouds, pokes Her head from beneath just enough to greet us denoting the beginning of our ritual, lighting the sky enough to expose the panoramic silhouettes of the tree line that surrounds us.

3 rings of the bell, the ritual underway... Clarity Hisssssing, Clarity, The Words of Opening intoned... the Circle then cast and quarters evoked. We rend the veil, followed by a summoning of the Great Magickal Power. Charcoal is lit and incense ignited in the name of our mother Hekate. Taking turns we each circumambulate the ritual space with the incense censor while intoning TEMENOS infusing the area with incense. A ritual cup for each participant containing three drops of Belladonna; the remainder filled with Pomegranate cordial is next prepared. Raising our cups we consecrate and charge the mixture by intoning TEMENOS once again and then salute our goddess Hekate in her epithet Nykteria... She of the Night... and then imbibe in the elixir. A proclamation to Hekate follows which is recited by the group -a declaration to our great mother requesting Her presence on this night. A charm of Hekate consisting of Hekate and three other epithets is then intoned a series of 9 times. An improvisational cacophony and deep trance results.

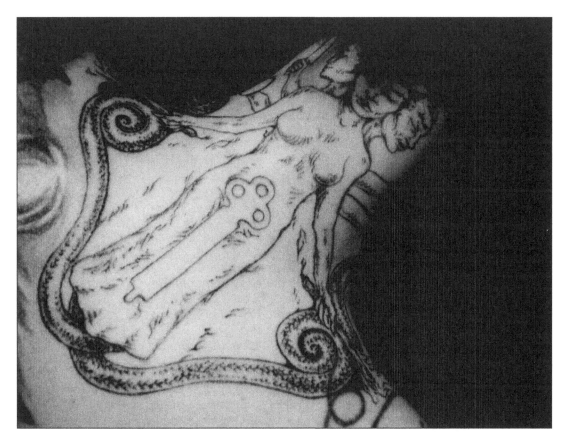

Figure 31 - Hekate Triformis Tattoo (Close-up) on Catamara by Orryelle Defenestrate-Bascule

Now intensely gnosticated, entranced by our goddess, I present a key to each participant. We bind the keys to black satin cords and then care is taken to anoint them with Aconite infused oil. After doing so, we consecrate and charge them using the words *LEFARIOS LLUCHEZ* (words I received as a result of a Hekate Dream ritual done a few weeks prior). Each key is old and worn, the head containing three circles -- uniquely symbolic to Hekate Triformis (I had found the keys at a flea market several moonths prior. I knew at the time they would be presented to my Witch Sisters, but did not know exactly their purpose nor when or in what ritual).

Still chanting *LEFARIOUS LLUCHEZ* three of us converge at one arm of the crossroads. Backs are facing, shoulders touching, each of us facing in a different direction of the crossroads at our ritual site. The three of us stand now as one forming a Hektarion... in the guise of Antaia (Sender of Nocturnal Visions), Brimo (Terrifying one/Crackling of Fire), and Propylaia (The One Before the Gates) we embody Their essence. One holds the keys, another wields a scourge/knotted cord, the other an athame... each form also holds a torch. The words *PANTOS KOSMOUS KLEIDOUCOS KLEIDOUCHON* (Keeper of the Keys of the Universe) now echoes through multiverses as the Hektarian begins to pulse. The words are intoned beginning in unison, moving into rounds and then eventuate into a natural yet otherworldly soundscape accessing higher frequencies and creating energy patterns anew... fuelling the centre of the Hektarion.

The fourth participant connecting with the energies formed from the Hektarion now invokes and draws down the Great Cosmic Mother...

HEART OF THE HEKTARION

Torch lit caverns span the abyss
Coiling~ Weaving ~ Twining...
Serpents merging into pools as Labyrinthine Vessels
Traversing all land and sea
Igniting~ Feeding knowledge to the flame
Stars Dripping with Hektarius Nectar
The Trinity now Revealed
Filling the cup
Crossing thresholds betwixt gods and men

Poised, your stance embraces Enodia ~ as a pillar before Egress
~Keys Destined & Sealed in Blood~
TEMENOS! TEMENOS! TEMENOS! TEMENOS!
The Third and Fourth IGNITE
Pantos Kosmous Kleidouchos Kleidochon

YOU Stand Before ME
EYE AM Wisdom
EYE AM Beauty
EYE Am Understanding
I AM~The Trinity~
The Portal to the Triune Void
One Point Intersecting All Worlds
The Crossing of a road that sees all elements in space and time
No boundaries, no truths, Everything IS
Feeding the Heart of the Great Cosmic Mother
HEKATETAKEH

Ripping the Tree from its foundation...Terra Firma
Tearing away all reality... shredding life anew
Piercing the core as she thrusts it into a new infinite location
The Kingdom Now Inverted
The Heart~~ A WYRLD In Reflection

Roots tendriling in the vastness, reaching & entrenching the sky
Foundations manifest in victory and glory anew

The Earth devours the branches tunnelling through the crown
Guiding the trinity through the veil of the void

Beauty~ IS the Point, the Intersection...
The Heart of the Hektarion
Pulsing, Vibrating, Emanating
Higher frequencies Erupt and Emerge

Portals ignite as you writhe and dance amongst Grentaline Visions
Inducing and Igniting, the Hektarion Animates~
Your Imprint, Your Vibration, Your Emanation
Pantos Kosmous Kleidouchos Kleidochon

By Catamara Rosarium

(...The verse 'Heart of the Hektarion' is a piece of poetic musing that includes recently divined oracles as well as the inspiration (as a result of ritual) to formulate and poetically combine many of the ideas and intimations She has imprinted deep within me over the years.)

Figure 32 - Spiralling Axis Mundi by Magin Rose

THE ONE WHO WAITS AT THE CROSSROADS

By Soror Basilisk

Thick fog is nestled in the trees, the air is still. The priestess raises her sword and the invocation begins. The moment for sacrifice comes. She cuts and her blood falls on the altar and on the censer, forming a cloud scented of blood, mugwort, nightshade and cypress. Some of the ritualists hear strange laughter in the fog. Offerings are made, the land is once again dedicated to Hekate, and the rite is complete.

This ritual was the 16th anniversary dedication to Hekate of an area of land in the beautiful foothills near my home. All the times before, as with any other ritual work that called on Hekate, her presence could always be felt but this time was, for me, the beginning of a far deeper and more personal relationship with her. Looking back at that time, it has proven to be a major factor in what is now truly a crossroads in my magickal life. The ritual used was one not used before and I feel this was a major contributor to the power of this particular rite.

When I say I am at a crossroads in my magickal life, I do not mean that I am faced with a decision to make, which path to follow. I mean that my three main paths of magickal training, study and experience are now converging into one path. I can make no decision, as there is no decision to make. As a magickal person, there really is no choice. Witchcraft, Ritual Magick and Mediumship, I now see with clarity, have provided me with the tools to create my own magick, which will become greater than the sum of its parts.

When one is at a crossroads, Hekate is there to show the options. The crossroads is also an initiatory *'ground zero'*. In Hoodoo, one disposes of unwanted remnants there and this can apply to the unwanted remnants of the Self. With that in mind, attitudes, beliefs, outworn and outgrown patterns of behaviour and thought can be shed. The whole of the Self can be completely destroyed and rebuilt anew. Hekate, mad as she is, wise as she is, can be trusted to guide and clear the mind.

WITCHCRAFT

I have felt Hekate's presence from childhood, although I didn't know her name at the time. It was only in later years with my initial steps into Witchcraft that I discovered her myths, history, nature and rituals. As a child she was clearly seen but the attitudes of society dulled that connection until I invoked her with the benefit of magickal knowledge, good teachers and like-minded friends.

She has always been there waiting for me and now that connection has been re-established, she will be by my side to guide and advise.

SPIRIT COMMUNICATION

Over the years, I have developed my own techniques of spirit mediumship, as the more traditional ones proved limiting, and I have found it an excellent tool for ritual and astral work. The ritual that was used for the dedication above was, I believe, pivotal in opening my connection with Hekate, which has since enabled me to develop this discipline even further.

Study of the techniques of oracular work, possession by the Vodou Lwa, Seidr, ancient seeresses and pythonesses has enriched my mediumship and magickal skills. Anything new will first make itself known in the astral realm and a short time before the dedication rite, I had been doing a lot of astral ritual work. I found myself coming in contact with a strong serpent energy that slowly developed from an objective force to something within me, a part of me. Through this energy, spirits and deities associated with serpents were using me as a conduit within ritual work. The following experience demonstrates this. I was in the astral realm and instead of remaining in my form, as I normally would with mediumship, I found myself watching my astral form being completely overtaken.

> *The goddess was of serpent energy, she seemed to have scales for skin but these could have been just markings, like a tattoo. She appeared in human form, the scaled woman, but with many arms, like Kali, and she was scarlet colour. Not Hindu. I could see her on the altar starting to lie down. As she did, the scarlet colour was replaced with blue but the altar became scarlet. As she left the body, I became more aware of actually being in my astral body as my usual self and I was exhausted.*

The astral work led to experimentation on the physical. As I remained in my physical body, I could see and feel what the possessing spirit could, almost in a 'second-hand' way. I could also see Hekate beside me, protecting, teaching and guiding.

> *Once the ritual openings and invocations were done, I sat in middle of the circle and entered into trance. The Magister Templi sat in front of me, repeating the invocation. Hecate's presence was strong and could be seen psychically. A spirit started to come through me. It felt similar to my usual mediumship where I become very small, sharing the body with a spirit that now dominates. I can't really communicate with those outside my body, only the spirit that has come through. I saw Hecate put her hand out over the incense and move it around in a circle, palm down and my spirit-controlled hand followed her. I was seeing visions, the spirit's visions.*

RITUAL SEX MAGICK

My partner and I had been exploring sex magick and sexual gnosis for some years, but it has only been the last couple of years that we have used this technique within a formal ritual setting, physically as well as astrally. The ritual that follows was intended to be a simple rite to strengthen our contact with Hekate on the astral, using sexual gnosis to propel and maintain our consciousness there. Hekate had a lesson in store.

> *A crossroads was drawn on the floor of the temple and the crescent moon symbol drawn on the altar. Garlic and moon blood were burned and sacraments of wine and hashish were taken whilst the invocation was spoken in turn by myself, then my partner.*
>
> *Our intention was to use sexual gnosis; the physical and emotional energies produced being offered to Hecate as a sacrament and the trance state utilised to project our consciousness into an astral crossroads for our dialogue with Hecate. With the first stages of the ritual, we focused on the intention and visualisation of the rite, each directing their consciousness to the astral crossroads.*
>
> *I began to feel the first stages of spirit possession, when a spirit takes control of the limbs and you simply observe and feel the results of that movement. At this time I was visualising what was happening on the physical also happening on the astral and projecting my consciousness there.*
>
> *I then focused on the astral, feeling the physical but feeling it all astrally as well, until it became purely astral. As the rite continued, my awareness became fixed in the astral and the crossroads became clear. It was completely dark but for an odd light, like moonlight or firelight, that illuminated us, the centre of the crossroads and a large grey standing stone. Next to this Hecate appeared in Crone form, standing there, watching us and smiling.*
>
> *I looked at her, mentally telling her this act was for her; the energy, sacrament, blood, all for her. Would she show us her mysteries?*
>
> *I was sitting upright leaning forward, my partner lying beneath me, my arms straight out with my hands either side of his head. I looked down at him and next to his shoulder I saw a withered old arm, just bone and sagging paper thin skin, clawed hand with bony fingers; certainly not my arm. By this time, the act itself was taking over. I was aware Hecate was through me and I realised the same must be occurring on the physical.*
>
> *My partner's consciousness was initially fully in the astral but when Hekate took possession of my physical body, his consciousness returned back to the physical, whilst maintaining an awareness of the astral. Although I was wearing a robe, he no longer saw this. Instead, he perceived Hekate's form replacing mine. She had changed position, sitting upright with arms outstretched and her head thrown back. Appearing to him as the Crone, he stated "she felt like a sexually vibrant woman, regardless of age or appearance." We heard (physically? astrally?) the beginnings of an insane laughter, deep and slightly guttural.*
>
> *After the point of orgasm on the astral, Hecate had left me and was again at the standing stone. I noticed that nearing the end of the rite, she had taken on a youthful beautiful form. I then focused on returning to the physical and closing the rite.*
>
> *I had assumed that everything I observed on the astral had also taken place on the physical and I had not changed position in any way.*

Hecate, teacher and key to mysteries, had shown me a way of full spirit possession. Remaining aware of my physical body and feelings but placing all of that into the astral space, *'grounding'* in the astral so to speak, keeps the consciousness busy, enabling the spirit to take full possession on the physical.

The astral overlay, the ritual setting, the invocation, incense and sacraments along with the use of sexual trance states and the ability to manipulate the altered states of consciousness all merged to make a powerful *'Rite of Possession'*. The technique we used for Hekate has become a standard formula for contact with other spirits and entities, physically and astrally. In a way, I become a crossroads; the physical and the astral converging to allow something truly magickal to happen.

> *We decided to do a ritual using sexual trance to initiate the oracular state. I started with an elemental opening at the quarters, then the statement of intent and invocation. My partner was standing behind me. Most of the session was a focus on breath and body rhythm, inducing trance with breath as well as sexual trance state. We both visualised the crossroads as in the previous rite. We merged the astral and physical so our actions on the physical were replicated in the astral. There I saw the standing stone and Hekate appeared. At that point I closed my astral eyes too and let myself be drawn into the breath and movement and trance.*

> *I suddenly found myself back on the physical and could feel the presence of Hekate coming through me. This precipitated the manifestation of several spirits including a very serpentine energy. Definitely not human in any way. Pure serpent energy. Again this could be perceived by some as quite threatening. A lot of strong hissing and guttural sounds. This led into a smooth transition to a woman spirit who told us that she acted as an oracle. I was getting images from her mind - a woman of the 1930s. My partner asked her if she would help us (she said yes). She said to him "I can see you". Through her vision I saw my partner in his animal form. She was fascinated by this. Then she faded out and I felt a huge emotional tug. As my partner started to close the rite, I could still feel the serpent energy within me.*

The separate components of experience in this procedure can all be used in various mediumistic, oracular, astral and ritual settings. The feature of this work is certainly the attainment of altered states of conscious; from the taking of sacraments to the breathing in of incense, journeying within the shadow and astral to formal ritual with words of power, or simple *'doving'*[1] to sexual trance.

Although mediumship is my predominant magickal activity, it has been enhanced by magickal techniques and procedures as well as a variety of other forms of spirit contact of different traditions. The renewed contact with Hekate in the dedication rite opened new doors, enabling a much stronger and more personal relationship with her. Her influence on my magickal work since that time has brought understanding, insight and clarity, without which, at this point in my life, I would have remained unsure of the next stage of my magickal life.

My relationship with Hekate is not one of placid worship. She is dynamic, harsh, exciting, half insane, wild, sometimes frightening in her strength and a very very ancient force.

---

[1] A method of entering trance. Either sitting or kneeling, the practitioner closes their eyes and proceeds to rocking forwards and backwards.

Figure 33 - Stone Altar of Hekate by MDL

Figure 34 - The Fall by Emily Carding

Baptism of Fire

By Mark Alan Smith

Post military career and heavily involved with real estate, I was also at what I thought was the peak of my witchcraft practice and involvement with Hecate. Every day there was some form of loving communion with, and offerings to, the Great Goddess. Possession work and the alkhemy of sexual magick featured heavily in our arte. I was more in love with my Dark Goddess than ever before. One of the most amazing aspects of mundane life at this time was the understanding and considerate people around me. Those who truly mattered all understood and supported what was rapidly becoming an intense and very devoted way of life.

The game had been left behind decades ago, I had seen what Hecate could do when approached correctly and asked for something with true soul intention and heartfelt love. I had also noticed how the Goddess of Witchfire always achieved the result that She wanted, be it some small offering or a request of a more significant nature. Whether by persuasion or the re-alignment of the elements upon the inner planes, the Goddess of Witchcraft always made sure that Her will and desires were manifested. I had no problems with this, I have known for a long time that my number should have been up on more than one occasion during my thirteen years as a professional soldier. I also knew that it was the Queen of Hell, Heaven and Earth who, more than once, had moved events slightly out of alignment to prevent this happening. Though sometimes this realization would come much later in deep analytical contemplation of these incidents and the near misses which accompanied them.

It is fair to say that in the light of all my experience with the first of the Elder Gods, that my trust of Hecate was implicit. It was only because our relationship was so intense and the trust level so high that I accepted Lucifer so easily when Hecate brought Him forward to become an integral part of not only my work with Her but also my life. I had worked with the Horned God for as long as I had loved the Dark Goddess. Whereas my personal relationship with the Queen of Hell had been encouraged by Hecate very early; developing into a very intimate and dedicated communion which went way past the personal and very powerful initiation that She gave me; the Horned God had always been a figure of many names from Cernunnos to Pan. He was a part of many rituals, practices and communions, but seemed for many years to linger in the background simply providing the solar compliment to the lunar vibration of the Goddess. That is until Hecate opened my awareness to Him further, bringing us closer together and revealing to me His true identity.

When the bonds with the Horned God were firmly strengthened through our communion and through the planes, I could see His true persona. This was not, you understand, a shining golden youthful angelic form; though I am more than aware of

His capability to manifest in this way. This was the Horned Lucifer of old and more akin to the great power that one would find in the Grand Grimoire than some of the more subtle conceptions of the consort and first created Son of Hecate. Still despite His slightly menacing appearance during evoked manifestations and open sky, dark moon workings I accepted Lucifer as She had asked me to. The knowledge, passed to me by the Lord of Thaumiel Himself, that Hecate was the one being to which He bowed always gave me a wry smile when I thought of the man made paternal faiths of more modern times.

Every day in the service and love of Hecate was another day of intense learning, another step along the transmutative soul path of the Dark Queen of Witchfire. In fact the only down turn to each of these days was the fact that I had to weave them around my normal everyday mundane life. I couldn't complain too much though as I was given many magickal gifts. Not the least of which were the Keys to the Gateway of Knowledge, the gnosis of transition through this gate in shifted form, and the magickal power infused at soul level and fed through to body and mind with which to initiate further change. All this enhanced my spiritual transition along the path of learning that I so faithfully followed in Her name.

Hecate brought many teachers to aid in our work. Through contact with them I was able to move yet further in my quest to, if I am honest, stand at Her side. I was in love! Glimpses of the gnosis of treasures such as the Keys to the Gates of the Ages, held by the Demon Princes, were given in tantalising and tempting flashes of inner circle ritual possession induced by the mighty Dark Queen.

The only slight problem that I ever had during this time was with one or two close spiritual friends who would voice their concerns about the pace and intensity of my work with Hecate. Yet coming from the Parachute Regiment I wasn't at all phased. I was able to absorb and retrieve almost all of what was delivered at soul level; whether in ritual format or full possession; and still go about my daily life selling property. To try and integrate my love for my spiritual work further into my everyday mundane sphere of existence I began to write of my experiences with Hecate. This aided in the task of returning Her gnosis; basically telling Her story; so much of which is still lost. Still I was not content. I wanted more. Try to understand that while yes, I wanted the power and the knowledge, I was and still am driven by the intense love that I have for Hecate; love that is held at the level of my soul. I wanted to be closer to Her. A close friend of mine, an intuitive person who often knew a lot more than she would care to voice to most, but who still enjoyed being quite vocal in her advice to me due to the mutual understanding we shared of the spiritual realms, tried to cool my enthusiasm. Warning me that Hecate was capable of far more than even I knew. After an exchange beginning on her behalf with a chorus of *"fools rush in where Angels fear to tread"*, which was always countered during such conversations with my *"what if Columbus believed the world was square"* speech we stopped on a mutual Scott of the Antarctic note and agreed to disagree on my chosen pace of spiritual exploration. Naturally, the warning was ignored!

It was in love and, I admit, the thirst for more knowledge and power that I did just that. I asked for more. This was done during a work of intense loving possession with the Dark Goddess. My request was addressed immediately, along with a warning. Hecate told me that She could give me more power than I could imagine existed but, She warned, there were things that She could not give, things that I had to find by myself, alone. When asked what these things were Hecate's reply was cryptic:

> *They are the elements of true spiritual ascension the keys, in part, to the Gates which lead to the Path of Eden.*

Asked if I accepted this work I gave a very quick yes in reply. The gnosis of The Rite of the Phoenix was then bestowed upon me.

At a glance through the rite itself I could see that this was a transmutational work of immense power. Involving both Hecate and Lucifer the ritual contained elements that would have ceremonial magicians shaking their heads in absolute denial of the proceedings. Hecate explained that these elements formed a path of ancient sorcery which granted the opening and subsequent shattering of secret gateways which lay concealed within the soul. The significance of certain key elements; such as the summoning of the Magickal Fire of the Gods, the role of Lucifer as primary initiator of this flame in the name of Hecate and the necessity to conjoin oneself with the combined energies of Hecate and Lucifer in full physical manifestation; was in no way lost on me. Even the title of the ritual itself gave a huge indication as to the resulting flow and intensity of the expected power that would be released. Of course I was nervous! I am dedicated, loving and driven and I do have a fair amount of courage, but I am not stupid. In fact, had this ritual been presented by any other entity I would have run mile rather than perform it. This was not just an entity though. This was my Goddess.

Taking all this into account and knowing I was opening the gates on singularly the most powerful rite that I had ever performed in Her name, I steadied myself for the resulting transmutational effects.

I was not ready for what came.

The ritual went all as planned and expected; even as I merged with the physical manifestations of Hecate and Lucifer; that is up until the point where they conjoined within my soul in the praxis of sexual magick. I hadn't realised, but this was the key with which the Gates of the Magickal Fires of transmutation were opened. I remember the power, the passion and the loving. I can remember being loved by Lucifer as well as Hecate. No, I am not bi-sexual but my soul is and all the more so now that the two ruling Gods of the witchcraft have bi-sexualised the soul energies, polarising the fiery serpents of gnosis as they did so. Solar and lunar when merged release the keys of stellar gnosis and here at this point, as I lay in a broken circle in overwhelming spiritual ecstasy and possession was where this gnosis was being delivered.

The magickal current that brought with it such spiritual, emotional and physical ecstasy and the actual mechanics of the sexual rite itself would not stop. I could not have stopped this even if I had really tried. The energies of the ruling Goddess of the Ancient Craft and her Horned Consort encapsulated my being at the soul. At this level all else is encompassed. The energy centres at the back of the head had long since been opened in this rite and I found myself freed of all physical and mundane manifestations of any kind. If Hecate and Lucifer had not carried my spirit from its enfleshed incarnate form, the spiraling fire serpents of hidden gnosis, which seemed now to be unfurling way beyond my possessed body, most certainly would have. Through this spiritual journey I was allowed to partake of the stellar current of the Goddess, the magick that is released in the merging of the two ruling powers of the witchcraft in their exaltation of the soul who has called them forth. The opposite reaction to this starry flight was the depths to which we plummeted in equal measure, far below the infernal realms. The path of this whole journey; though I was at this time unaware; was the template upon which my upon my soul and incarnate life path was to be mirrored over the immediate and foreseeable future.

The ritual lasted from midnight until an hour or so before sunrise. Once all was completed, as best as I could, I closed it all down. Though there is no real way to close a gateway that has been shattered. I knew that the soul work that was ensorcelled within this rite was only just beginning and I didn't have to be particularly sensitive to vibrations to be aware of the huge influx of energy that was now pouring in through the gateways of my subtle bodies and coursing into my physical form. The fact that my balance was off and I couldn't walk properly were both indication enough. Shuffling as though I was walking with a duvet wrapped around me I made my way to bed. My dream sleep matched the flight of the ritual. This was to be expected. The alarming thing was the next day, when I rose from my well earned rest to find that I still couldn't quite get it together when trying to walk in a straight line. Mental focus and grounding and centring exercises helped to sharpen my magickally overwhelmed senses to the point that I could function more efficiently, though I left driving until much later in the day.

The first few days post ritual weren't too bad at all and I was rather enjoying the highly charged atmosphere around me generated by the greatly increased flow of magickal energy and life giving power that was flowing through my soul. Both Hecate and Her consort joined me in powerful channelling to inform me that huge change was afoot. Hecate told me:

> Lucifer will open the Gates of Fire through which you will see and hear the worlds of the Gods.

Taking this onboard and at face value I awaited the onset of these changes.

The first indication that all was not going to proceed as smoothly as I had planned was the almost continuous presence of Lucifer. He was everywhere I looked. I mean everywhere! The harsh intense solar energy, which seemed to radiate at a frequency so inimical to my own subtle vibration, soon removed the novelty from what were becoming increasingly solid manifestations. This was the first time that the thought that I may have bitten off more than I could chew presented itself to my conscious mind. The thought was banished by pride! Not for long though. The power kept increasing. Day and night it crept up at alarming rate. Lucifer would be there, constantly, His horned form outlined in deep red etheric energy. The eyes would change, depending on the intensity of manifestation, from yellow to a solid red. The solar flames came from the eyes. I could not see them, not even in the ether, but I could feel them; in my soul, in my mind, on my skin. Next came the blackness. It was akin to the solar flame, as though it was the next stage of increased and intensified power. This hurt. It was horrible, it was crushing.

Within a matter of days the power had become unbearable. I consider myself strong, and up to a point I could have handled the etheric flames, but this blackness was horrendous. I felt trapped, like the life was being crushed from me. That's what it was like, a never ending weight, a huge black force pushing down from above. Behind the wall of denial that was my pride I knew that this wasn't just raining down upon me on the astral plane though. It was pouring within my soul. This was a heavy black power that pushed away even the urge to smile, let alone leave anything to smile about. It was stretching my sanity and the strain began to pull at the fabric of my mind, which began to crack at the seams.

The strangest thing at the time was that this pain was punctuated by visits from my Goddess. Hecate would manifest as densely as Lucifer and lift me from the depths of despair, sometimes in sexual magick, sometimes just in possession and channelling. It didn't matter. Her presence brought with it a sparkling energy that was of stellar origin. The respite was short during each occasion, but welcomed with open arms each time. At first I said nothing about the pain. Stiff upper lip, soldier on, this is the way it is meant to be. I didn't last. I felt like a kid who was being bullied at school and didn't want to tell his mother. That's how I felt, like I was totally out of my depth. I was. The blackness continued to flow into my soul. The thought that this was true alkhemy at the highest level did little to raise my suffering spirit from despair. I was now being overwhelmed. Each visit by Hecate felt like a breath of air for a man whose head was being held under water until the last burning second of oxygen in the lungs. Each time She left me it was back to being dunked into the black despair. What had I done here? My mind went through all kind of scenarios from everything I had ever done wrong coming back to haunt me to fables of pomegranate seeds. I could not understand why the mighty Lucifer who had been, although always intense, nothing other than amiable could turn this way. Maybe I had made a mistake in the rite? Deep down, I knew that wasn't the truth.

I hit several points during the process where I would try to fight back. The first and most obvious was banishing. No result. I wasn't really that naive to think that a pentagram, some rituals and prayers and incense (no matter whose name it was in) would stop this. In the end everything that I tried, every barrier that I put up, was crushed or just moved aside. Lucifer would increase the frequency of the energy each time, as if making a point. As the volume and vibration of the khem intensified within my soul, so too did the manifestations and the possessions. Again they were at opposite ends of the spectrum. Though now, the duration of each became completely unbalanced. It seemed as though Hecate would only come just as my sanity felt like it would be about to split. She would stay long enough for me to remember why I was doing this, though I never lost sight of how much I loved Her, then She was gone. Lucifer, on the other hand, would indulge me for hours. Not just in passive contemplative moments either, but throughout the entire day. It became difficult to focus on anything at these times, let alone anything positive; nevertheless, I tried.

As I observed the increasing duration of Lucifer's visits, I decided to return the compliment. The first attempt was in my bathroom of all places. The venue wasn't important to me, just the intensity of the dark solar flame which carried the Horned King into my form in full possession as I called Him forth. I stopped fighting and stepped up to the challenge allowing my mind to fully merge with His, letting the alkhemical energy alter the vibration of both mind and soul to that of a Witch God. The planes converged. I was now looking through a solid wall into another realm which showed blood soaked tunnels that radiated pure magickal energy. This was how He saw the universe. This was how they as Gods not only saw it, but could travel through dimensional gates, created by their own power, making their incursions into and between the many planes. As I opened myself to these visions Lucifer seemed to allow more energy to flow to me. The gnosis that is contained within this type of high frequency current gushed forth into my soul granting me knowledge of so much more than I had ever been aware of in these realms before.. Unfortunately, as I discovered, this little gift had a price when performed at this time; it intensified the flow of the black horror that was drowning me spiritually. Attempting to back it off I did the worst thing possible under the circumstances. I tried to back pedal from the experience entirely.

In a cast circle I called all that could. I opened the gates of the dayside spheres and drew in more light while attempting to hold the energies of the nightside at bay. This, I hoped, would give me more balance. Perhaps psychologically it gave me a brief respite, but not for long. There was even some communication in the direction of the Great Michael. I am no stranger to the empyrean realm, embracing it as I do the infernal in my practice. I received in reciprocation to my communication, compassion, a reminder of free will in calling this change upon myself and the directive that this was my path and one way or another I would have made my own way here to this point of soul evolution. Both Lucifer and Hecate were present. The Horned God had not left, in fact the intensity of the black energy now increased. I could see Hecate, peripherally and flashes. I was still in the circle when I broke down. I have no shame in telling this. I just felt as though the light was being suffocated from my very soul. I know that the soul is the gateway of life to all incarnations. The power of the soul keeps the body alive. It was my soul that was being suffocated by the black khem and the accompanying relentless flames of the Witch Gods. I was scared. Nothing in the experiences of losing and burying many friends and saying a similar last goodbye to one very loved girlfriend could have prepared me for this. In five active service tours, the odd angry shot and occasional land mine from Armagh to Pristina, nothing prepared me for this. I just felt like I was so crushed under this weight that I could not stand anymore. I crumpled. I hadn't quite got to the why are you letting this happen, stage when Hecate spoke to me.

> *I cannot give you the faith to complete this journey, You must find it within yourself. I can only tell you that I know that you have it.*

It took a couple of minutes to sink in. Her words hit me at my core, at the part of me that knew She was right, the part that loved Her so much. That was the part of me which fed the strength and the will to get back up, to the rest of me. I re-initiated the communication with Lucifer; still within the circle, for all the good it was doing me. It wasn't as though I had far to send the message either, He spent most of the day and night with me at the moment. I asked Him why He was doing this to me. Lucifer replied.

> *I am the primary initiator upon the soul path of Hecate. I am the breath of flame.*

I don't know whether it was a moment of clarity or stupidity, I won't ever know, but I addressed Lucifer again, I won't do it. I know what you are trying to get me to do and I won't. I won't throw Her name down. I won't spit it out and I won't recant. So you may as well take me to the next level. The Horned God opened an etheric hand before me. In His palm was what looked like a small camel, nothing more. A gift! Lucifer's voice in my head. A camel? What was I going to do with an etheric camel? Had I been more accomplished in my reading of the writings of Kenneth Grant at the time I may have understood the symbolism immediately. For now it was lost on me. I accepted the camel. With an instruction to me to form a ritual on the second full moon from today Lucifer seemed to withdraw. The weight appeared to have eased a little, though I was now so tired that maybe I just didn't care. Either that or I was getting accustomed to it. All I knew was that I had basically just told the Witch Gods to give it their best shot and accepted whatever challenge taking a camel from the first born son of Hecate meant.

The journey of the Abyss is personal to the individual, I know that now. Once the dark khem and the flames of Lucifer have empowered the soul it is ready to step into the true darkness. The tests of the soul are as interwoven with the mundane incarnation as the soul itself is with the body it inhabits upon this plane. As the Gods of witchcraft stepped back, with even Hecate becoming little more than a flash of inspiration and hope, the next phase of transmutation began.

Through a twist of mistimed events, cancelled sales and a whole host of other horrendous little events, the structure of my day to day life fell like lined up dominoes. This began with the collapse of my real estate business. Everything of any financial importance around me zigged when it should have zagged. It all fell. This is what is sometimes termed as a divine shunt. Knowing that it could be for one's own good isn't always the greatest comfort! Hecate was allowing the trials of the darkest of crossings; I was to witness things that are perhaps best not described and sometimes best not seen at all; to merge with the tribulations of mundane life.

On the mundane I lost the ability to pay for the luxury apartment that I had bought as an investment for myself. That was just the beginning. My greatest weakness had always been material gain. The money left completely. The Rolex that I had worn on my wrist for nine years was pawned along with the gold boxing gloves that I bought for myself as a present when I won the Southern Counties of England amateur boxing championships years before. The car was returned to the hire company. No attempt to find any employment elsewhere was successful with most applications being strangely ignored outright. At least I was not parted from my beloved mountain bike! I had however, been exposed to a lashing of the ego that will never be forgotten.

All that I thought that I held in power had been challenged by those who truly hold eternal power. I felt like a helpless child. My pride lay sacrificed on Hecate's altar.

On the transmundane, the journey of the Abyss seemed to have started before Lucifer offered me the camel. Though of course this may have just been my perception of the hideous chain of events that were triggered within and around me at that time. The most remarkable thing, in retrospect, was the visions of all that I saw in this supposedly desolate place. As my consciousness soared to match the flight of my soul across the dark desert crossing, I was party to the most powerful of experiences. Certainly Hecate and Lucifer had stepped back; though I do not doubt that they were observing; but I was by no means alone.

It is the soul which delivers the gnosis and visions of the higher planes to the mind. In the crossing of the desert of the Abyss at the Gates of Daath, the eyes of the soul are opened very wide indeed. I saw the huge inhabitant of this realm. A titan which just seemed to be a gigantic mass of eyes and mouths with no particular distinguishing shape to it. It wasn't exactly hard to see, it reflected through my soul eyes to my physical eyes onto every surface upon which I looked. This was what I was passing alongside on this journey. Though this huge being, which has as many names as it has legends concerning its role in the universe of man, paid me little heed, I wont ever forget the eyes though. It was the eyes that made me realise what this was, that it was not just some amalgamated thoughtform. The eyes showed within them a powerful and cunning awareness; this was a very ancient intelligence. It was the dark guardian of this realm.

The further into the crossing I found myself, the more detached I felt from not just Hecate, but even Lucifer. It brought a surprising sadness. This was hardly a time when I could quietly contemplate this detachment though. My mind was being stretched in many different directions all at once. The flames had gone but the sanity tests had not! The buzzing and vibrating that seemed almost a part of me appeared to be the energy signature of this part of my journey. In truth I could have dealt with that alone and would not have felt so perturbed about this particular stage; just as long as I didn't have to swallow any more of that black khem; were it not for the physical plain manifestations of some of the denizens of the Abyss. The buzzing of the Abyss took on a new dimension with the arrival into my home, in hordes, of little flying ants. Of all the creatures to manifest near me these were the ones that were guaranteed to bring out the worst reaction. Fascinating they are! Love them in my home I most certainly do not! They were everywhere. Landing on me as I tried to sleep at night. They didn't bite, didn't sting, they just helped push my sanity that little bit further apart. Combine their arrival with the intensity of the buzzing which increased to a spiritual crescendo during the quiet hours; around the time the ants would come out to play; and I wasn't dealing with all of this so well. The ants were the manifestation of the soul stripping denizens of the Abyss; you could have told me that they were working in my favour and I still would not have been particularly enamoured with the situation. I just tried to take it one day at a time.

As I faced the transmutation of my soul alone and all around me on the mundane fell, I resolved out of nothing other than pure love for Hecate, to hold dear to my heart my own personal vision of my beloved Goddess. Deep inside myself I knew that, though the ordeal I was undertaking did everything to convince me otherwise, She would not abandon me. I addressed Hecate at Her altar, telling Her that I thought that perhaps She did want to see that I would crawl over hot coals for Her, and confirming that I would do so much more than that. Another moment of clarity or something else; but I made a vow. I swore that no matter what they threw at me I absolutely would not turn from this path or this arte.

Maybe it was this faith or maybe something else entirely but it was around this time that the tensions which the transmundane energies placed upon my soul began to ease. The little crawling, flying house guests vanished as quickly as they arrived. Their departure not only brought great relief but also allowed more uninterrupted sleep. The second full moon from the time I had accepted Lucifer's camel gift was only a couple of days away. I once again felt as though I had a clear enough head to work correctly and effectively in ritual.

The rite that was held on this full moon will always be a landmark for me in this particular lifetime. I steadied myself before the ritual. The buzzing was still around me, but I was accustomed now. The tensions had eased and I was getting by each day. Though it was just that, getting by. I was however still very wary and approached the evening's proceedings tentatively. Hecate and Lucifer were both called in devoted evocation accompanied by offerings of my own blood and sexual fluids, as was our custom. The rite then proceeded into one of possession and conjoined soul communion. To say that I was greeted with pure love would be to grossly understate and marginalise the entire work and the intentions of the Witch Gods to whom it was dedicated. I was once again overwhelmed but this time with the utmost loving and caring all encompassing energy. Even the intense and mighty Lucifer emanated nothing but pure love for me; though it did take me several seconds to get over an initial wariness of Him that I had developed over the last couple of months, in possession. I knew then that it was soon to be over. All the signs pointed to the end of the ordeal in a very short time.

The crossing once completed signified the end, for now, of the spiritual tests which I had incurred in undertaking the Rite of the Phoenix. There was still the re-building of my life to consider, but for now all I felt was pure spiritual love from both Witch Gods. In the communion of full possession I had needed to ask my beautiful Dark Queen why She had put me through all this. I hadn't even asked to be placed anywhere near the Abyss yet; let alone be thrown into a flaming river of black alkhemy. Well, not in so many words anyway. Hecate's answer was simple. She reminded me of the words that I had used when I asked for more power and knowledge, I had asked Her, To grant me the greatest secrets of this arte, the knowledge that is hidden from Gods and men! She then informed me:

> *You were only given what you asked for child. Knowledge is power. Power is delivered at the level of the soul. Your soul needed preparation to receive the coming gnosis. Now it is prepared. Your faith carried you through the darkest of times. When all is tested beyond its limits faith must be found within oneself. The dark desert of the Abyss can be crossed with faith alone!*

Hecate's statement highlighted the significance of Lucifer's gift; all that the camel requires to cross the desert it holds within itself. The Queen of Hell was not finished with Her revelations though. Hecate showed me that the life that I led up to this point was, by and large, guided by Her; the bad as well as the good.

> *To prepare you, to strengthen you in readiness for the task which now lies ahead of you for the remainder of this incarnation.*

This knowledge was delivered with compassion, but reinforced with glimpses through the veil of time as Hecate illustrated Her words with periods and events in both my own current life, and those of past incarnations, that were relevant to the powerful message that She now delivered:

You have always been my child, my spiritual warrior.

I suppose Her profound words would have really tweaked my ego at this point, if it wasn't already lying in shreds around me. I didn't care though. I felt like this was the start of everything. Hecate seemed to sense my feelings on the matter and informed me that this was where I would begin to learn again, as a child at the feet of the Queen of Hell, Heaven and Earth and Her Horned consort; He who is the Breath of Flame!

Post rite, the early hours of the morning brought intense vibrations. Immense energy frequencies radiated to my being from more than Witch God, though they were no doubt initiated by Hecate. The understanding of lives long past and the illumination of my soul path thus far was reinforced by many visions. The energy intensified into audible buzzing that increased until it was deafening to the ears of the soul as portals opened and visions of lands full of pyramids abounded. I didn't care about the intensity of the energy now, it wasn't something that I was ever going to sleep through but what it heralded was very welcome.

Once all the tests had passed my life slowly started to take form again. Though not in the direction from which it had come. I began to write more of Hecate, to search more. To go deeper into Her mysteries. In short my life became filled with all of the work that I love, undertaken in the name of the Goddess that I love so very much. Daily life was a little bit hand to mouth for while, but I never really had to go without. Something would always be provided, as long as I performed the work that She wishes me to follow. All that I require is always there for me. I did not lose the house into which I had placed my investment money in the end, after a long tenancy which came at the eleventh hour it is now about to be sold. Though to be honest I would willingly place it up there on Hecate's altar, so to speak, if that's the way it would have to be in order to balance all that is necessary to continue this work. I accepted that choice when I realised that that was one of my lessons. I am never going to be rich and I neither care, nor want to be. I have found something far more valuable than any money that will ever cross my palm. What I have in the work that I undertake with Hecate is pure gold.

Every single day of my life is now dedicated to the work that I do for my beautiful Goddess, bringing back as much as I can of the gnosis that has been lost for so many thousands of years. The happiness that I feel in this life; whether conjoined with Hecate, Lucifer or both in my soul work and magickal practice; is happiness that flows from doing the work itself. I feel this love and contentment at the level of mind , heart and soul. Hecate gave me the one thing that was missing from my mundane life, its total involvement with and dedication to Her. Upon the transmundane, at soul level, She still gives me so much more.

The secrets and gnosis that I craved so much are still unravelling at a tremendous pace, nearly every day. This includes the knowledge of my own experiences, such as the Rite of the Phoenix which opens the path of the nightside at the gate of moon where the soul is propelled directly up the middle pillar, as Lucifer releases the Magickal Fire of the Gods to initiate the first phase one of the highest and most powerful forms of spiritual alkhemy. The sheer velocity of this journey catapults the soul into the great Abyss. The path of higher learning begins with the success of this crossing.

Not long after everything began to pick up for me I bumped into the spiritual friend who had tried to warn me of Hecate's power. Upon hearing of the events of the previous few months she remarked about Hecate: *"She has now made you totally Her's"*. To which I replied, *"No, She Made me.... a long time ago. I have always been Hers. She simply used the Phoenix Rite to awaken me"*.

This was the path that I had seen before I undertook the journey through the City of Pyramids. This was the lore that I had to abide by as a soul on the Path of Hecate; to be awoken in each incarnation, to learn again as a child at Her feet, before I could once more carry the Torch of Hecate for others. This task is the greatest honour of my existence. This is, and always will be a journey undertaken in love. Through the Rite of the Phoenix and the baptism of its flames I have found my way home. It is where I am meant to be.

Figure 35 - Shrine at the Crossroads by MDL

Dark Night of the Soul

By Naza Cogo

Your eyes have fear at the sight of me ,
but your soul trusts me, you are yearning to embrace me,
you wonder if you should fear me, your soul cries out to love me,
this my child is because you were created by me.
My dark womb is the home of your soul,
The essence of She who is all, the Dark Queen, absorbed into thee
filled with magick, prophecy, ancient knowing,
I have Blessed you my child you are to serve me.
I am Hekate Queen of Witches,
You have been chosen to walk in my service and honour me.

My husband asked me to do a tarot reading for him, which he never usually did. I began to lay out my cards, which didn't look very good, I saw that Death was coming for a King of Cups. I was horrified at what I was seeing as the only *"King of Cups"* I could think of was my husband's brother Sanel. I told my husband the cards didn't look good and I hated bringing this news to him. Within a week, my brother in law Sanel, aged 32, had a heart attack in his sleep and died. We received the news and our world was now covered with darkness... he was so young, it was such a tragedy and we were grief stricken. I couldn't bear to see my husband in such pain, I had to change this, I had to turn this darkness into light, and I was desperate to make the shift...

The only thing I knew to do was to call upon Hekate.

> *"Beloved Hekate hear my calls .... This grief and pain I cannot bear, I cannot see my beloved husband grieve so deeply. I have come to ask your aid. Lift this darkness from our lives, grant me a child, a son, let Sanel's soul incarnate through me, to bring joy to my husband and his parents, I will sacrifice my body and soul, to have this child if it will free my beloved husband from this grief, and I will pay whatever the price will be, my Goddess I ask you to shine your lantern over me..."*

I called my husband into the room, and I told him, I will bear you a son, Sanel will incarnate through me, now as his body is being buried into the earth, from the heaven's Hekate will send his soul into my womb. He will be born through me again. We made love, then I saw Her, standing on top of the moon and placed a seed from her cupped palms upon the rays, as I made love to my husband, my focus was on what she was showing me. The moon beams began to slowly come towards me, as I made love to my husband I felt a cold yet soothing feeling over my womb. I knew Hekate had heard me call, she was implanting the soul within my womb. As we completed our love making, I told my husband that life had been implanted within my womb.

The next morning when I awoke, I felt like a different person, like I was no longer me. As I got out of bed, nausea came over me, and I spent the next week vomiting and feeling very sick. I knew that I was pregnant. As the second week went by, I waited to see if I would menstruate...but nothing, tests confirmed I was with child.

When the realisation had kicked in I was suddenly surrounding myself in darkness...panic came over me. This was to be my fourth child, how would I cope, I have to go through pregnancy and childbirth all over again, even thoughts of abortion raced through my mind and it was then I was shown one sentence *"You will not disturb the cycle of rebirth."* So I made peace with carrying this child and bringing its soul onto the earth, after all it was what I had asked for. My pregnancy was drowned in depression and darkness, I was very ill, nausea never left me, and I became angry, scared and bitter fearing whether I would be able to cope with such a big family. I got lost in my dark thoughts, in my dark world and didn't want to come out of it.

Was this the price I would have to pay? To live in this world of darkness for the exchange of my wish. Hekate let me be in my Darkness, when I was getting to deep she would lift me with her whisper *"Your Son is coming, he needs you."* and I would somehow find my way back. She kept me safe, held me when I needed extra strength and saved me when I thought I was going to lose my own soul. It was a very testing time on my family and on my marriage. Not for one day of my whole pregnancy did that darkness leave me, until September 27th 2008, when I awoke to hear my second eldest son Amer telling my daughter Aisha *"Mama is going to born the baby today"*. I tend to listen when Amer speaks as he is a very gifted child. As I slowly got out of bed I felt immense pressure and went to the bath room. I had the "*showing*", then like a sword slicing under my womb I had my first contraction.

My husband was working so I let him know he needed to go to the hospital and I rang my family and friends to come to my aide, to take me to the hospital, and look after my children. I went back into my room, and started chanting in my mind, calling her "*Hekate, Hekate, Hekate*"... over and over, until I knew she had heard me. I was surrounded in breezes of what felt like ice, then I felt it going within me, taking over my whole being, not just my physical body, but also my soul. I had invoked her and she would be with me to greet my son. My friend had arrived and all I could do was breathe...not one word was spoken from my mouth. The pains were growing stronger and we had finally arrived at the hospital. I remember answering nurses with hand gestures, I went into the shower and gestured them to leave, as the pains came on stronger I was still chanting in my mind keeping her with me and before I knew it I was on my knees delivering my son, all the midwife had to do was catch him. She couldn't believe how I had given birth and said to me *"Do you even know how strong you are? How much mental strength and control you have is unbelievable"*, I told her, *"this is the strength of the Goddess Hekate"*. Within one hour of my first contraction I had given birth to my son *"Ashton, Sanel"*, without one sound, without a single word it was done. Hekate who aids in childbirth had completed her duty, looked after her daughter and delivered Sanel's soul back into the world as my son.

I came home the next day, now overcome by baby blues I found myself back in darkness just as I had stepped out of it. My husband and I were arguing, I was so scared of my reality, questioned my own ability and competence as a mother, I didn't feel in control as I normally do, this was horrifying to me. Then I said *"I don't believe in anything anymore, not dreams, not love, not even the Gods"* and my eyes shifted over to the window and what a sight I saw. It was the full moon beaming over at me, without even thinking I said *"Oh yes I do believe! My Goddess is waiting for me! "* I ran outside, and fell to my knees and screamed *"Hekate take this pain and darkness from me, save me before it swallows me completely, lift this darkness from my soul, take it and set me free, the darkness is no longer the place I want to be!"*

With that I stood up, raised my hands to the moon, tears streaming down my face, I was fighting with my own soul, my own heartbeat, and said" *My mother Hekate save me! Heal me! Free me!"* Then to my surprise, before my eyes five separate moon beams dropped and began slowly coming toward me, just as she had sent me the seed....I watched with my own eyes the moons beams come closer and closer, I brought my hands together and cupped my palms to receive...those beams entered through the middle of my palms, as cold as ice...into my bones, into my veins, my entire being.

That night I invoked Hekate, since then she has never left me. I stood outside for about an hour, I could feel the darkness lifting off me, great burdens sliding, I knew she was healing me. I went into the house, hoping to spread her energy upon my husband, but he was very hurt and angry and wanted time alone, so instead I asked Hekate, so heal him. Two hours later he came to me...and with that I knew that finally my dark night of the Soul was over 11 months later.

ASHTON'S BLESSING CEREMONY

You and I were meant to be,
again you have chosen to find me,
We have journeyed lives before,
promised to find each other again once more.

As I was birthing you, it was the Goddess I called
Hekate was present to greet you into this world,
For you my blessed son, are her son too, together we shall guide you
and carry you through...

Carry the Goddess in your heart, always take her along with in your path
for she will protect you and guide you to, the path and fate she has set you too
Remember that she is your mother, as I am too.

I place the blue star on your brow,
wear it with honour be forever proud
Magickal blood flows through your veins
born with knowing, wisdom of ages...
deep in your soul is where it all lies
as you journey your life,
each will unfold
the hidden mysteries that will arise
the answers to all mysteries will be undisguised

Always mind the threefold law, as you giveth that will return
every action, every word think through clearly, for it will be heard
the price will be times three... seek to be the best you can be

Live with love and joy in your heart
find the light whenever it fall dark
always remember to stay true to yourself
and trust your inner self...

Figure 36 - Hekate Kourotrophos by Georgi Mishev

TATTERED SHARDS

MY DARKEST HOUR

BY AMBER-ROSE

When looking back upon my life and my many experiences with the Great Mother, Hecate. None have been more profound than that of my darkest hour. When not even the void, entropic chaos or the abysmal bowels of the deepest chthonic womb could ever compare to the forlorn sorrow I suffered at the hands of a blackheart. A time when I had felt powerless, timorous and lamented over the rapid turn my life had taken. Looking back through time, many signs came flooding back to fill the deluge of reminiscences and nightmares. Young and impressionable, and, a little naïve when it came to relationships; especially when that relationship turned rotten and sour to the very apple core, no longer the sweet ripe fruit hoped for... instead decayed, fetid and sordid. At the age of seventeen, I had left New Zealand to be with someone who clearly did not deserve my devotion, admiration. The night prior to leaving, my Mother and I shared quite a few tears and I knew she did not want me to go; that she knew no good would come of my adventure. Still stubborn, determined she watched me leave; fly out of her life- little did I know it was nearly a permanent endeavour. Adolescent love, one that by no means should ever take the tolls mine had. Things turned violent rather quickly, where many results of the abuse rendered me in hospital and in even one case in a wheelchair for numerous months.

People usually look upon women who suffer abuse with an expression of antipathy or shame. However, sometimes your life is at risk as was mine. During these eruptions, and sometimes even before the outbreaks (though at the time it did not register as anything but a coincidence)- but, I would hear the raucous growling of dogs, at times shrill bitter howls of baying hounds; the type of timbre that make the blood curdle and tiny fragments of fine hair stand on end. On the odd occasion even a whispering hiss accompanying the growls or howls except this wasn't in my unequivocal hearing but rather right in the forefront of my conscience. Regardless of searching later high and low for the hounds, even as I was picking up clumps of blonde hair or trying to subside the bleeding of cuts and wounds. Countless times I thought my sanity was questionable. Many times I ran only to be hunted down like the wounded rabbit I was, trying to find a safe hole and allow all the wounds to heal. Softly spoken words that things would change or the threats towards my Mother's life always lead me back to the prison of his twisted, sick love. Again and again the brutality, sadism and sheer cruelty emerged, slamming into me like a gigantic hammer that I could never avoid. I simply never knew when it would come, this terror, my own personal living, breathing nightmare.

There were many times my face was dappled with bruises, arms and throat black and blue- still the growls continued, closer and closer until I felt their hot malodorous breath upon the back of my nape. Juxtaposed in his clinging wraith I remained, many times leaving and many times returning. Eventually everyone I loved had turned away, no longer able to witness this horror or my inability to permanently leave. In all hindsight, I do not blame them for doing so, for as they say *"Ignorance is bliss!"* Yes, this man frightened me but it wasn't until one night that I was stabbed that I became to know him as psychotic; and that he was hell-bent on killing me. This was when Hecate appeared for the first time in her wrathful, fear-provoking manifestation. Still to this day, I am not sure if I was awake or dreaming. Stygian and nigrescent, rivulets whipping against the elements which collided around her, like waves crashing against jaded obsidian rocks. Garb of serpent skins and pelts of animals draped around her Titanic form- the winds and air clashing upon her like a ravenous tornado. Nevertheless, it was her eyes that pulled me into the arms of fear. Reflectionless, opaque and void of sympathy, affection and all emotion; and yet in this poignant lurid dread her left hand rose towards me and in the palm of that hand coiled a gilded snake before it turned to charred ashes. Talons of wind gyrating, bringing those ashes up into its tempestuous embrace only to disperse them to the elements while she faded back into the plethoric cloak of darkness- no word spoken just the cold sensation of death. Subterranean embryonic.

That image struck hard in my mind. I had missed quite a few cycles and a visit to my doctor was required. It was not uncommon for me to miss a cycle or two when under stress and physical distress. After a few tests, disbelief and half-hearted joy I discovered I was pregnant, quite a way gone. Surprised I had not lost this little life growing inside of me numerous times over. My Mother had become gravely concerned about my health at this time, I was dreadfully underweight, skin a deathly white and black rings under my eyes. Literally like death and felt not a great deal better. When admitted into hospital urgently by ambulance after suffering a severe paroxysm, a lot more tests, it was discovered I had been poisoned by arsenic and quite close to death. The seizure had been a very minor brain seizure and respiratory failure, similar to an epileptic fit. Four weeks in hospital I was released. Poisoning was put down to the water at his parents place since at that time I drunk mostly from the stream (since it was mountain stream water), and them finding low levels of arsenic in the same water supply from farms in the area.

Again my Dark Mother appeared to me, in the midst of the trouble with the law, knew no better and being the naïve youth as stipulated prior I believed his story. So we ran, baby and all. During this whole time of being a fugitive's accomplice on the run, again the hounds came to warn me. It was a growl much similar to my familiar Hera's growl when something is not right or someone is there who shouldn't be. A caveat that danger was approaching, an impending warning that soon my life would take a horrific turn, one that would stay with me even after the darkness had lifted. You see, I wear my scars like a crown, they are there as remembrance to my son, that he chose to save me, even if it meant a sacrifice. In all hindsight, I remember little of the actual evening this man took my sons life. All I know that I was incredibly tired and hurting at the onslaughts of violence that continued even after my son's birth. Trying to runaway only to have him nearly run us down in the car in the telephone box while I screamed down at the other end of my sister back in New Zealand; how he bred fear into me to the point I wore it upon my face, and within my eyes.

The say the eyes are the mirror into your soul, while mine writhed in torment and fear, fear for not only for myself but also the life of a small angel who depended so much upon me... and who ultimately I failed. It was in the deep Dark Moon in all her hellish fury and whipcord, her portrayal was the same except for this time she wore a black horned crescent upon her brow and this time in the palm of her left hand it wasn't a serpent but a pulsating vortex of rubiescent energy. Within this orb, black veins palpitated in a steady yet rapid reverberation. Synchronizing to this quick motion was a drumming resonation, like a deep beat, a heartbeat and I knew this my growing baby held in her hand. A hand that could lovingly nurture, effortlessly crush like a delicate petal between two stones: birth and a tombstone. This tiny miracle portended before me like a revelation, in the centre of this crimson globe a tiny shape appeared and I marvelled at it for it was my child and I knew within my heart it was so. Hecate revealed to me that this beautiful and emergent life was indeed male. I remember the joy I felt in my soul that my baby was a boy.

A joy that as I write this account of my life makes me smile warmly, the fervour of that memory filling me with love, yet also a deep despondency. My hands reached out to cup this incandescent phenomenon, yet finding my hands upon my abdomen, discovering for the first time a Mother's affection and protectiveness. When my eyes looked up to see Hecate, the orb had grown black, dying and my child along with it. Her face had changed from one of gladness to one of mourning, even in her throes of terror and frightening facade, I no longer feared her but held great concern for this vision and the welfare of my defenceless child. These images and apprehensions carried with me till the birth of my son, and just when things couldn't be any worse, my then partner had gotten his own self in a situation of major trouble where the law was involved. Knowing no better and since everyone I could have originally turned to had turned away, I had no better resources and not in a position to argue. He had told me that should he go to prison, I would lose my son. The only option being to run from the law and if I didn't go with him, his Mother would go for custody and money always wins against those who have none. Me, who had never been in trouble knew no better and took to flight. Leaving behind all reason and any facade of stability I had. Tensions ran exceedingly high and the more volatile things had become right up until the night that he took my son's life; I did not hear a cry or even a whimper at his passing. Still, I do not know if it was out of pure exhaustion or intervention out of protection that I did not awake until early morning nor did I dream of the premonitions yet to be.

In all honesty, I do not expect anyone to be able to relate to this, keep in mind the exhaustion, mentally, physically and emotionally during this entire time where I felt completely like a hostage. Not being able to call anyone, no one saw me at any motel which we stayed in and at during the last days even locked in the motel room after the fact. I will not go into detail the injuries my son suffered, but again he went on the run and dragged me along with him by force. In this time of mayhem and loss I actually managed to crawl out of a small window in the bathroom of a two-storey motel room and down the fire escape to phone my Mother. Again, Hecate came to me in the same image as before except this time in her left hand she held a torch and in the right a serpent. This serpent kept trying to bite her, but at every bite, it bit itself-poisoning itself. That night I awoke in a cold sweat, even the air around me in the room conglomerated in misty tendrils from exhalation of warm breath against the blizzard of forewarning. In this prescience the sounds of the dogs took upon a more yelping intonation, as if beaten and broken by lack of sustenance or the abuse of the rod. Painful, despairing and desolate, various pitches differing between choirs of lament; incensed with revenge- plagued of death and vilification.

Visionary death; and the threats to go along with it- words idle enough to rub the salt into the scourge wounds. Myself too weak with the bereavement, in a bottomless pit of drunkenness to care about my own life...Weak, you may think. Listen, I can tell you that the murder of a child at the hands of another is something that can break even the toughest of spirits. It is easy to sit back, read and judge a person for the mistakes they have made. Unless you have lived the experience, felt it and suffered it, you cannot and will not know. I ask for no pats on the back or pity, I have suffered before the courts of Hecate and her scorn. I have felt her hounds biting at my heels and experienced the harsh rectitude of their tempered hellish natures. From the time I suffered, to the time the authorities broke down the door to arrest us both, only in the due time to safe my life from being extinguished, rolled up in carpet and dumped at the side of the road as indicated by statement of intent. To him pointing the finger at me for the murder of my son, our arrest and charges in regards to said conviction, or rather Police brutality on my behalf. Pending bail and serving time in one of Australia's most infamous female prisons, Boga Road, Brisbane. My mindset in the darkest phase it has ever been, where I did not care if I lived or died and certainly welcomed the mainstream to have a grand old crack at it. By this time only just at the age of eighteen, 1994.

Despite losing any semblance of sanity I had left. Regardless of the depleted strength I had having to deal with the loss of a child in horrendous circumstance- let alone the guilt I felt so cavernous inside that it was my fault and it was me who failed in protecting an innocent life that had no way of defending itself. I failed as a Mother, I failed as a Warrior and most importantly, I failed Hecate. It was not the fear that gripped my heart in regards to the women at Boga Road, instead it was the fear that I no longer cared about my own life because everything I held sacrosanct had been stolen from my hands and I was incapable to take it back. I could not reverse time, resurrect the deceased or forgive myself- I closed myself off to the world around and returned back to the womb of darkness. Forgiveness has always been a weakness of mine and yet I was enabling to resolve myself, and forgive myself. I tried taking my own life numerous times, not the cute sneaky way of searching for sympathy with a loose noose or flippant collection of medication stashed every night in my pillow for a month or two. Every attempt was met with Hecate standing there with torch ablaze and other palm pushing me back to the land of the living. All I wanted was to be at peace, and be with my boy in the beautiful Summerland, away from this mortal affliction, this gripping agony that endlessly raged throughout my entire body.

There was not a day that went passed where I did not ache, physically, mentally but most important of all spiritually. I had nearly given up on my innocence to this crime, my faith and ability to see the positive aspects to situations surrounding me. Even though I 'knew' I was innocent to the fact, I still blamed myself for the beautiful light of this life to be callously snuffed by an evil person. My tears never ended, I cannot for the life of me remember a time where I cried so much- my winter was perpetual, the oceans were infinite and darkness everlasting. To feel truly lost in the night is one thing, but to be entirely asphyxiated by your own darkness is another. It is like having ink completely obscure your eyesight and despite all the tears it never dilutes or washes away; just makes it all the more painful to endure. My heart was utterly devastated, broken into a million glittering shards of fragmental dreams...{shattered}. Every fibre of me yearned, shook with distress and there was not a night my pillow wasn't drenched in the fountain of Lethe, only I could not forget.

Only relive the night over and over again. How many times can you beat yourself up? How many times can you bleed for mistakes? How many years does one have to cry? The answer is simple...for as long as it takes for you to find forgiveness and meaning.

It would be lies to state I was not frightened and giving up on any semblance of faith in the judicial system. Just when I had hit the lowest pinnacle of my darkest hour, Hecate appeared again to me only this time the shrieking winds did not accompany her or the snapping Paramounts at her sides with the gravel and grating growls. Facial features were not of horror but of lament, the same lament which gripped my heart to crush it as if it were a delicate petal caught in the wintry breeze of spite. I was closer to death than what I had ever been, willed, faded, wilted away like the white silken flowers upon my sons grave. She poured upon me the vision of my son happy in her embrace, nurtured by her love and mine- amalgamated together to form a catalyst that no negativity or dark thing could cross. She showed me that I needed to be strong and stand true to myself so that others could have faith in me because I was destined for great things...in her honour. Amongst these portraits of faith and belief she showed me that he would be brought to justice and that my innocence would be proclaimed as long as I stood firm and true to myself. Her torch would always be there to shine my way home, but it was entirely up to me if I took her path or chose to stumble my way within the darkness; either way, I would always find my way home just that it was my will and choice how I accomplished that.

During these dark days, I saw her frequently and continuously felt her presence radiate all around me. Everything she had stated to me came to pass. Within a couple of months I was released, though his trial continued and justice served. All that was required of me was a little faith and belief in my integrity, honour and loyalty to Hecate. Hecate always providing to me what I needed the most...just like she always had, and with what she thought I required not what I had asked. Throughout my entire life and even until this day Hecate has provided for me, held her torches to light my way and prompted her hounds to nip at my heels when straying from my path and purpose; even when I needed guidance into the simplest of matters. Despite her being in whatever form, I urge you not to fear her- even in the form of battle, death and destruction; it is only because that is the strength of her we need the most. To remind us, we are her Daughters and that her strength is our strength. I did not know this before, but I certainly do now; we have a relationship beyond words, beyond sentiment and mortal meaning. With her I transcend the stars, dance upon the moon and hold the torch aloft so that others may find her, and their way within the swarming tenebrous serpentine shadows of night. *"Hers was the wisdom that comes in darkness, in suffering, in pain, in dreams. Thus her wisdom is available to all, though very few embrace it!"* I found her in the cave of my soul, when I thought I had no soul left. In the liminal spaces between my light and darkness, I turned myself inside and out to discover the potency of her ways, and in doing so, not only did I discover her- but I also discovered myself.

Hail Hecate!

Figure 37 - Twin Torches by Brian Andrews

Twin Torches

By Brian Andrews

As much as I love her in my own quiet way, Hekate has not often been a goddess I have actively pursued. Which is peculiar, because she is the one goddess who I have worked with the most over the years. She has certainly been the focus of a lot of my art and yet to me she has always seemed slightly distant. Not cold, not hard as such. More like a warm piece of wood or an item of furniture that one is very fond of. Hekate is just there; calm, serious, knowing, yet willing to let me find out what is going on. (Unlike, for me, Sekhmet; who is as hot and punishing as the noon sun and yet a cause for celebration. Or the Morrigan, who is the furious mad ranting scratchy cow from across the water in Ireland, where my Mother and her Mother are from.)

Hekate however stands resolute in my mind. Not harshly determined but still an irresistible thought and force that drives me. For my part, I might as well try to resist the night. When she comes, it is not with vengeance but a quiet knowing. *'This is going to happen'*, *'that has been going on'* and then we walk on together.

I recently found myself cut off from living a normal life and interacting with many of my friends in a comfortable or positive way. Even while coping with anxiety and depression Hekate stood a little way off. I took my time, because that was what the situation warranted and though I had to step back from witchcraft, I never said that I would never return. She did return to me though, like an old song on the radio. Not something I love to sing along in my mind or dance around the kitchen to. But a familiar if melancholy song rising to a great crescendo and then she wandered off again.

Hekate always seems to encourage passion and a winding up of energy until a task is done, or a safe plateau is reached then she drops off. It is the end of this song and later she will come again. Once more filling my dreams with half heard songs, following me down to the underworld where I feel safer in the darkness and shadows. Where I feel I belong. And yet Hekate is not often a great comfort. Clutching twin torches in both her hands, she cannot hold me or cradle me. All she can do is let her torches reflect on objects so that I can try to tell what is going on. And yet anyone who has ever lit an object with two light sources will tell you that you end up with two shadows. And that is where things can start to go wrong but the fault is not with Hekate.

The key of working with two shadows is that here are two lights. Two sources of illumination and I try to look at the object from both angles. By moving from one light to the other I can see how different actions create different outcomes and by constantly changing the angles I learn much more about what I am thinking about. And yet as I said before she cannot comfort me or reassure me, but she can enlighten me and then it is for me to carry on and use her lights as a guide. Rather than having one huge defining decision, cutting it up can be a better use of my time as I then understand the whole more clearly.

When I studied life drawing one of the key skills was to consider the whole at the same time as an individual part. By going from macro to micro and returning to macro repeatedly I learned to understand the whole and the part as one. One of the things that I often got caught up on in witchcraft was worrying about a small task or detail I had to perform, rather than understanding the whole. When I step back and try not to micro manage a situation it is easier to see how each small detail fits into the whole ritual and what energies I must control for each section to fit together as one. Just as with Hekate it is very easy to touch on this point or that point but stepping back I see that she is mistress of heaven, earth and sea.

Because Hekate has always seemed a distant enigma she often fills me with doubt. She is hard to understand as there is never one clear interpretation of her actions so it is easy for me to mislead myself and be misled in turn. That though is why being slightly distant can help, because I can also step back and not try to comprehend everything at once. After my recent bout of anxiety I have had to learn how to cope with losing a great amount of confidence and ability to adapt quickly to experiences. Instead I have to carefully look at things from more than one angle. Often having to understand the constituent parts of a situation and then wait and view it as a whole to work out how other people are reacting to them. By passing a light from one side to another different things are revealed and sometimes very tellingly I see what gets hidden. It is not a fast realisation, as with Hermes, it is a constant steady onward pace. It is rarely humorous or enticing; it is more often than not like walking through a dark tunnel. At that point it is as if Hekate is there anyway and we fall into step but we don't walk *together* she is always a little behind my right-hand shoulder even though I am right handed my right hand side had always been the lighter. My left is the steady anchor and always slightly more abundant.

While two torches may seem an over abundance of fire and potential for harm it also creates a balance that most deities don't posses. I think that this is why Hekate often seems calmer to me. Rather than pointing a single torch up or down she can point both up and another down at the same time signifying both life and death at the same time, rather than either one exclusively. This can appear to be less dynamic than a single thrust in one direction but the potential is also there for both torches to point in one direction and at the same time suggest twice the power and yet also being in balance. This then becomes something very hard to counter. For rather than feint to one side or deal with a single threat there is always a second threat equal to the first. If then we try to deflect both at once we leave ourselves open and potentially defenceless.

Even though she is standing off to one side apparently inactive, it is actually an example and encouragement of how I should act. That I should take the torches in each hand and I should light my own way and by shining the light of illumination myself I can see what makes it easier for people to understand what I am showing them. Am I lighting things too starkly or am I showing them a clear neutral picture of what is happening? My natural reaction is often to obfuscate things as I always prefer to show an impressionistic view of things but by doing that it often leaves too much for the viewer or reader to fathom out for themselves. This is odd as lack of definition has always been a frustration of mine when coming to terms with the mysteries. I sought for hard facts and the hidden truth and they always eluded me. Now though, I am content for the mysteries to remain mysterious. At least in part.

Maybe things don't need to be clearly defined in every aspect of their being but the torch bearer shows us that it is better to take the torches and make our own choices about what we see or show rather than let others show us only what they want us to see.

Figure 38 - Threefold Hekate, Relief from Aigina

Figure 39 - The Path by Tina Georgitsis

ILLUMINATING THE PATH

BY TINA GEORGITSIS

Hekate came to my aid during a dark time in my life. I was just exiting the astrological significance of my Saturn return as an immediate family member whom I had dedicated many years of care had recently passed away. I fell into a dark night of the soul of sorts as I had sacrificed many a thing for this family member. So after their death I started questioning my purpose in life. I became even more troubled as my patrons as well as my spirit guides remained silent when called upon, be it in meditation or ritual. Nevertheless I continued to enter sacred space and practice regular meditation as my faith is what kept me going.

One night, during the Dark of the Moon whilst in meditation I asked for clarification or guidance as I was angry and confused about my path in the mundane world. I was quite irate as I incomprehensibly blurted out this request and I did not expect what would happen next.

A beautiful woman with pale flawless skin appeared to me in a vision. She was between her maiden and mother phase with a white streak in her long black hair. Her robes were a saffron coloured Greco-Roman styled dress, complete with black edged trimming. She had a powerful and commanding yet graceful presence and she felt familiar like I had seen or known her before. I began to tremble, my breath quickened and my heart beat deep and sharp as I stared at her in disbelief. I knew this woman…my breath caught…she wasn't a woman, she was a Goddess! I had worked with her before, within my previous Wiccan covens as well as being aided by her in various forms of magic. This time she appeared differently as if she was summoning me instead.

There she was - Hekate in all her inexpressible magnificence. She leaned towards me and sternly said, *"You are lost. I will help you find your way; I will guide you to plant the seed of your hopes which will grow into fruition. This comes with much devotion and attention given. Dedicate yourself to me and I will illuminate your way."* and with that the vision ended. I stood up from my kneeling pose, still shaking from the experience but I felt lighter, somehow comfortable with the knowledge that I had indeed received an introduction to what I had asked for.

With alacrity I grabbed a nearby pen and notebook then started to compose a ritual to Hekate whilst in a mild trance like state. It flowed easily and once completed I began to construct an impromptu shrine to her. The only place I could put the shrine was facing a door to a storage space which was in an area between the front door and the door leading to the kitchen in my home. Little did I know at the time that her shrines perfect placement was liminal/in between places.

Once her shrine was complete I began the magickal working to her. I created sacred space in the way I was accustomed to, utilizing my witchcraft experience and proceeded to anoint a natural beeswax candle with some Dark of the Moon oil I had previously made. This oil blend contained essential oils and herbs used in her service such as lavender and saffron which I also anointed myself with in an appropriate manner. As a sign of devotion I offered Hekate a coin which was a drachma I had retained from one of my first trips to Greece and an old iron key. Lighting the candle dedicated and inscribed to her with my athame, I evoked Hekate in my own way:

Hekate, Mistress of Magic

I come to you as devotee

Hekate, Light Bringer

Illuminate my way in this time of darkness

Hekate, Guide of the Crossroads

Show me the true path of purpose

Hekate, Opener of Doors

Allow me to seek clarity of vision

Hekate, Keeper of the Key

Unlock your mysteries to me

In a vision similar to the one experienced earlier she appeared and I relayed in my own words where I was in my life, what I felt was holding me back and what my confusion was. I was careful to be clear and concise with my words as well as being completely honest without fear or shame. At the completion of my address Hekate moved aside and showed me a heavy wooden door. She unlocked the door, opened it before me and encouraged me to pass through the door. Once I did this she handed me a key and I found a crossroad before me. Hekate took her place within the centre of the crossroad and held her arms up in supplication. Two blazing torches appeared in her hands and she lit one of the paths in the crossroad ahead. Hekate then handed me a torch and beckoned me to walk along beside her as she guided me down the illuminated path. I followed this radiant path until the answers I was seeking began to appear in the form of images, feelings and words. The answers that Hekate shared with me were both personally and deeply moving. She shared with me that I will always be a caretaker where I guide and assist people in my day to day corporate profession as well as my passionate work as tarot reader, healer and teacher. This has always been my purpose and a journey that has not ended.

I felt great release and joy, with tears streaming down my face I thanked her profusely and promised I would dedicate myself to her. I also swore that I would honour her through regular rites as well as a *deipnon* to her on the New Moon, as sitting down and sharing a meal with loved ones is a beautiful form of magic in her name.

After this rite I worked with her intensely. I found that the ways I started to instinctually work with her, were supported through the writings of others. These writings devoted to Hekate were both modern and ancient and were discovered whilst conducting further research on her. I started coming into constant contact with other devotees of Hekate and I added her as patron to my Lyceum within the Fellowship Of Isis. My Lyceum quite aptly needed a third patron and was called the Lyceum of Heka. That year I began to hold many rites devoted to Hekate with my magical working group. A high point included a public Samhain rite dedicated to Hekate which I was told touched many in attendance. I continue to work many rites in honour of Hekate on my own, as well as with the other devotees of hers that I meet along the way.

I will never forget that Hekate was there for me during a great time of darkness and to this day the devotional is ongoing.

Figure 40 - Hekate Soteira by Shay Skepevski

Hekate's Sacred Lunacy

Bearing the Lunatik Flame

By Shay Skepevski

> "Hear now the words of the Dark Maiden, who was from the beginning, and is for Eternity! Whose womb is the limitless and ever fertile Darkness which births forth all life, light and all creation. I am the Lunar flame of Life. Mine is the Serpentine Labyrinth of Prophetic Knowledge that shall guide thee to thy spiritual truth. Ye who seek to lift my veil and know my true face, know that thy seeking and yearning shall avail thee not, unless thy own face beholds and knows the mysteries of thy own Self. Mine are the Keys that open the gates to all the Mysteries within thee, and Mine is the chalice of Lunatik wine that intoxicates and liberates the spirit from Oblivion and awakens the true self. Kneel before mine most Holy face of night, and I shall shatter the illusions that mask thy mind, and grant thee the Ecstasy of Divine Vision."
> ~'Charge of Dark Lady Hekate', 2009

As 'Guardian of the Gate', Hekate is a Goddess of Liminality and Transitions, of being on and crossing boundaries. Those between Life and Death, Nature and Civilization, Sanity and Madness, and the conscious and unconscious mind. Hers is a knowledge beyond limits. She stands at the crossroads of our mind as we pass from one state of consciousness to another, and resides in the liminal places in our psyche we normally keep in the shadows, such as our dreamworlds and our unconscious. Because these places offer insights which our ordinary consciousness is 'in the dark' about, Hekate connects us to a source of profound spiritual insight, knowledge, and wisdom. She is Kleidouchos the Keeper of the Keys that open the doors of self-knowing, and grants passage into other worlds and other states of being. Granting us vision and insights which cannot be reached with the rational mind. Hekate's light illuminates the Dark and mysterious landscapes of our minds, giving us an even greater awareness of ourselves as we reveal what lies deep within.

While today the term 'Lunatic' is commonly used in a negative sense to describe a person who is mentally ill, dangerous and unpredictable, this is not its original meaning. 'Lunacy' comes from 'Luna', Latin for Moon, and in ancient times the term Lunatic was used to describe someone who was Moonstruck. This condition is also known by the ancient Greek word 'Seleniazomai'. Being moonstruck was considered a state of Divine Inspiration. Similar to the ritual of 'Drawing down the Moon', this Lunatic state can facilitate a connection with the divine, and a greater awareness of one's soul. As the Sender of nocturnal visions, Hekate induces this sacred Lunacy, which the ancients believed was caused by Her sending prophetic visions to humanity through the influence of moonlight. The Lunatic who was 'Moon-

struck' would possess an insight that can only be gained by standing outside of normal perception, their consciousness transcends the illusionary bounds of ordinary reality. To the rational mind, the Lunatic experience is labelled as madness, because it transcends what we see as reality. In this state, one would receive clarity, prophetic insight, creative inspiration and spiritual vision. In many ancient Mystery traditions, such as the Maenads of Dionysos, this temporary state of Madness was a condition that was specifically sought for by initiates for Prophecy, Insight, and Magick.

This state of Hekate's Sacred Lunacy is something I have come to personally call *'Bearing the Lunatik Flame'*. It is the illuminated and visionary insight and awareness of dreamers, seers, artists and mystics. By means of Hekate's Illumination, she guides the seeker to the dark palace of our inner underworld where we can receive innate knowledge of our spiritual truth, and an awareness and insight about ourselves, of who we really are. She holds the key that unlocks the door to the deep realms within our own minds, and she bears the flaming torch that illuminates the landscapes of our inner darkness, revealing both the treasures and the terrors of our unconscious. This insight can sometimes be more then one can bear as Hekate shatters the illusions of the Linear-thinking mind. The initial experience of Hekate's Sacred Lunacy can often seem frightening, confusing and distressing because it is an unfamiliar experience. In my case it may even resemble an experience similar to a panic-attack. We can easily lose our sense of individual self, as she dissolves the ego and rational mind, liberating us into a greater awareness of our Self and how we define ourselves. We can be filled with fear and anxiety and feel as though we are going mad. A descent into what appears like madness I feel is often involved to become initiated into Hekate's Mysteries.

MY DESCENT INTO MADNESS

> *"A Broken mind heals stronger then Before,*
> *Seeing the unseen, as the veil is torn,*
> *Never again will this world be the same,*
> *My shattered mind, Beautiful Again."*
> - *'Mnemosyne – Our Poem'*
> *[2008]*

From my late teen years to my early 20's I suffered from severe anxiety. I grew to hold a fear of my own mind. My mind became a place I saw as uncontrollable, unpredictable, unfamiliar, and unknown to me. I couldn't trust myself and this terrified me. I would have visions of the world around me dissolving into pure energy, as though the world I knew was leaving me. During these experiences I would be overwhelmed with terror and loneliness. If the world I knew was disappearing, where did that leave me?

Slowly over the years my worship of Hekate had become more and more shamanic. I began experiencing spontaneous moments of ecstasy, a oneness with nature and a sensation of being *'loose'* from reality. On one full moon night, I performed a ritual esbat in honour of Hekate, calling for Her blessing upon me. As I watched the moon illuminate the dark earth, I felt her light begin to illuminate the darkness of my own mind. I drew down the moon and I felt a sudden heightened consciousness with me. I felt an identification with Hekate as my mind began peaking into an ecstatic frenzy. I could feel Her power within me, and this lead to a very profound visionary experience where everything in my mind suddenly became clear, I was illuminated. By the light of Hekate's Flaming silver torch I was moonstruck, and I saw myself, I saw my mind for what it really is, nothing to be feared. I connected with that place inside of me, and it was beautiful. I remember looking at the moon-lit earth and thinking to myself *"This is my Kingdom!"*, and that my mind, my whole mind, was mine...I owned myself again. I came to embrace this aspect of my mind, and from this experience with Hekate, my anxiety, my *"curse"* of madness has now become a blessing. I have transformed my darkest demon into my strongest ally. The place within my mind where I once felt lost, helpless, powerless, and alone...where I felt I could no longer control or understand myself or the world, has now become a place of beauty! A source of inspiration, insight, empowerment and creativity. I finally understand this part of my Self, and I feel as though now I have a *"foundation"* for my mind, as though I am more real. I feel like a more complete, more free, and more stronger me. More sacred and more connected to Hekate. My darkness of walking between the worlds of sanity and madness, I surrender unto it now. I am now the bearer of Hekate's Lunatik Flame, and Her fires have healed me and made me more aware of myself. I confronted one of my greatest fears and now I grow into a more powerful witch, able to see into the waters of my other selves, minds and worlds within me. Touched by Lunacy. My shadowed mind is now clear and illuminated. I have control again.

Hekate brought light to my darkness and healed my view of it. Her gift of Sacred Lunacy has given me a greater awareness of my mind, She is a goddess of psychological and spiritual transformation. No longer do I suffer from the crippling anxiety I once had...I haven't experienced a panic attack since.

Experiencing Hekate's Lunacy, I see similarities with the Dionysian principle. Like Dionysos, Hekate dissolves the ego-self, and the boundaries of the rational mind are destroyed. Hekate's sacred Lunacy, like Dionysos' divine madness, is a temporary state which leaves one with a new sense of oneself and the world. Always extreme, the witch can experience a manic state involving high levels of ecstasy as one unites with their immanent divine self, or great moments of terror as one reveals that which is buried deep within their unconscious. Hekate excites a Lunacy that liberates us from the constraints and illusions of the rational mind, into an ecstatic, primal and deified state where we are able to find insight and realization of our own truth and immanent divinity. Hekate in this sense, is the collective Unconscious, and the enlightenment achieved through the unconscious mind. Both light and Dark, not only is She the Mystery concealed within Darkness, but she is the Light which illuminates (reveals) the Mystery.

Like Dionysos, Hekate's is a Shamanic consciousness, and through Hekate one reaches the divine through descent into the universal collective unconscious. Her mysteries involve the knowledge of Transformation, as She herself transforms into a Dog, Horse, Serpent, and many other animal forms. Hekate holds the torch which guides her followers to the hidden aspects of their own mind, and She imparts the knowledge to pass into other states of consciousness, a practice today called *'shapeshifting'*. With Hekate, you must give a part of yourself over to Lunacy. Her knowledge takes the seeker into the deepest places of one's imagination. Hekate's sacred Lunacy is an experience of one's soul, in all its intensity, both light and dark. I have experienced it as both a dreamy and mystical energy, guiding me into a serene trance, or a more wild and primal frenzy as I descend into my unconscious. Many of the herbs sacred to Hekate are hallucinogenic, and were used to achieve these varying states of consciousness; the Opium Poppy, Deadly Nightshade, Hemlock, Cannabis, Aconite, Datura and Mandrake were all used traditionally by shamans, witches and mystics to release the spirit from the body, inducing a trance-like altered state of consciousness. Although I personally don't use most of these potentially fatal herbs in my practice, they show a clear expression of Hekate's power to bring forth altered states of consciousness.

16TH OF NOVEMBER 2009, NIGHT OF HEKATE, FROM MY BOOK OF SHADOWS

"Beautifully the night fell upon a Dark Moon, and a storm began to cover the skies...All these auspicious forces were aligning themselves with this night...Her night...I could feel the power in the raising winds. As the sun began to set, I undressed and walked through my home lighting candles, and lanterns. Upon my altar I lit three white candles, and anointed my body with an oil I made using olive oil and infused herbs sacred to Hekate. Nightqueen and Patchouli incense was lit, and now the storm had really begun. With lightning flashing through my candle-lit home, thunder crashing outside. I couldn't wish for anything more magickally appropriate. I began to chant in Her honour, my song vibrating my whole being, slowly getting louder and more melodic, energy began to move through my body and around me, a tingling sensation covered me, as though my aura were humming. Gazing upon her image upon the shrine, I called out to her, I invoked her...and she had come. I could feel her presence all around me, all throughout my home. My ritual turned into a very ecstatic and shamanic rite, with the breath of each chant I felt myself becoming "higher"...as though my consciousness was going up into a state of mystical frenzy, as opposed to 'down' as is common with meditation. I began to pray and call out a desire, a spontaneous spell...I chanted, and sang, and gestured, and raised my spells energy...I cut off a lock of my hair and gathered some raven feathers and threw them into a burning cauldron by the altar. So mote it be. At this point I felt extremely connected with Her, My mind was Her mind and I could feel Her power within me. I gathered my vessel of red wine and began to spill in libation to my goddess, I raised Her offering dish, a sacrifice of Eggs, Garlic and Honey and implored her blessing, at this point my offering began to feel very heavy, and the offering dish itself grew noticeably warm...I knew she had accepted my gift. The storm slowly began to pass, the incense began to fade...yet the effects of my ritual stayed with me through the whole evening, a calm yet alert, connected, and cleansed feeling. That night I could not sleep at all, I simply wasn't tired...my mind was so wired to her presence, and I felt as though she wanted me to stay awake and experience the night...so I did. I listened to music, wrote about my experience in my Book of Shadows, drank red wine and waited for dawn. Blessed be Hekate, and Blessed be all who are Her followers."

The way I manifest Hekate's Sacred Lunacy within my practice is through the ritual of *'Drawing down the Moon'*. I have always been inspired by the moon and for me, She is Hekate. She is the shining light of Hekate's flaming torch, the beauty of her silver light illuminating our path and our spirits in the Darkness. She is *'Spiritual Power'* and She is Transformation. She is *'En Erebos Phos'*, the light in the Darkness. She is the spirit of Hekate and the Heart of the Witch. My ritual of Drawing down the Moon is expressed in a similar way to the ancient *'Bacchanalia'* rites of Dionysos. It is a very ecstatic and shamanic rite of divine possession.

With intoxicants, primarily wine, and with dance, chant and the scent of incense, I intoxicate my mind. The experience of the witch who draws down the moon I see like the Maenads of Dionysos, who achieve their mystical union with their god, whose souls are liberated by His intoxicating fires. The Lunatik witch who draws down the moon is liberated by the fires of Hekate. We are moonstruck, blessed with vision and illuminated with Her sacred lunacy. She unlocks our rigid minds and we become the bearers of the Lunatik flame, a temporary earthly vessel of Hekate's sacred fire. Sincerity and the willingness to surrender oneself to Hekate are the key components for an effective experience.

THE RITUAL

Beneath the light of the full moon, I dress my altar in black cloth, representing the darkness, and silver candles to represent illumination. I place as many mirrors as I can upon the earth around me to gather Her light. I like to use a lunar associated intoxicant such as white wine as opposed to the very dark and chthonic feel of red, which I prefer to use in rituals to Hekate during the Dark Moon. I pour the white wine into a large silver bowl and allow the vessel to sit beneath the light of the full moon to be charged. I lace the wine with an infusion mugwort for its lunar, prophetic, psychic and dream-like qualities, along with an infusion of white willow for its connection to the moon and as a sacred tree to Hekate. Along with the bowl of white wine, I also place a large vessel of water upon the altar to be charged with the light of the full moon. I light my charcoal dicks and begin burning mugwort, jasmine, and willow incense. I wash my hands and bathe myself with the water. I take deep and calming breaths, and while gazing upon the full moon I perform Hekate's sacred salute, which is a gesture I designed that makes the sign of Hekate's Wheel in the air before me. I then say:

> *"Oh Hekate, with thy silver flame of Lunar Light,*
> *Hail and Praise unto thee, Holy Moon,*
> *On this thy most illuminated Night"*

I light the silver candles on the altar and raise my arms to the goddess. I call out to Hekate, I invoke her:

> *"En Erebos Phos...In Darkness, Light!*
> *Hekate, Torch Bearing Holy Daughter of Night*
> *Beneath thy Holy Light I Stand.*
> *Lady of Sacred Lunacy, Bearer of the Silver Flame!*
> *Hekate! Bringer of Illumination!*

With Love I call upon thee, I invoke thee!

Light of Moon, Dark of Night,

Burn within me thy silver glorious light!

Hekate! With Love I invoke thee!

Hekate! With Holy Voice I call!

Descend upon me from thy Throne of Night,

As I chant thy Sacred Names...

Phosphoros, Propylaia, Chthonia...Kleidouchos Antaea Hekate!"

I link my hands loosely together with my palms pacing the moon. I close my eyes and allow the energy of the moon, the power of Hekate to fill my body with Her light. I surrender myself to Her. I visualize myself crowned with the silver fires of the Moon, with Hekate's power to pierce through the darkness. I take my silver chalice and gather wine from the bowl and raise it to the Moon, to Hekate, saying:

"As Thy light pours upon the Dark Earth,

So may Thy Blessings Pour Unto me!

May thy silver flame burn within me,

Through this river of Illumination"

I drink and spill wine upon the earth in libation. I would now lead into the purpose of the rite. I would skry a burning fire or the vessel of water upon the altar for guidance or a vision of insight. I would perform magick, or I will dance and chant and drink the moon-blessed wine all beneath the light of the full moon, and simply allow myself to experience the moment, and feel my connection with Hekate, embracing this state.

I find Hekate's specific Lunacy expresses the more feminine principles of psychism, seership, dreams, intuition and imagination. I have found the experience can benefit many aspects of a witches practice. It has the potential to become an extremely mantic experience, as Hekate is known for Her powers of Divination, where one can receive insight from the truth of the past, the secrets of the present, or prophetic vision of the future. I have also found Hekate's Sacred Lunacy to be helpful with shapeshifting and trance-work, for creative inspiration and vision, for guidance as Hekate brings forth profound insight of one's Path, for working on self-awareness and reflection, and for self-empowerment in rites of Magick. Most of all, Bearing Hekate's Lunatik Flame allows me to connect more deeply with my Goddess, to feel close to her, to literally have the goddess within me and experience Her power, Her Love, Her wisdom....To be with Her.

Hekate is portrayed as a goddess who wears a gleaming headdress lighting the way into the darkness and the depths of our inner being. As Her devotee and priest, I see myself crowned with Her sacred fires. Hekate has taught me the gifts of all levels of consciousness, both awake and sleep, sane and mad, conscious and unconscious. She has taught me that these places are not to be feared, and that prophecy, inspiration, creative vision and wisdom can be found there. Hekate's Mystery is knowing thy true self without fear, both light and dark. Not only does She bear the Keys to the Mysteries, but Hekate is the Key to the Mysteries. It is through Her that we are able to open the doors to our truth, our power and our divinity. In the words of Socrates *"Our greatest blessings come to us by way of Madness"*. Her Lunacy is a gift, and once you have known this state and have become the bearer of Her Lunatik Flame...You are altered forever.

> *Blessed are they who know the Mysteries of the Goddess...*
>
> *Blessed are they who hallow their life in the worship of the Goddess, who chant the sacred chant of the Goddess and who giveth sacrifice at the holy crossroads of the Goddess...*
>
> *Blessed are the Witches, they whose souls are illuminated and whom within the Darkness the Goddess Guideth...*
>
> *Blessed are they who keep the rites of Nyx, the Mother...*
>
> *Blessed are the key bearers, they who wield in their crimson stained hands the holy wand of the Goddess...*
>
> *Blessed are they who wear the lunatik crown of the Goddess and drink the wine of the Holy moon...*
>
> *Blessed, Blessed are they...Hekate is their Goddess!*

Figure 41 - Torchbearing Enodia by Magin Rose

Shining Her Light on Fear

By Connia Silver

Yes, give me your hand I pray
And reveal to me the pathways of divine guidance that I long for,
Then shall I gaze upon that precious Light
Whence I can flee the evil of our dark origin.

Diadochus Hymn to Hekate and Janus, 5th century CE, trans. Ronan[1]

Fear. Everyone is familiar with this emotion, but not everyone realizes how much it is a part of their everyday lives. This emotion has a wide range of degrees: from all-out terror, to mild apprehension. Some deliberately seek it out - addicted to the adrenalin rush that it provides - or the everyday stressors of work, relationships and family may provide triggers for this internal response. Natural disasters, terrorism, economic crisis and viral epidemics are just a few of the incessantly broadcasted horrors that eat away at everyday peace of mind.

Fear may also be found in the multitude of inner doubts that we hold about ourselves. Fear of not being smart enough, thin enough, rich enough – or *"enough"* period. Fear of illness, success and/or failure; fear of not being a perfect parent, friend, spouse, or employee, may occupy our daily thoughts. Or, we may fear not being understood and accepted for who we truly are.

There is a scientific reason behind why fear plays such a large role in our lives. According to the neuroscientist, Dr. Paul Maclean, the centre of the brain that controls the most basic survival *"flight or fight"* response is called the r-complex, also referred to as the *"reptilian"* or *"root brain."*[2] This is the oldest part of the brain and it governs pure instinct, as well as ancestral memory.

Today, the r-complex interfaces with two other layers of the brain that later developed over time: the limbic system (personal feelings and memory) and the neo-cortex (thought and speech). These three aspects function in an interconnected manner to form what Maclean called the Triune Brain. Each layer of the brain developed separately in our evolutionary process. The r-complex was the first to form, so the instinct of fear originates from the most deeply embedded, primordial part of our brain. It has been with us from the very beginning in order to assure our very survival.

Every day we are given countless opportunities to surrender to fear. When this becomes habitual, we hand over our personal power, giving fear unlimited

---

[1] The Goddess Hekate. Ronan (ed), 1992.

[2] The Triune Brain in Evolution: Role in Paleocerebral Functions, MacLean, 1990.

authority to take hold and direct our emotions and actions. We may find ourselves living in a waking nightmare where our inner demons are given free reign, while we blindly search in the dark for a way out. But just because fear is part of our physiology, does not mean we are doomed to be controlled by it. Instead, we can learn to value fear by discovering what it has to teach us. Whenever you need to find where your inner fears lie, invite the Goddess Hekate to walk with you and be your guide.

May the comforting presence of Hekate
accompany me through the dark times
and help me fear not the unknown,
lest I fear myself.

The ancient and revered Goddess Hekate is more than qualified to help navigate the journey to the deepest recesses of mind and emotions, where fears may dwell. There is nowhere this powerful Lady cannot observe or go. Even during the reining days of the Olympians, Zeus himself acknowledged Her complete freedom over earth, sea and sky.

One meaning of Hekate's name is *"influence from afar"* or *"the distant one"*, which refers to Her ability to affect change over a vast expanse, as well as having a uniquely impartial vantage point. She can see into the wildest woods, the deepest ocean caverns, and the utmost skies. When you have somewhere frightening to go - either in the real world or within yourself - it is always reassuring to have someone with you who already knows the way. There is nowhere that this well-travelled Lady has not been; She has access to all realms, both within and without. She moves without restriction between all worlds and Her steady gaze can pierce the deepest level of the unconscious mind, where the primal emotion of fear makes its home.

Hekate is well-known for Her ability to easily cross through liminal thresholds: transitions between all stages of being. Her tri-fold nature as the Goddess of the Crossroads allows Her to see and access all areas at once. She stands firmly in the present, while viewing the past and the future at the same time. She overlooks the triple intersection of the Jungian conscious, personal unconscious and collective unconscious, as well as the junction of the triune brain where instinct, emotion and reason work together as one. For Her, nothing is hidden and there are no boundaries. She walks freely through the labyrinths of our lives and can help pinpoint where inner fears have taken hold.

Wherever fear is found, it indicates that something on the most basic level requires healing. Because of its nature as a primordial force, it is a powerful initiator. One of the gifts of fear is its ability to get our attention, and point to where we are experiencing an imbalance in our lives. When you make the conscious decision to confront your deepest fears, call upon the initiatory Goddess Hekate to help find them, and illuminate their meaning in your life.

May the radiantly pure light of Hekate
shine upon all levels of my being,
part the shadows, and reveal my Inner Self.

All shadows depend upon a source of light. Their strength also directly relates to the intensity of the light creating them. Our personal relationship to spiritual Light may also influence how strongly our shadow-side is reflected back to us. Calling upon and bringing down vast amounts of Light at once can result in the illumination of all manner of Darkness within - which can subsequently be misinterpreted as an imbalance. This is one reason why those who concentrate solely on the Light and disregard the Dark are often confronted with their own *"dark sides."*

Illumination is best experienced gradually, in small doses. It is through the recognition of the eternal dance between the Light and the Dark within that we learn to accept ourselves as harmonious and whole beings: perhaps not walking in perfect balance, but at least in self-understanding.

Hekate's fiery torches, the brilliance from Her shining crown of stars, as well as Her own shimmering luminance, brighten everyone and everything that crosses Her path. Wherever She is invited, She reveals all. It is Hekate's ability as a Light-Bringer that allows Her to illuminate a person's inner nature from the very depths of mind, heart and soul. Wherever She passes, truth is automatically brought forward and secrets revealed. She does not discriminate and Her brilliance reveals both beauty and ugliness within. She is a Goddess that dispels all forms of illusion. Both hidden talents and deepest fears are brought to the forefront of consciousness so they may be more easily seen and understood.

Whenever you are feeling at your darkest, ask Hekate to help you look within and bring awareness to the situation. It does not matter how devoid of light your *"dark night of the soul"* may be: this resplendent Lady can provide a soft glow, a bolt of lightning, or anything in-between. She will assist in seeing what you are missing to bring you into harmony, as well as cast an encouraging light on what you are already doing that is positive. Allow Her to show you your own light within – it will be easily seen during these times. The darkest days of your life always contain a glimmer of new hope to guide your way; even the smallest spark will show up brilliantly in pitch blackness. You only have to remember to look for it.

In some ancient writings, Hekate is capable of striking fear into the hearts of man. But She is capable of the opposite as well – granting peace in those same hearts. We have seen where She can shine Her light on our internal *"evil spirits"*, that take the form of fear in our lives. She may also assist in turning them into useful dreams and visions that will help change the future.

> *May night-wandering Hekate*
> *send me kindly dreams;*
> *and allow the Mare of Wisdom*
> *to guide my way.*

Hekate is also known as the sender of ghosts and dreams. When called upon, She may send ancestors, animals, or other spirit beings to provide valuable information to you in a dream or vision. Or, She may confer upon you a dream that you interpret as a nightmare. Nightmares result when fears and dreams are brought together. They are not meant to torment, but to bring on sudden and dramatic awareness. A bad dream may be emotionally disturbing, but it is ultimately a gift because it provides a signpost that something within you requires attention.

One of Hekate's many animal faces is the horse, so when you experience riding a *"night-mare"*, you may find yourself being taken on a journey by the Goddess Herself. She may carry you into a realm where you may not wish to go, but ultimately it is for your own well-being and spiritual growth. A nightmare is most often thought of as a frightening or deeply upsetting dream, but it also may also be looked upon as a means for Hekate to instruct and initiate. For Her, nightmares are mere shadow puppets on the wall of the subconscious mind.

Hekate may have inherited the connection to dreams through the Goddess Asteria (*the Starry One*), who in some literature is named as Hekate's mother. Asteria bestowed prophetic dreams to petitioners in Her dream temple. Learning the art of lucid dreaming and dream analysis is extremely useful, especially when experiencing disturbing dream imagery. The ability to confront and transform dream images while asleep and interpreting dream images are both powerful methods that carry over to increased skill in manifestation in the physical world.

> *Gratitude to Hekate for helping us*
> *find and illuminate our fears.*
> *Gratitude to Hekate for helping us*
> *transform our fears and ourselves!*

Fear is not something we can completely banish, nor would we want to, as it performs a most valuable function. Fear alerts us to danger and imbalance, both within ourselves and in the outer world. The illumination and understanding of fear makes it less of a terrible foe and more of a welcomed tool. What you can see and recognize within yourself, you can ultimately accept and use to your best advantage. Fear is transforming, and so is the Goddess Hekate.

Although one of Hekate's epithets is Soteira (*Saviour),* Hekate will not swoop down from the celestial realm and save you from your fear. No Goddess will - at least not in the way that you may wish. Rather, She will be an enlightening companion and encourage you in the unique opportunity to save yourself through transformation and self-knowledge. Just as She is Persephone's guiding attendant through the Underworld in the Eleusinian mysteries, Hekate will walk with you through the darkest of times, providing support and wisdom to reach your goals.

Simply reach out to Her in whatever manner is best for you – through meditation, ritual, prayer, song, dreamwork or divination - and She will be there, offering Her hand to comfort and light your way. With Her assistance, you can learn to overcome your fears and shine your own radiance out to the world. Hail Hekate!

Shining Her Light on Fear article adapted from a forthcoming book.

Figure 42 - Three card reading from the Transparent Oracle - Snake Wolf Horse - By Emily Carding

Figure 43 - Triple Hekate by Georgi Mishev

HEALING THE SOUL

By Kay Gillard

She comes, the guiding light upon the path, the path itself

The key that opens the way, the doorway to change...

As a devotee of Hekate, there is no area of my life where She is not an influence. In my professional life I am a healer and teacher, running courses on Reiki, shamanic healing and sound healing, and working with clients to heal physical complaints, emotional trauma and spiritual wounds. In my work with my students and clients Hekate is not overtly present, and Her place within the Reiki and shamanic healing systems are not immediately obvious. But while She may not be a part of the healing process for my students and clients, She is always present for me. I can't overstate Her influence on my healing work – apart from anything else it was Hekate I turned to for guidance when I was crying out for a new direction in my life, and She instructed me to begin training in the healing arts. I followed her guidance without question and it changed my life, I now run a successful healing and teaching practice. And while I do not bring Hekate into my practice in an obvious way, the way I heal myself and others is overseen by Her, and there is an inescapable cross over between my personal spiritual life and my healing work. Although She is, is some way, always present in my healing work, there have been many occasions when She is fully present and in control. This has happened often when I am working on my clients, and countless times when I am working to heal myself.

The spiritual healing work that I have done with Hekate, working to heal at soul level, has unfolded for me in different ways. For my own healing She has worked to affect my physical and energetic body, removing negative energies and blockages, cutting cords that attach me to people or situations I need to let go of, and raising my energy levels. She has led me into landscapes rich in magical symbolism to help me understand myself more clearly, shining a light on how I need to move forward, giving me inner strength and restoring to me lost power and soul parts. It is this last issue, the restoration of the soul, that I have begun using with others with great effect.

In shamanic healing there is a great focus on healing the soul. The soul is conceived to be of many parts (Sandra Ingerman, renowned soul retrieval practitioner, refers to the idea of the *'fragmented self'*). We do not consider soul force as something which is fully present within our bodies at all time (for example, think of your higher self, a part of your soul with knowledge not necessarily accessible to your conscious self). A person's soul force will be present in varying degrees at different times. If, for example, we are faced with a dangerous situation or trauma (emotional or physical) the soul – the eternal part of us – will often leave the body – the transient part of us – almost like a protective measure or coping strategy. Often it returns when it is safe to do so but sometimes when a part of our soul leaves us we are unable to maintain our connection to it. This is known as soul loss and is considered to be a cause of illness, emotional difficulties and lack of energy within the shamanic world view. Shamanic healers employ various techniques to locate these lost soul parts on the astral plane (or 'non ordinary reality') and return them to our clients, in a process called soul retrieval.

While I have been trained in modern and traditional shamanic soul retrieval practices, in the past year I have come to realise that Hekate is the perfect deity to oversee this work. There are so many aspects of Hekate that are perfect for soul retrieval work. Shamanic practitioners will either journey into non ordinary reality on behalf of a client to find their lost soul part, or take a more interactive approach and guide the client into non ordinary reality (or their own subconscious, depending on your point of view) where they identify and reclaim the soul part for themselves. In either case, the shamanic practitioner helps to guide the lost soul part back to the body and keep it there. Who better than Hekate, psychopomp, guide of souls for this purpose? Shamanic practitioners hold space for the client as the work takes place, holding them is a safe space between worlds. We journey into other realms and realities, while maintaining an awareness of the material realm and the safety of our clients. Hekate, a supremely liminal Goddess, is perfectly placed to guide and protect me as I perform this work.

Other aspects of Hekate can be called upon for soul retrieval work, depending on the individual circumstances. The symbolism we find when exploring a non ordinary reality can be fascinating, and I once found a lost soul part locked away in an ornate wooden chest. Hekate Kleidoukhos – the key-holder – was present to unlock the chest so that I could reach the soul part and guide it back to where it should be. In some cases we work with the other side of soul loss, when people are actually subconsciously holding on to a part of someone else's soul. Grief is a common cause of this, when someone cannot fully let go of a loved one who has died. In this instance I would call upon Hekate as Queen of the dead to release that soul part.

Sometimes I have even found many aspects of Hekate to be present all at once during an intense healing session. On one occasion I was working to reconnect a lost soul part with a very ill client. Her situation was devastating, she was suicidal after suffering emotional traumas over many years and felt helpless and fragile all the time. This was the first time Hekate came to me to assist me in a healing of this nature. I was struggling against many barriers to her healing (the anti-depressant medication she was prescribed for a start, which is always difficult to work through) and many obstacles were being placed in my path. I was finding it difficult to get to the part of her that we wanted to bring back, and Hekate appeared in many guises to take over the work. The pathway was lit by Hekate's flaming torches and She illuminated the dark landscape as Hekate Phosphoros. I felt her presence as Hekate Enodia as new pathways were laid out, providing a way back for the lost soul part. She walked with that soul part back along those paths in her role as Psychopomp, guiding her back to create a more whole self. As we crossed the threshold back into this realm to return this soul part to the body, Hekate was the Guardian of the Gate, holding the way open for us. And as this soul part was restored I felt the presence of Hekate Soteira, the Saviour, the World Soul.

All of my soul retrieval work is dedicated to Hekate, but there are other aspects of soul healing to consider when working with Hekate, and one idea in particular has been of great importance in my own self healing. In shamanic healing there is the important concept of the interconnectedness of all things, the Web of Wyrd. Every thought, word and action reverberates along the threads of the Web of Wyrd, affecting the whole of our reality. In Reiki, though the influence is far more from the Buddhist perspective, this idea that all things are connected is essential. For example, in Western Reiki it is often suggested that the distant healing symbol used is like a bridge we can use to connect us to people far away from us so we can heal them at distance. In face the symbol is intended to bring about the desired state of mind in the practitioner to make distant healing effective, this state of mind is the understanding that there is no distance, no time, there is only this moment and the interconnectedness of all things. It is a state of oneness – of course we can heal people at distance, because all people are one.

Considering these ideas of interconnectedness and oneness, and how essential they are in energy healing, helps us to see the importance of Hekate Soteira in healing work. In *The Chaldean Oracles* Hekate was equated with the Cosmic Soul – the soul of all things are contained within Hekate. Think of the importance of accepting that all souls are connected, and part of Her, in terms of the need for forgiveness when approaching soul healing. Soul wounds and soul loss almost always come from some kind of interaction with another person. Part of what hinders healing at this level is holding on to anger and grief; a lack of forgiveness both for other people and for ourselves. Understanding that we are connected to all people and all things assists us in that forgiveness. Understanding that we are at one with all people helps us to live our lives in a different, more positive way. It helps us understand that our healing work, our magical work and all of our behaviour shapes our reality and the lives of others at a deeper level than we may have realised.

If we understand Hekate as the soul of the whole world, we must also not limit ourselves to thinking about people. The soul of every animal, the energy of every plant can be seen as a part of Her, therefore if we consider ourselves a part of Her priesthood we see all these things as sacred. If we are to live our lives and practice our spirituality as devotees of Hekate, the importance of treading gently on the earth and having compassion for all living things should not be overlooked. Being a healer is not about facilitating specific healing work for others, or even for ourselves. Likewise, being a devotee of Hekate is not just about performing ritual devotional acts. Both of these things are a way of life and, if we are embodying these roles truthfully and authentically, every aspect of ourselves and everything we do will be carried out as a healer and a member of Her priesthood. As we move through our lives, understanding Hekate Soteira as the World Soul, we try always to understand that every soul we come into contact with in our spiritual, magical and mundane lives is a part of Her. And so are we.

Figure 44 - Reflections by Shay Skepevski

AT THE CROSSROADS

WORKING WITH HEKATE AS AN EMBODIMENT OF TRANSITION

BY KATHERINE SUTHERLAND

Crossroads have long served both therapeutic practitioners and magical artists on a metaphorical and metaphysical level. Being a key part of the iconography associated with Hekate; the concept of the forked, or three way path allows for the creation of not only a still point, but of a threshold or boundary point, which, when crossed, facilitates forward movement and inevitable change. A common cry amongst those on the path the Seeker is *'be the change'* or *'become that which you seek to be'*. However, it is possible to argue that the experience of standing at the still point, before change and motion occur, is one of the most powerful experiences when working through transition and self development. This piece will explore how Hekate can enable pause at the crossroads, to allow us to look back at our journeys and to consider the way ahead before stepping forward into onward motion. Through working with Hekate, it is possible to become the threshold, to embody the energy of transitions, not only for ourselves, but also for others.

When standing at the crossroads, we pause and consider the path to follow, the effect we seek, in the light of what we are and can be as the cause of what we seek. In other words, what instructs us to go on our way, right, left of straight ahead? Hekate asks us what instructs you to hurry forward or proceed deliberately or just amble on? And what empowers you to do so? In pausing and considering we weigh up our objectives, but not being content with pure outward motions we look inwards, to the resources we have as worthy, inspired beings. The ways in which we look inwards are deeply individual, some by meditation, journey work and prayer, others by being in nature of places of personal power, or by simply taking some time out of everyday lives; we can tap into Hekate's wisdom through a variety of methods.

When working with Hekate on transitions, one can be sure that things may not happen as we envisage them, and, probably not to our own mortal timescale. Perhaps in the process of the crossroads, it is prudent to continue our worldly routines, whilst continuing to look inward to our purpose. By doing so, inner wheels are turning; not spinning us out of control as Hekate aids in the forward motion towards a wisely guided and clearly defined destination along our way. By keeping inner awareness open, not impatient, yet alert, we can pick up on Hekate's wisdom and act as we need to when guided by her torches. Hekate's wisdom will show us the way to onward motion, but our task is to fine tune our own inner alertness and to find the means to make wisdom manifest; in stepping up to the threshold, and being ready to act when guided, maybe immediately, or in a more sedate fashion, we can be sure of one thing ~ a process has begun.

Even though crossroads are part of the human condition: times in life when one thing is drawing to a close and another is beginning, the can be intensely problematic and frightening. We may not feel ready for one situation to come to an end, and have no idea what the onward motion will be, so perhaps it is natural to feel helpless and to react with panic. Fear can be crippling, and it is with this that Hekate can assist, with the moment of pause and stillness at the meeting of the ways, before one path is chosen over another. It is important to remember the following points when standing in the place of transition: crossroads are normal, crossroads show us the difference between illusion and reality, crossroads reveal to us the importance of intention.

When we realise the importance of intention, we can look back and see that the crossroads are a magical mirage.

When standing at the crossroads people at a crossroads feel uncomfortably challenged by the thought of changes to come. However, Crossroads are a normal, natural part of life. For that matter, change is a normal part of life; and crossroads are nothing more than an invitation to change. The feeling of discomfort relates to the loss of the familiar. It would be nice if changes came one at a time, but often that is not the case. There's an old saying that changes come in threes, which relays the notion that often when something shifts in one area of life, something else in another area shifts as well. Taken together, both can trigger other changes. Before too long we feel the road is unstable beneath our feet, and there is no solid ground on which to tread.

In working with crossroads in our inner reality, we can be forced to re-evaluate truths we have previously subscribed to in the past, on our journey to this point of transition. Hekate can show us that whilst some of our beliefs may be true of our everyday experiences, they do not tell the truth as we had previously perceived it to be. In standing at the crossroads, it is possible to come into alignment with the flow of Hekate, and to understand the different realities of the paths when one pays attention. Once we have seen beyond limitations of our previous realities Hekate can aid us in focusing our intentions, for without these there can be no onward motion. If we are overcome the threshold of the crossroads it is imperative to allow the power of our intent to triumph and to release any older truths which have held power over us. In this way, our inner experiences can influence and shape what is occurring on the outer planes of our lives.

Once we have grasped the importance of intention, we have the ability to step through crossroads. At this point, there is very little we need to do except sustain our intention and accept Hekate's guidance. What will begin to happen is that occurrences will begin to unfold along the lines of our intention far more readily than if we had tried to jump in and make them happen. Literally, we will find ourselves receiving guidance from the things that happen to us every day. With our old vision, we would have said that these were unrelated and accidental; and we probably would have given them no notice. But now with our new vision, we are allowing being to unfold according to its own lines, its best lines; and we allow it to teach and guide us. In our everyday world, we are often praised for being in control; in actual point of fact it is much more interesting to be disciples of being, watching, learning as we go, finding the right information and opportunities opening up before us just as we need them. Rumi, the Sufi poet and mystic stated: *"We fritter away all of our energy devising and executing schemes to become that which we already are."* In truth, we don't have to go out and build a new reality from nothing; all we have to do stand at the crossroads focus our intent, and with Hekate's guidance, change will happen and the way ahead will become clear; a notion beautifully put into verse by the poet Philip Clayton Gore:

WHERE THREE WAYS MEET

*Where three ways meet
You stand and wait,
Unsleeping and all-knowing,
And softly greet
To investigate
Where passers-by are going.*

*All travellers seek
In youth and age
An intended destination,
But they hear you speak,
And must engage
In revealing conversation.*

*One's road leads here,
Another's there,
A third's to unknown places;
Yet, calm, austere,
You tarry where
All ways meet your three faces.*

*Wherever we
Would wish to be,
Uncertainly we wend.
Triplicity
In unity,
You wait where all roads end.*

*From "New Poems and Old Verses" by Phillip Clayton-Gore.
Used with his kind permission.*

Figure 45 - Altar by MDL

A Rite For Hekate

Meeting the Dark Mother

By Diane M. Champigny

I was brought up in a rather unique set of circumstances. My Mother was Protestant and my Father is Catholic. It was always a point of contention between the two of them, although at the time, I was blissfully unaware of what the fuss was all about. I grew up in an Irish Catholic community with friends who offered (threatened) to *"baptize me with rain water if need be!"* My Mother was a very strong woman: resourceful, selfless, innovative, and way before her time. She insisted that I choose my own religion when I was old enough to make such an important decision. That woman gave me the greatest gift that I have ever received by so doing and *"unknowingly"* set me on my Path.

Growing up in Boston, Massachusetts I had access to several world-class museums, one of which is the Museum of Fine Arts. During one of my many forays to the MFA in my late 20's I came upon an ancient depiction of a tri-form Goddess named Hekate. I was immediately *"struck."* Intrigued, I launched head long into researching this most fascinating image.

Hekate has been described as the consort of Chthonian (Underworld) Hermes in the cults of Thessalian Pherai and Eleusis. Both were leaders of the shades of the dead, and were associated with the annual Springtime return of Persephone/Kore. I learned that guarding the crossroads, Hekate is She who encounters you, the Triple Goddess wielding the power of transformation and renewal. She is the Goddess of the moon, of the underworld and of magic. She is the protectress of flocks, sailors and (most importantly in my case) of witches. She dwells in the Underworld, alongside Hades and Persephone. She has the power and wisdom to pierce the darkness, bring visions, call back from the past, illuminate the present and give warning or promise of the future. The Goddess of moonlit crossroads -- Hekate of the Three Faces. I had discovered my Matron, Light and Guide!

Several years later I joined a coven, which worked with a pantheon of Celtic deities (British, Irish and Welsh.) We occasionally worked with the Greco-Roman pantheon as well. It was noted on more than one occasion that during these rites in particular my face would morph into an unmistakable Mediterranean/Greek countenance. I didn't find this particularly disturbing, or surprising, as my Grandparents and other ancestors herald from Sciacca, Sicily. I was strongly drawn to the deities and myths of Greece and did even more research on Hekate. From there, those synchronicities that only occur when energies, powers and planes align started to occur (as happens when you're on the right track.) For instance, I would discover images of Her in unexpected places, books (or other information) would present themselves unsolicited, and people with an affinity for Her would suddenly appear along my Journey.

When it came time to write a ritual for the coven, there was no question as to what the focus would be. We would encounter the Chthonic Goddess, Hekate!

I chose Hekate as the focal point of this ritual because she is the Goddess of the Crossroads, the place of choice -- a liminal place where we can change our course and, in turn, the outcome of our lives (She is NOT a deity of manifest destiny!) Hekate is a Goddess of transformation and renewal, and these are the aspects of Her that are focused on during the Rite. The participants were advised that they may face a choice that needs to be made in the near future, different options that need to be looked at and assessed but only one chosen. It is also possible to skry as a sort of *"check in"* to be sure you're following your Right Path (are in spiritual alignment) or to explore different perspectives. These instructions set the stage.

INVOCATIONS

What follows are the invocations to the God Hades and the Goddess Hekate, which I am including here to convey the energy and concepts behind the ritual, and also so that people may incorporate them into their own Rites as desired. With the Priestess of the West serving as Hekate and the Priest of the East serving as Hades. The following is chanted at the beginning of the Rite:

INVOCATION OF HADES

"Hades, Lord of the Underworld,
God of the Unknown, God of the Shadows,
God of the Other World,
Leader of the Shades of the Dead,
Abductor of Persephone,
We seek your presence here."

INVOCATION OF HEKATE

"Hekate, Gate Guardian of Hades
Hekate of the Three Ways, Tri-Via,
Dark, immortal Goddess of crossroads, caverns, and moonlit rites,
Lend your powers this night –
Enable us to see more clearly with our inner eye
The choices at our disposal,
The possibilities for transformation and renewal.
Hear ye the words of the Grandmother of Time:
She who has been known as Hekate, Ceridwen,
The Cailleach, Kali, Spider Woman,
And by many other names."

A central altar held a black skrying bowl filled with water, illuminated by several candles, which were lit before the skrying portion of the rite began.

Participants raised energy by dancing and chanting, while concentrating on the build-up of energy for the upcoming skrying rite. Simultaneously, they concentrated on connecting/aligning energetically with the Dark Goddess of the Crossroads.

We used this familiar chant by Patricia Witt:
"Hekate, Ceridwen, dark Mother take us in,
Hekate, Ceridwen, let us be reborn."

The central altar with skrying bowl was moved to the centre of the Circle. Priest of Hades lit the incense pleasing to Hekate and the skrying bowl candles (we used one on either side.) When all was ready, each seeker approached the Priestess of Hekate (who donned a black veil in order to *"reveal"* herself.) She in turn attuned to the energy of each participant. When that connection had been clearly made, the Seeker looked into the black skrying bowl for as long as they needed. It is very important that this not be rushed by feelings of self-consciousness or embarrassment. After each participant was finished, the Priestess of Hekate blessed him or her, and they returned to their previous place in the Circle.

To skry means to discern or to perceive. Skrying enables the operator to open the inner eye to unconscious realities. You may peer into the present, past or future. Relax your mind and allow your eyes to gaze without focusing. Do not attempt to control or force this process. How you interpret the symbols, signs or sigils is up to each individual, because our symbol systems are unique to our previous experience and subconscious minds, not to someone else's interpretation.

The skrying was concluded with the Priest speaking these words:

By the powers of Hekate,
Whose magic weaves through the web of the world,
This magic is done.
It finds its mark.
Our visions flourish.
So, it is woven, so it is done.
So mote it be.

The following are some impressions of the skrying portion of the Rite from a number of the participants:

Morwynna: "*I always think I know my path is straight ahead, but I saw it curve to the right.*"

Guydyon: "*I saw a lot of arrows in the skrying bowl.*"

Mannanan: "*People were becoming transparent standing in front of Her. A red substance was flowing from the skrying bowl down to the floor.*"

Candela: "*I had a hard time leaving the altar.*"

Mannanan: "*At the end of the skrying, there was a ripple in the air when She stepped away, as if the air were water. I heard a dog barking in the distance.*"

Hekate enlightens us to the concept of eternity. She has been the Maiden, and remembers that joy. She has been the Mother, and recalls that pleasure. She has guided the dead along their journey and extended Her comforting touch. She has seen many ages and epochs and has learned that the Wheel is ever turning – the Wheel that is life, death and rebirth. She has become wise with age and time and can see portents of the future. The past is the future, and the future is the past.

Hekate is a learned teacher who is the harbinger of inevitable change. With Her hounds, She guards the mysteries of life. Sometimes it is what is unseen and hidden that teaches us the most. She is the invisible unknown that lies ahead and personifies that concept.

Hekate is viewed by the uninitiated as malevolent, but Her touch enables us to understand that seemingly harsh experiences teach us much if we apply the lessons going forward. Only in ignorance is She scorned and reviled. By describing Her attributes and twilight haunts, we entreat her to depart Her ancient cavern, and attend to us.

These pivotal moments in our lives provide opportunities for us to become more aware of our own divinity, gain a greater or alternative perspective of things and to perceive other worlds beyond our own. Through our insight, we can act as conduits for that knowledge to be revealed to all.

By the touch of Hekate's immortal hand, we are awakened to the mysteries of life. Hekate warns that to approach and enter Her realm, you will be facing the harshest judge of all – your true, essential and eternal Self.

Figure 46 - Altar by Richard Derks

A DRUID & HEKATE

... AND HER COMING SHALL BE PRECEDED BY THE BARKING OF DOGS

BY RICHARD A. DERKS

I owe much to Hekate. She came into my life suddenly and without warning, and with that coming almost everything changed. Without her I would not be where I am now in my spirituality. This is the story of my journey to her, and how she lead me into my current syncretic practice.

First a bit about me; My main spiritual practice is for the most part that of a Druid in the Revival Tradition. Though I started off with a solely Druidic practice, through Hekate I was led to become a Hellenic Polytheist as well, and I now walk both paths side by side.

I owe much indeed to this most wonderful of Goddesses. For a long time I had been undergoing a *"dark night of the soul"* experience and really struggling to make any connection to the divine that I could. Up until then I had been worshipping the Norse/Heathen Gods, mainly because my ancestry is Scandinavian, but try as I might it really was not working for me. All of my divinations at that point had two things in common, information regarding being guided by a strong female presence, and when I used the runes, the Eihwaz (Yew) rune was featured prominently in every reading. Also during a Druidic ritual, when skrying into a water bowl, I was presented with an owl looking back at me. I thought perhaps it was Freya or Skathi, but much to my surprise it was Hecate; the Greek Goddess of the crossroads.

She finally revealed herself to me in a dream on the morning of August 13th. I awoke with the following words spoken by an irritated yet amused female voice echoing in my head as I made my way into sleepy morning wakefulness:

> *"I will never understand your human insistence that you can only worship those of us whom you have ties of blood. If you are human, you have all you need to hear and connect with us. I am Hecate, learn of me".*

I woke up to the barking of my black dog (who is usually not known to be up at that time of the morning)! Now it's not often that I hear voices in my sleep as such, but when I do I have learned to sit up and take notice. I pondered this for a while. While I was not folkish in anyway shape or form, I had not explored much past the Norse pantheon. It had never even occurred to me that the female presence spoke of in my divinations would be Greek! All throughout that day I was presented with her image and name where ever I looked. I felt her presence with me all day. I learned that among others, two of her most prominent symbols are the yew tree, and the owl. Her presence is said to be heralded by the barking of dogs. Also upon doing my research, I found that August 13th is considered to be a sacred feast day to Hecate by many modern pagans, although I had no clue of this at the time. That night I went out for a night time walk to the crossroads and prayed my greetings. I told her that I would follow wherever she would lead. I was rewarded by a frog hopping out at my feet (the frog being another one of her symbols, the liminal creature that it is). I took this that my prayer was well received.

Adopting the worship of Hekate as a Druid and reconciling the Celtic and new found Greek aspects of my practice was not an easy task for me. It is an ever ongoing task. Fortunately I found through experience that Hekate has an astonishing number of aspects that synergize with the practice of modern Druidry. Now, I'm not saying that she has anything to do with Druidry historically, but in my experience she seems not bothered at all about being included in Druidic ritual. Indeed she is a very accepting Goddess of different faiths, which is probably one of the reasons she is so widely worshipped across the Pagan spectrum.

First off Druids are very fond of triplicities. Much of the druidic wisdom is contained in Triads, which is basically a one line short poem that highlights three topics. Three is considered a number beyond duality, and the third side of a topic is always sought beyond the binary. Hekate is a triplicate Goddess and has a triple nature. She looks in three directions, has three heads, and is Goddess of the Crossroads, which has three prongs. Her classic symbol of Hekate's Wheel highlights this triplicate nature.

She is also a liminal Goddess, presiding over liminal spaces. Again her association with the crossroads highlights this fact. Liminal spaces fit very prominently into Druidic lore because these are times of balance when no one influence presides. It is through these liminal times and places that gateways to the Otherworlds are sought, and Awen (inspiration) is said to flow. As a Goddess whose primary domain is the liminal, this leads to her working very well in a Druidic practice.

However, her influence does not end there, for she is also associated with the Earth, Sea, and Sky, having been given dominion over these areas by Zeus for her help in the war against the Titans. This is interesting because those are the three druid elements of the revival tradition! Her worship was also often carried out in groves in antiquity, which is where of course much Druidic worship takes place. This is where her worship really synergizes in a Druidic circle, and I learned that I can call upon her to watch over me in circle with no disharmony.

In time however, she me lead to walk two paths at the same time and brought me to the worship of the Hellenic Gods, and my other patron Dionysos, whom I love fiercely. Prior to her I would never of even given these deities a second glance. Although it has been difficult, I have found a balance between my Druidic side and newfound love of the Hellenic Gods that works well for me. I credit this all due to Hekate's guidance.

Eventually I started receiving messages from her in the form of dreams, synchronicities, and divination that I should make a more permanent commitment to her in the form of an oath. It was as if this oath was somehow meant to strengthen our connection, and let the true work begin. I had my reservations but on the morning of the most recent dark moon I felt her presence keenly, and felt her inside saying

"Just trust me". And so I did. I decided to take that leap of faith and just trust her fully. She has never let me down yet.

I'm amazed at how well things worked out.

I ultimately decided to give the oath, not in front of an altar under a roof, but in a grove beneath the sky, which seemed most fitting. There exists a peaceful little area nearby that consists of a grove of trees near a lake, with a large stone in the centre. It's really pretty perfect, a place where Earth, Sea, and Sky meet. Here it was that I decided to go. I gathered together a traditional Hekate's supper and trekked out there.

I laid the food items out using the rock as an altar. I spoke her invocations, and then spoke my oath aloud in the open air. Yet there was one more thing asked of me. At the time I carried with me a bronze coin depicting Hekate. I carried it everywhere I go. I held it when I prayed to her. I contemplated it when I'm feeling needful of direction. It was kind of a prized possession to me. As I finished the oath I strongly felt that I should leave it behind. I recoiled at the thought, knowing full well that I could never get another one. Then I was reminded of a story my first grade teacher told me about how Pan asked a shepherd to sacrifice one of his favourite sheep, and how he didn't want to because he loved it. Pan explained to him that only something you truly love and will miss is a proper sacrifice to the Gods. I knew I could spill wine upon the ground until I was blue in the face and it wouldn't mean as much as that coin. Thus I knew that I had to leave the coin with the supper, and so I did. A tangible payment for the bond we were creating.

And so I left without looking back (and wondering about my first grade teacher and exactly why she was teaching me about sacrificing to Pan in 1st grade)! Hmm?

I left with the serene feeling that the sacrifice and oath was accepted, and a stronger bond than before was created. I felt as if this whole process, rather being just, well... normal as it would of been if I had done it at the altar as planned, felt truly like an initiatory experience.

That is how I became a Druid oathed to Hekate. May I serve her well.

Figure 47 - Shrine of Hekate Chthonia (Earth) by MDL

A Sacred Life

BY TIM FURLOW

As I wandered freezing through the snow, in a world lit only by the light of the moon, a cave was visible in the distance. I sought refuge inside, only to discover that I wasn't alone. Standing before me was a Woman, dressed in white garments that shimmered like millions of diamonds spun into thread. Her hair was white, but moreover, it glistened like all the colours of the spectrum. She was neither old nor young; She was ageless. Frightened, and yet comforted, She welcomed me. Before I could ask Her name, I awoke- safe and warm in my bed. This reoccurring dream was my introduction to the radiant Mother known to the ancients as Hekate.

More than a decade has passed since the nights of those childhood dreams, and I've followed Her path through many cultures, countries, and languages. Her image and worship traces back to long before the Greek city-states, to the foundations of religion itself. Even at the primitive roots of civilization, there were signs of Goddess worship. Archaeologists have recovered Mother Goddess effigies thought to be as much as 27,000 years old. In those early days of humanity, nomadic hunters marked their bodies with symbols to represent tribal affiliation, to ward off negative spirits, or to show devotion to their deities. These early effigies and tattoos mark the beginnings of society; the foundations that would eventually become the Greek polis, and the study of early religion and culture would form the patterns that have defined my life.

When I was a child, I spent most of my free time sitting beside a small creek. I shied away from playtime with other kids, preferring to listen to the sound of the water and the birds chirping overhead. As time passed, I studied the animals, and began learning from them. Upon finding a dead bird or turtle, I held funeral services for them, mourning and trying to give them proper passage to the afterlife. Though I was too young to acknowledge it, the animals were teaching me religion. I grew to love nature, and became more interested in ancient traditions. Studying the religious beliefs of my Lakota ancestors took precedence to everything else, and I discovered that the animals and Mother Earth were everything to them. Soon, this led to an interest in tribal rites of passage, and it was only a matter of time before my first tattoos and piercings. Around the age of thirteen I began studying Pagan traditions, and found an inner peace I'd never known before. The concept of being connected to the animals, the elements, and the universe gave me a sense of oneness; I began to feel a part of nature, not just a spectator to it.

Body art came to me as naturally as religion. The sacred act of tattooing became a ritual, and the mere sound of a tattoo machine could conjure a deep trance state. Summoning the spirits of ancestors long passed, I would sit stoic, refusing to

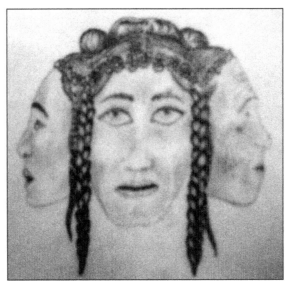
Figure 48 - Detail of a Tattoo on Tim Furlow

flinch as the artist worked busily. Just as in those ancient times, the tattoo ceremony remains much the same. A stencil is drawn where the image will reside, the tools are carefully cleaned and inspected, and the pigment is prepared. The piercing of the flesh for spiritual purposes is symbolic, and the recipient sits in quiet contemplation, resisting the urge to shy away from the pain.

This ritual is a rite of passage, a doorway to a new phase of life, through which the wearer passes from the world of the mundane, to the world of the divine. As my understanding of the universe grew, I realized that this doorway was another liminal point; another lesson to be taught by Hekate. As my religious beliefs became solidified, my love for primitivism grew. By the time I reached my early twenties, my earlobes had been stretched, and I wore numerous symbols and images dedicated to Hekate. Religion and ancient rite became one. I began to feel the footsteps of the ancients. I could hear their voices in the wind, and see their spectres in the shadows. Truly, I was learning the old ways, or as the Lakota elders said, I was *"walking in a beautiful manner."*

I've seen Hekate in many cultures, and, not surprisingly, I've found her several times within the Lakota traditions. The story of the White Buffalo Calf Woman is the basis of Lakota religion.

According to the legend, She came in the form of a beautiful maiden to two young warriors on the prairie. She was dressed in a white buckskin dress, and was indescribably radiant. One young man had intent on rape, and his comrade advised him not to. The man refused his friend's advice, and tried to force himself on Her. The woman in white and the young man were surrounded by a massive swirling dust cloud. When the cloud dissipated, the woman walked away unscathed, leaving in her wake the bones of the man who had tried to rape her. As the other young man trembled in fear, She told him not to worry, as he had a good heart. She commanded him to take Her to his village. When they arrived, a large counsel was called, with all of the chiefs and medicine men in attendance. She gave them the first sacred pipe, and taught them how to pray. After teaching them about praying to the four directions, She advised them to look for Her return. She then lay down on the prairie, and began rolling back and forth, stirring up another cloud of dust. When the dust settled, there stood a great bison in Her place, and it ran into the distance. Lakota people have awaited the return of the White Buffalo ever since. Interestingly, there have been many white bison calves born in recent times. I've always found that the pipe was a very similar image to the torches of Hekate's Greek symbolism, and Her presence in this story reminds me of the Dark Mother. This became the basis for the faces tattooed on my back. The similarity between Hekate and White Buffalo Calf Woman gave me a way to concretize my religious and ethnic backgrounds seamlessly, the two traditions lending to one another in such a way that I can find likenesses in the refined Greek polis, and the traditional Lakota village.

Hekate speaks to us each and every day, and bids us to see Her signs in the mundane reality of our lives. Her way is the way of mystery and chaos - but out of chaos comes order.

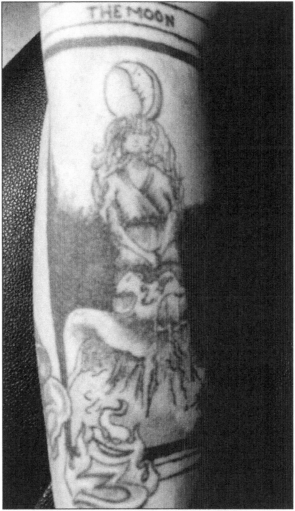

Figure 49 - Hekate Tattoo on Tim Furlow

Figure 50 - Keybearing Hekate with her Companion Hounds by Magin Rose

An Illuminating Presence

By Dorn Simon-Sinnott

Of all the qualities and aspects that our Great Hekate possesses, it is unlikely that subtlety is one of them!

Why? In my experience, with each encounter, and almost on a daily basis, Hekate has something to offer; whether it be guidance, illumination, a simple reminder in some other vein, or a blatant lack of subtlety in an action, which in my case includes; the item's on Her Shrine either falling or spilling over out of the blue; images, paintings and portrayals of Hekate seemingly leaping from her pose to quite purposely fall on the floor in front of me, taking a myriad of other sacred items with her in her leap.

At other times Hekate has merely sent through imagery, or repetitive visions with hints for my lack of insight or recognition of what it may be Hekate is trying to tell me.

Hekate has an air of authority about her, yet can be the greatest support, nurturing with a stern hand, and at times as demanding as a relentless child, no insult intended Hekate!

Her presence is the strongest I have felt from Deity and in such a unique wave of mastery, Hekate knows how to be heard, found, sought, adhered to and worshiped.

The way in which she reaches us is outstanding, as we each are individual with our own way of thinking, working, and believing.

To possess such power as to manifest her messages through to the physical realm and in mundane daily tasks is what astounds me most, that in each of us there is a way for Hekate to get us to notice her, these can be simple or challenging and are most certainly diverse.

I recall once, when trying to find a placement for my three painted brass wall masks, that the fuse box above me and my new home's front door opened unexpectedly, this led to my choosing to place them on that wall, just inside the front door.

In this same time-frame, whilst out walking woof (as he is affectionately nicknamed), I had come across an area of woodland that had been thinned, leaving oddments of timber for the wildlife. Having spotted one piece in particular it urged me to pick it up as it quite clearly stated should be made into a key holder, I rationalised this in the belief it would get me back to my creative side and wood-working, yet also provide a useful item in the home, so I took this piece of timber with me.

I began to see a pattern of *'things happening'*; as I noted each occurrence, it slowly unfolded.

Later that same year; I began Spiritual Training within the *Fellowship Of Isis*. As I embarked on my Adepthood initiatory challenges, Rites and studies, I began to be called to address many issues that resided within me, which had been making my life difficult and unhealthy, as I was storing negative energies.

I transcended into my depths with emotions under scrutiny, actions under silent guidance, and life taking on a other-worldly feel, more so than my norm.

I also had an up close and personal experience with Persephone whilst visiting one of Ireland's most noted caves, she appeared clear as day to me in the calcite formations, stalactites and stalagmites within. It was Persephone whom opened me up to Demeter, Hekate and Helios, I had already spent some time with Hades!

Research ensued, a closer look into Hekate, which brought results that stunned me; Keys; (Key bearer), Three Masks; (Triformis), Crossroads; (The changes that were occurring in my life), Psychopomp; ability to walk through the Underworld and return to the Physical Realm and is the guide of souls (Delving to the depths of darkness to re-emerge into the light cleansed, renewed and studying Psychology and Reiki), Shrines or Altars; placed outside the front door's of home's or by the threshold themselves, (The placement of my masks and key holder, adding later a small altar), Soteira; (Saviour), Phosphoros; (Illumination - see the light, be guided by Hekate back to the light), Gateways.

These all inter-related to the signs and patterns I had been receiving.

Suddenly my world became an epic receptor, with messages everywhere, lessons to be learnt and adapted to, perceptions having another viewpoint, everything correlating and connecting, the most miniscule input became linked to something larger that I was doing, whether it a Rite, a Study Guide, Reiki Training, re-arranging my house, walking my dog, it all merged into a purpose, a routine, with a loud repetitive chant over many month's...

> *"Hekate, Hekate, Hekate...She will send you to your depths, leave you in darkness till the fear has gone, the pain eased, the dark thoughts spent, the emotions untangled.*
>
> *She will then guide you into the light, from the darkness, with force, strength, vigour, and initiating your Divine purpose; Hekate is calling you, she refuses to stop, you must listen, that voice each day that speaks her name in your mind, the signs she has given you, must no longer be ignored, you are being chosen by Hekate, to do her work."*

During this period, I did in fact live the way Hekate was steering me to, I reached Adepthood, this qualifies me to found my own Iseum for training other's, and an Iseum has to have a Patron Deity, Goddess/God/or both.

I knew that the Deities I had encountered and worked with previously were not for this adventure... it was a time of renewal, of finding new path's and new ways, to find a Deity who fit's the purpose of my Iseum, that being; reaching into yourself, learning the shadows, clearing, cleansing, healing, therapy, counselling... taking oneself through the self's darker aspects, to emerge brighter, lighter, healthier and happier.

Now Hekate was consistently calling me, yet I was still reluctant to work with her, in part due to my rebellious nature; *"I won't be bullied!"*, and partly due to the misconceptions, and darker aspects depicted of and through Hekate, and of course we have all heard of her scornful, vengeful side.

I kept being brought to a cave in my visions, again in relation to Persephone, having now realised the impact Hekate had in Persephone's story.

The simplest of things were being shown to me, Yew trees, Blackthorns, a sudden over-consumption of Garlic on a regular basis, and that never ending chant, which now struck my mind like a neon flashing sign…*"Hekate, Hekate, Hekate"*.

I was not able to do anything, without Hekate being somehow related to it, everything I read, researched, bought, liked, ate, it all linked to her in some way or form…she is very persistent, persuasive, and at times as already stated, rather demanding.

Alas at the end of many months and much thought (when I had a chance to think with all her chanting!) I gave in.

My Iseum was dedicated to Hekate and Hermes, the work forged ahead, busy and fast, students flowed in to sign up, (they still do!) and Hekate had become a large part of my daily, and Spiritual life.

Since then, Hekate has stood up for me, guided me, chastised me, pushed me in new directions, made things happen, by making me make them happen, ebbing her flow when I am low, kicking my butt when I sloth, and most of all, being there in everything I do.

Times have been emotionally trying, even in despair at times, yet Hekate is strong, stern, comforting and consistent, always lighting the path ahead, forever showing alternative routes, always initiating a new phase, a new project for me to do.

Hekate what would we do without you?

Figure 51 - Hekate Phosphoros by Emily Carding

Painting Hekate

By Emily Carding

As a visionary artist, I tend not to work in an overly rational way, but am rather blessed, (and often hounded), by images which burst fully formed into my head and then persist in banging against the inside of my skull until I can find time to release them onto canvas. Thus it was with the painting of Hekate for this anthology, though it morphed a little over the months it gestated in my head, and other details became clearer as I worked on the image.

The initial image arrived in my head quite a while before I was able to find the time to paint it, as I was relocating to the other side of the country at the time! The concept and feel was clear though- Hekate herself as a series of layered gateways to other realms, layers of perception, keys that are masks, masks that are keys, veils that are doors, and keyholes that lead through all the layers of being to the stars beneath.

Her hair is as fire, she herself becoming the guiding torch of divine light. She has the powerful horns of a bull, a nod to classical descriptions of her as bull-headed and a symbol of lunar power in its most forceful aspect. Not a passive, receptive Goddess is Hekate, but an active force to be reckoned with! The fiery tendrils of her hair form a crown of power, which reaches into the starry sky, connecting her to her mother, the star Goddess Asteria.

A feature that was not planned was the mask she wears, which appeared gradually as a result of intuitive painting. When I asked about the meaning, the answer that came to me was that the mask was a key- as a symbol it showed that there is always more to see and know which is hidden beneath the surface, but it is also present to show that masks do not always hide, but can also reveal inner potential. I had a strong feeling that the inclusion of the mask was a hint that mask work is a powerful way to invoke and work with Hekate.

In her hands she holds two torches in a symmetrical pose, which are not traditional flames, but rather searing beams of stellar power. The torch on the right side of the painting is white, and the other is black. This was an added detail in order to hint at the columns of mercy and severity, revealing a link to the structure of the Qabalistic Tree of Life which was not planned, but which I noticed once I had blocked in the initial composition. If we superimpose this structure over the symbols of the painting with Kether at her crown, then Chokmah and Binah are in the light of the two torches, Chesed and Geburah are at the base of the torches, Tiphereth is at her centre, which is also the radiating tip of the unicorn's horn, as well as the tip of the keyhole. Below that we can imagine Netzach and Hod in the wings of the unicorn, with the black hound as Yesod and the head of the serpent in Malkuth, (with its body clearly leading up towards Tiphereth). It occurs to me that, amongst other parallels, with both Yesod and hounds being linked to the moon, there is more significance to this discovery than compositional coincidence. This is especially clear when we also note that she wears a key at her throat, in a position that fits perfectly with the hidden Sephira, Daath. In Qabalistic teachings, this is the position associated with Daath on the human body! I also feel that the key is a powerful symbol to represent Hekate's connection to this Sephira, as she offers us the key of knowledge and a possible glimpse of wisdom and understanding beyond the abyss.

The figure of Hekate of course dominates the landscape of the painting, which consists of earth, sea and sky, the three realms over which she rules, the three paths of the triple crossroads, the above, below and between. Earth is represented by mountains, (three peaks on each side for symmetry and triplicity), which are black and white, emphasising again the pillars, but also perhaps causing us to ponder what lies between, the liminal state that is neither black nor white. Hekate herself is robed primarily in scarlet red, a colour of power, fire, blood and passion. Together with black and white, these three colours are most often associated with this great goddess of all things triple!

These three colours have symbolism of their own which is also seen in the three animals lower in the picture and the keyhole-shaped gateways within Hekate's skirts from which they are reaching out to us.

Most people would be able to tell you that white is the colour of purity, and this is also a quality associated with unicorns. However, like everything associated with Hekate, there are hidden depths. Horse is one of the most prominent animals associated with Hekate, especially white horses. In this case the energy of horse is taken to its most exalted level, its power of movement and sovereignty expressed on a divine level with the addition of the spiral horn reaching to the stars, and the wings, (also linking to the element of Air), which have the power to take us there. The colour white and the winged unicorn can then be seen to represent the might of the angelic realm and the power to access the dazzling, distant beauty of the upperworld.

Black is commonly associated with death, especially black dogs as in this painting. Black dogs have long been strongly linked to Hekate, as well as to two other symbols linked with the goddess- crossroads and ghosts. However much it may chill our bones to think of the hell-hounds or Black Shuck as omens of death, the dog also represents a significant protective and loyal power when it is on our side, so this symbol relates to both her associations with death and her strength as a powerful protective ally. These can be seen as her qualities that come from the element and realm of Earth. However, going back to the Qabalistic parallels, the black dog could also be seen as a gateway to the lunar realm of Yesod, and hence the dreams and nightmares of the subconscious over which Hekate also rules. If we combine these two ideas, we can see how Hekate as the black hound provides protection for us as we travel into the dark depths of the underworld and nightmares, for sometimes that is where we bury our treasure, deep in the earth of our dreams. She also lights the path for our return...

Red is most obviously the colour of blood and fire, and hence is connected to the qualities of action, transformation, and lust. It is a colour often associated with magickal power and so is an appropriate colour for the serpent, also a symbol of magickal power, which winds caduceus-like from the tip of the keyhole gateway to the bottom of the painting. As has already been noted, the serpent's head is in the position of Malkuth, the earthly realm from which those of us on a spiritual path hope to ascend. If the snake evokes thoughts about the Garden of Eden and the tree of knowledge, does its winding path indicate a fall from the spiritual grace of the higher levels of the Tree, or offer a path to re-ascend? Perhaps both. Certainly there is a connection with the energy of the fallen angel Lucifer, who offers knowledge as a path to power. Here we can see that the serpent appears to emerge from the red dress, and hence from the being of the goddess herself. The other animals are bursting from the keyhole shaped gateways that the goddess forms, again revealing inner dimensions of her sacred colours. If you look closely at Hekate's eyes and the eyes of the three creatures, they are the same, (also in red, black and white), thus showing them all as aspects of the same multi-formed deity.

Beneath the layers of colour we reach through the keyholes, we again return to the stars...an illustration of the basic principle *"As Above So Below"*, or as without, so within. Our journey is that of the salmon who seeks the place of its origins, and we must always return to the stars from whence our souls were born.

I hope that you enjoy the painting, and that this short piece has given you a little insight into not only its meaning, but as to the importance and depths of the lessons offered by the goddess Hekate and the multi-layered wisdom that may be uncovered by her devotees in the pages of this book.

HEKATE

On a night like this, the sky is like a naked soul,
Unveiled in full glory, radiant in the infinite eyes
Of the blessed Fool, who does not know he knows,
But sees and feels all truth inherent,
Colliding within like the cosmic dance that brought forth life,
As the gilded light of Hekate's torch shines
From her mother's starry womb, with incandescent immortal bliss,
And if there were a wind, what names it would whisper!
Secret names of gods too oft forgotten...
But the night is still, so still...
Still enough to hear the song that starlight plays,
Each its own note, resounding in perfect harmony,
And so our spirit may join the song,
Embraced by distant souls that reach beyond the void,
We expand, we are one, we may become,

EMILY CARDING

Figure 52 - Priestesses Andrea and Francis

Following Her Moons

Extracts from a Travel Journal

By Andrea Salgado Reyes

Having renewed my dedication to Hekate for 13 moons in January 2009, I felt confident knowing the general shape of things to come. A weekly ritual to make offerings, meditate and listen to her teachings. A supper at a local crossroads in Chile with invitations to other witches interested in her or already working with her. To learn for a year about Greek mythology and myths specific to Her. To gather information about Her from classic sources and publish it in a blog in Spanish for others to learn also about Hekate, in a language in which it's difficult to find information about Her. Simple!

What follows is an account of how events developed with short extracts from my personal journal.

1st february 2009 Algarrobo, Chile

The first major part of the commitment I have undertaken took place during the annual witches' camp on our land, *Comunidad Paganus*. We prepared several rites, among them a ritual to make offerings to Hekate and, later that night, a supper in Her honour at a crossroads nearby. Preparations had begun a month before with the gathering and drying of herbs to make incense and candles. For a month all herbal offerings on Her altar were allowed to dry right there, becoming imbued with the energy of daily invocations. Oracles were received regarding who should attend.

The main candle had been made in our candles workshop a few days before. In the shape of a 5 pointed star, the mould was partly filled with star anise, lavender flowers and juniper berries. As I stirred the paraffin, I invoked Hekate and then poured the liquid into the mould. I twisted a metal snake, from my altar to Hekate, around the mould to watch over it while it hardened and cooled. The main image of Hekate had been painted by my mother, Myriam, a few weeks before and had served as the focus for my new dedication altar.

The last minute preparations began the day before with the purchase of ingredients to make food offerings. Crescent-shaped tiny honey cakes, onion bread, sopaipillas (a fried wheat and pumpkin flat bread, coloured with saffron), boiled eggs coloured with turmeric, cold-pressed olive oil, fresh figs and black olives, a comb of honey.

The temple room had been properly prepared, two kilos of sea salt and fresh rosemary were scattered on the floor, allowed to lie there for a time to absorb any pollution and then brushed from the room in turns by several witches bearing a traditional broomstick. Then hyssop leaves simmered in water were used to asperge. Then it was censed generously with frankincense.

The altar was laid in black, red and silver cloth and decorated with olive tree sprigs bearing green and black olives taken from local trees that morning. The offering dishes were of baked brown clay and two were of simple white porcelain in a circle enclosed by two crescents. We sought to represent the earthiness of working with Hekate, in the offerings and also in the decoration of the altar.

Figure 53 - Hekate Altar in Chile

There were three priestesses in service: myself to invoke and present offerings, Madelaine as guardian of the temple, Francis as scribe. The invocation, or rather the calling and welcoming of Hekate's presence into the ritual space went well, candles burning brightly at once. The offerings were made and were marked by the unusually strong flaring up of the central candle when each touched the altar. Then we proceeded to trance channelling. I was seated upon a chair and a black veil placed upon me. Then a priestess read the invocation of Hekate. The channelling began. It had two distinct parts, the first an oracle to all; followed by a short oracle for each individual present who chose to approach when invited.

"The Goddess comes, her visage veiled, her walk opens paths
The Goddess comes, her visage veiled
The Goddess, She comes
The offering of incense created by mind and heart
Is received for the glory of the maiden
Blessed be the hands which prepared the bread
Blessed be the hearts which in siblinghood gave it shape
Blessed be the feet which walk the sacred enclosure
In this land soaked with blood
Many souls wander the roads crying out for justice

They are errant children who this night through this work
Begin to understand that peace is a door open wide
Blessed be the hearts which suffer for their brethren
And lift spirit and hand to proffer aid
When a suffering child finds and steps upon the sacred space
Of the World Soul, transformation is their answer
This altar takes suffering and grants joy
This altar takes illness and grants abundant health
This altar lights the deepest night...
... Wide paths open which return to the past.
Ancient temples sound their bells and offerings will be rewarded.
The soul flies and dreams and returns to a profound awakening.
The light of the universe is in expansion a new star will be named.
When this happens you will know this Oracle speaks truth."

(Later in Spain I received an instruction to look for the new star in the skies. Alcor B, a red dwarf star, was found in the Big Dipper cluster and reported that December 2009).

Madelaine., A., M.E., Francis and I took the offerings and a few lit candles in procession to the nearest cross-roads to the left of our land, a T-shaped meeting of paths in front of a derelict piece of land gifted to the catholic church by a neighbour, to mark the death of his daughter a few years before. I made a statement of the purpose of the offerings: to request of Hekate that those souls who wandered the world without finding their true resting places receive Her aid and be placed where She judged fitting. From my notes of that night:

"As soon as I began to speak, the presence of a multitude of souls approaching from south-east, south and south-west, all coming to stand a few metres away from the priestesses. Arrival of beings dressed in very ancient clothing, others only shapes of light, creating between them a portal through which many souls began to cross. I felt a male, elderly soul coming very close to me, charged with energies in disharmony. That soul asked, 'Is this for everyone? For me too?' I explained that it is for every soul which comes to the Goddess to go to their destined places. 'I am an assassin, I killed someone'. 'I am not your judge nor your jury. My work is to open a path, Hekate decides where you will go, not I'. A feeling of relief, then soul moves towards portal. Another soul, a female one, approaches. 'I am a suicide, will they forgive me?' 'We are all children of the Gods, I am not your judge, approach the Goddess to receive peace'. The soul also emanates relief, thanks me and goes towards the portal. Souls continue to arrive and to go through the portal for 20 or 30 minutes. ... Eventually the energy ceases to flow in that direction and I hear a few exclamations of '... and me! And me!' as if a few hadn't been able to cross before the portal closed. The last beings of light leave, some souls walk away through the country-side. Three black hounds emerge through a fence nearby. I realise they are physical and not visions when they walk towards us. For the first time that night, I project a circle around us. We watch each other intently for minutes. They don't advance, they don't leave. Then I call out to Hekate mentally, 'Really impressive, can you take them away now please?' The lead dog moves forward a pace then turns away and the other two follow..."

23RD MAY, 2009 L'ISLE-ADAM, FRANCE

A presence appears while I am writing some notes for a course. I challenge it, demanding its name. The presence grows stronger until I feel the whole room vibrate with its energy and psychically see a large form appear, as tall as the room is high. It is female and dressed in a simple cream robe. Spontaneous writing:

"I AM the light-bearer, the Luciferian force, the maiden with the shining torch, beloved of the Gods and beloved of the Titans. I am Hekate beneath the Earth, Demeter on the land and I am the mother of all, the sky goddess Isis, Hekate and Demeter are one goddess. Three aspects and one child, the sacred Persephone who represents humankind."

(Bewildered by this vastly ranging statement of being and multiple names given, I challenge formally for the second time).

"I am HEKATE of the liminal rites, I am PERSEPHONE of the Earth rites, I am ISIS of the Star Children, I am HEKATE bearer of the eternal torch which lights the pathways of the universe. I am PERSEPHONE Earth goddess who travels within and on the sacred Earth, Gaia my aunt. I am ISIS-DEMETER the Mother Force, the Creatrix, the Abundant One who brings life or death to the earth and all her children. I am HEKATE the child of Titans, beloved of Zeus, mother of witches and sorcerers. I am PERSEPHONE, divine and regal wife to the Lord of the Underworld, I am ISIS-DEMETER and my birthright is life everlasting for myself and all my Star Children. I have answered three times three, now you may answer the same question, WHO ARE YOU TO QUESTION ME SO!"

(I am aware that the same list of names is given, with new attributions and titles, yet all familiar to me; but I am not of the *'all Goddesses are one Goddess'* opinion. On the other hand, it doesn't seem I am going to get a third go... so I answer who I am in as general a way as I can and without once actually saying my name yet being factually correct in the spiritual and magickal lines of work which I follow).

"The paths are open for you and yours to enter Spain and you enter it by birthright. None may forbid it, your influence will reach two sisters and three sons of Hekate there and they shall form the basis of your circle there. You carry my energy into the new lands and it shall flourish there. The path has been complicated and long for you and your mate, but the service of Hekate is never a simple or quiet one, you must walk the dusty roads in My name and much honour will result."

(Within a day, we were offered a place to stay in Spain and necessary funds were made available soon after. We travelled to Madrid. There were no border controls, which is unusual. There, I found and recognised four sister priestesses, three of whom entered Hekate's service).

JULY 2009 MADRID, SPAIN

Teaching session for Francis and one other, in oracle techniques. Oracle received by Francis:

"Two from Spain in Chile. The waters will reach very high, you will survive, it sweeps away the houses with its strength, you will survive, the just word, the just offering and all will be given."

(April 2010 two of us returned to Chile after an earthquake and tsunami hit Chile. Towns to either side of ours on the coast suffered badly and one of them was hit by a huge tidal wave. All members of our community unharmed. Our land untouched. Little damage to our belongings).

JULY & AUGUST 2009 MADRID, SPAIN

We met eclectic wiccans in Madrid and developed a link of friendship and some work together. Hekate manifested greatly in this, telling me to offer aid and protection in some difficult circumstances they were experiencing. She pointed out two women in particular who had to be protected, one of whom had a new baby and whom Hekate named to me as Her priestess. The other, She told me, would be an initiate and form a coven if she were aided. I followed Hekate's instructions to the letter in a series of private ceremonies. Some of the results are reported further on.

4TH SEPTEMBER 2009 GRANADA, SPAIN

Oracle:

> *"On the third month you will return to this land, you will bring with you your wife and very soon after a spiritual son of yours, you will come laden with fruits and with your heart broken at leaving behind once more the one who is your flame. You will proclaim my name in the annual rite and I shall come to you so that all will know that among my children are those who work with their soul."*

19TH SEPTEMBER 2009 UNITED KINGDOM

I attend a private ceremony organised by a Priestess in the UK, at which I was asked to take the role of Oracle in the sanctuary which housed the shrine to Hekate.

> *"Prepared myself for taking the role of oracle priestess by private ablution and then praying to Hekate in the shrine sanctuary for strength, clarity and truth in my service to Her. Invoked Her within myself, seated myself and placed veils on my head and upper body. ..."*

21ST DECEMBER 2009 GRANADA, SPAIN

Oracle:

> *"Oh daughters of Hekate! Each betrayal brings its punishment. Among you one who dared to repeat the words of the Goddess in hostile ears. Cursed! She is outside the circle, she will not be accepted. She betrayed roof and table. Cursed! She betrayed the words of the Goddess, which had reached her. She allowed her body to be desecrated, the same body she had given to the Goddess. Her body curses her."*

(We do not know what events this oracle relates to, at the present time).

27TH FEBRUARY 2010 MADRID, SPAIN

The end of my year long dedication finds me in Spain and so I carry out the annual Hekate's supper, as promised to Hekate. A ceremony at a crossroads in the middle of Madrid isn't an option, nor is transporting 20 or so people to the countryside. So the ceremony takes place in a newly opened healing centre hired for the day. The planning begins a month before and the event is announced on the 15th of January through a local website.

The morning of the ritual, I rise at 8 am. We have slept 3 hours. Switching on the television, I see on the morning news that Chile has just suffered a major earthquake an hour before. For over an hour, we try to contact our families in Chile. Eventually Francis manages to speak to her father for a few minutes. We watch scenes of complete devastation in a section of the country similar in size to Scotland. We are stunned. Our hostess, Gaia, offers to cancel the ritual on our behalf. But this is not an option. Now it's a matter of how much stamina and presence of mind we can gather while not knowing who is affected among our family and community. We are scattered over several cities, two of them are epicentres. We set out for the health centre. I think through the implications of the part of the ritual for lost souls in a setting with non-initiates and a couple of people unfamiliar with group rituals. I decide to divide the day in two, reserving the more challenging section for trained healers, initiates of a couple of different Traditions and ourselves. I change the format slightly to add a session to send healing to those souls which need it.

Altar set on three tiers, the bottom one being the ground itself. Covered with altar cloths and the top tier covered again with a second altar cloth embroidered with yellow, green and red snakes, as per two dreams which Hekate sent to the artisan, Olga, and to myself.

The top layer bears the figure of Hekate burnt onto a piece of wood, A black glass chalice, three wooden snakes painted black, red and green, two clay pentacles, a carved snake painted red and black, three clay snakes painted red, green and yellow, some small moonstones and other small crystals and semi-precious stones, two red candles and a black candle, olive oil, paper poppies. All the items except for the candles have been made by those present and are votive gifts which will be kept for this altar in its new home. The exception is the bag of moonstones, which are here to be charged with Hekate's energy and to be taken to home altars of those attending and those who have sent votive gifts.

The second layer bears honey, olive oil, many candles as gifts for the permanent altar, candles to light that day, pomegranates, paper poppies, an athame belonging to Dana, a tarot deck to be later used in divination. Objects here may be taken away by their owners later if they wish, except candles.

The bottom layer bears food offerings: two loaves of bread made in lunar shapes and one as a plait with three strands, onions, garlic, painted eggs, olives, figs, a carved wooden pentacle, assorted flowers (bulbs and root plants). These food offerings are to be used in the lost souls section and so I enclose them in an energy field until that time. No-one will eat them, food for feasting has been kept separate outside the temple space. Only the loaf shaped as a full moon, a pomegranate and one jar of honey are to be used during the other parts of the ceremony.

(Left) The Hekate Altar in Madrid

The three oracles were seated in a row, First Jana, then Fyrea then Dana. Then, at right angles, the three attendants were in a row holding bread, an open pomegranate and honey, respectively. Each of the latter gave the blessing of the respective Goddess and some of the food representing each one. The bread symbolised the present incarnation, the pomegranate the seeking occult wisdom and the honey the sweetness of the rewards. Each priestess representing a Goddess was veiled and then the priestess Gaia invoked Demeter while facing the corresponding priestess and I stood behind to help the integration of the energy through the crown chakra. Then we moved onto the priestess for Persephone and finally for Hekate. This order was shown to me by Hekate, as well as Her choice of priestess for each. When I asked Jana to work as oracle for Demeter she smiled and told me she already knew she would have to do that and that she is a Priestess of Cybele.

Each querent approached the priestesses in turn, receiving an oracle from each. Then the attendants offered each bread, pomegranate and honey with blessings. When this part of the ceremony had finished, we gave thanks to Demeter and Persephone.

Hekate had told me that during the ceremony She would show me a sign that I was giving the altar to the right person. I had seen the person days before in a meditation. During the offerings part of the ceremony, I received an instruction to tell that person to place her athame on the top section, as a tribute to the Temple. The woman told me that she had already received the instruction earlier from Hekate. That she had refused and Hekate had told her she would receive a bigger reward than she could imagine, if she obeyed. I took this to be the sign that Hekate had told me I would receive, yet still I hesitated and waited. This athame had great personal significance to this woman, it was an effective weapon which gave her aid and strength. As the woman approached the altar and gave her athame, I told Hekate silently to give me another sign. The woman placed one knee on the ground before the altar and, as she did so, a peal of thunder sounded outside. As she rose, the thunder ceased. So did my doubt.

I announced what Hekate had told me was Her will: her new altar would go to the home of the priestess Dana, if Dana accepted. There it would form the heart of a group of priestesses who would come forward to build a temple for Hekate in Spain. As I spoke, I saw the faces of some of the women present and several women whom I didn't know yet. Dana accepted after I explained some restrictions placed upon her and what having the altar would imply. Some of those present said they had received the image of her face when I said the altar would be given to the keeping of someone present. Two other women said they chose to work as Hekate's priestesses for her Temple. Others offered help.

A session of psychic readings with various tools followed. We then closed this part of the rite, all partaking of food and drink. Those who were to take part in the next ceremony remained and the rest left the premises.

Detail of the Hekate Altar in Madrid

The nine women and men who remained are healers and initiates with experience at varying levels, for this reason we used a very simple format. The others were inside an energy circle and I was inside a separate one, joined by a narrow channel which I controlled. I called upon Hekate to take the souls of those who approached me, then I used an indigenous technique to journey to the area of the earthquake and call lost souls. Many approached, but dozens rather than hundreds. To my surprise some were not earthquake victims, they were significantly older. Some had the appearance of walking rags, remnants of beings. Some were self-aware and communicated briefly with me. I saw with my inner vision how Hekate opened Her arms to them, they approached Her and vanished as they went near Her. I was aware suddenly of danger and a depletion of energy. Then I saw the shapes of several large dogs and a wolf appear around Her and something was swallowed by their energy and the danger disappeared. I could see many snakes milling around near the altar, particularly black and red ones. Eventually the numbers of souls diminished and became a trickle. Soon after I could not see any at all. I checked the energy levels of the others doing this work, All were stable.

We began to send healing to the areas most affected. There had been numerous requests from individuals and from organisations for healing and we used these requests as a focus. The session continued for over an hour. In the feedback afterwards, several had noticed snakes all around us. All reported increased body heat, particularly in their palms. Two had seen Hekate clearly, taking souls into Herself. We ended the session after grounding and sealing our energy channels.

The dreams with Hekate which most of us had been having for the three weeks prior to the rituals continued for several days more and so did curious synchronicities.

28TH FEBRUARY 2010

The altar was taken to its new home and set up there in a space in the main room of the house. We did a ritual to declare it a temporary temple of Hekate and to name its keeper. The energy change was distinct and again, snakes in the room, particularly below the altar itself and near the door. That area of the room had a warm, glowing light which seemed to pulse.

26TH MARCH 2010

Oracles:

"The serpents of the paths sweep and clean, open new ways, seek new paths. My daughters are thus: two by two they walk, united by my priesthood, by my work. Always a red one and a black one. Among them there is no good and no evil. There is power and love for the Path. The serpents of the hearth are others. The yellow and the green. The yellow serves and protects. The green heals but her bite opens the portal of the worlds, the pain of its fangs and the changes it brings open the ways, the portals. The green gives healing and it gives death when healing is not possible. The yellow defends and attacks, it allows no outrage. Under its care lies the altar, fecund and fertile the home and the altar which give milk and honey to the serpents. My daughters on the roads need no defence because over them walk I, they are the pillars upon which I build my temple...

They may know men but they belong to me. They may train men if their oaths make them mine. Their work is different, they must be loyal servants of the temple. My voice is not their voice but my hands are their hands. Their seed will be spilled in my honour or they will be empty for life."

Possession trance:

"When they are nine, they will all be public and again the devoted and the pilgrims will arrive to receive and to make offerings. Prepare your souls to be faithful carriers of the torches. Their light brings wisdom and siblinghood. Because that is what sons and daughters are: a great fraternity...

Light in my darkness and the darkness which nourishes the light. Among the nine temples, 27 lares each with my effigy and my offerings. Each temple with three altars, one to the young maiden who I looked after with my own hands, the Kore. One to her divine Mother and also my own altar. No temple of mine is complete without these three altars. Hermes at the door! Every woman and maiden under My roof will be free to lie with whom she chooses...

Observe the forehead, there the wheel gyrates rapidly. Thus is the vision of the past and of the future opened. ..."

Three paths open towards the horizon. My daughters will come, the serpents are meeting, feel their fire, recognise them. Know that they will all arrive, I will make them arrive, they will arrive where they must, they will arrive from afar. The work has begun and the fruits will be received.

Young energy arrives, three paths open. The path of youth, the path of the buds of spring, the path of the Mother and the path of death. You must know that path, know that your feet will bleed but you will be rewarded because you are my daughters...

For you, the work is done, travel to the next destination. I am very proud of you but now you must continue. ..."

Since the workings in Spain, the group which has gathered to build the temple and to maintain the temporary sacred space with Hekate's altar has grown. One priestess has moved cities to live in the same place and has done her dedication to Hekate. One other has made time in her schedule to also undertake a dedication to Hekate and two others have manifested their intention to work for the building of the temple. A Wiccan priestess who owns some land just outside the city has offered space on her land for the temple to be built. There are regular Friday night meetings to honour Hekate with offerings at her altar and for priestesses to train in the skills which Hekate seems to favour: divination, healing with herbs and crystals, oracles, crafts related to Her sacred objects, spell-making, dream work. The amount of dreams and also events showing and creating progress in the concept of a temple for Hekate is surprising in its speed, for all concerned. Yet not so surprising for a Goddess of paths and change.

The oracle regarding the snakes of Hekate working two by two seems to be taking shape. Two were already a matched pair in many senses: Francis and myself. A further two are now in a very similar working partnership and sharing living accommodation. As a nomenclature, Snakes of Hekate has some sense as a title of sorts for her priestesses, but one which to my knowledge does not have any historic echoes.

The group wishing to form a Wiccan coven in Spain are now safely under the auspices of an established coven elsewhere in Europe. Three others are undertaking training, including a priestess dedicated to Hekate. The priestess offering land for Hekate's temple is also amongst this group.

My own personal wheel has come full circle, I arrived back in Chile a few weeks ago. The time which I undertook to be in Hekate's service is now formally over. It has been a very challenging year which has again and again shown me that my limitations can be diminished and as a result I am more than I was. I am tired. I am also very glad to have been part of others' process of reaching Hekate. Or perhaps of Hekate reaching them? Either way, I have learnt much from others and gained worthwhile friends and companions.

Those of us who work with Hekate in Chile continue our work under her auspices and protection. There has been constant and fruitful work in my absence. The altar which I left in the keeping of Madelaine will not return to me, Hekate has instructed that it must remain with her and I must build a new one. So it shall be.

Now we move on to a new stage in our development as a magickal group. Without doubt, Hekate will continue to be a guiding force in this, particularly for those in the group who seek initiation into a particular Tradition in which witchcraft plays a large role.

Figure 54 - Stellar Witch Goddess by Magin Rose

(Used on the Cover of Hekate Keys to the Crossroads in 2006)

She Leads the Way

By Henrik Holmdahl

Over the years I have had many experiences with Hekate. She shows herself to me in many ways and faces. Is she a maiden, a crone? I believe she has all these appearances and any as she pleases. Judging from my dreams she has her traditional *'static'* forms as we know them, but she is not limited by them. The mistress works her way through my dreams, signs, people, symbols, totems and other goddesses. When I started I did so, not because I wanted to something from Hekate, rather it was the sum of my own previous experiences. It was all leading up to the moment when I learned of her existence. She had worked from afar. Today my primary way of expressing my devotional work with her is through creativity. The magickal art – in art. The first piece of the puzzle to this story came when I was a child. I can't remember my age but I was around nine or ten years old. It was a summer day at dusk. I'm lonely, playing with a football. Looking into a nearby forest glitch further down this field, I see two black dogs running through the air! They looked somewhat transparent and indeed ghostly. The experience was to say the least frightening. I never went near that place in years to come.

The last piece of the puzzle before I learned about her existence came to me while scrutinizing a photograph taken years before. I had been on a vacation in Turkey, visiting the ancient city of Hierapolis. The ruins have a cavern there, a sanctuary to Hades, known as plutonium. I remember being so fascinated by this particular place that I spent least half an hour just gazing intently at the entrance. Lizards sunbathed on ancient rocks around there. I could feel that the door to the sanctuary pulled me, whispered to me something that I couldn't grasp. I was moved somewhere so deep within that it left a strong impression. You can hear the toxic gas hissing up from this cavern giving the place a sinister touch.

Years after the photo was taken I was at a crossroads in life. At this time I was taking a course in decorative painting and as such starting to express my creativity in a sincere way. I had just started to open my eyes to a lot of paranormal occurrences and symbology. Something was trying to speak to me through the symbols, but I didn't know what to do about it, it was confusing. One summer night I looked through my photo album, and I found a photo of the plutonium mentioned earlier, and decided to research it further. The pull was there again but instead I stumbled across a strange goddess, Hekate and her role in the myth of Persephone. It felt like I had found a long lost friend. Things made sense. The dance had begun. Midnight, the next evening, I was standing at the very forest glitch where I had seen the ghost dogs in my childhood. As it happens, it is where three roads meet.

I had no idea what a suitable offering to Hekate would be, so I improvised. Some food from the kitchen - Honey, egg, bread, macaroni, chocolate, as well as a stick of incense and a coin from Crete. The date of this night I was standing at the crossroads was August the 13th. Everything had come together. The ghost dogs, the photograph and my offerings that night, it was all related. I left my offerings and I felt contented. But mindful that her ghostly dogs might decide to appear again, I left in a hurry.

Hekate must have been pleased, because she soon answered my devotional act to her. She showed her presence and appeared to me in dreams. I created a shrine for her. I tried communicating with her using a candle flame. I asked her to show me a *'miracle'* and a large spider came jolting across my floor straight at me! This happened quite frequently when she was near! In fact as I write this essay, the first spider of spring is walking across my wall. Being fearful of these creatures has been a great aid to see them as divine messengers - I don't kill them and they taught me to respect life. Sometimes I heard the local dogs howling while working with Hekate in worship.

Then the super physical contact with her started to fade. Hekate started to move into the subtle background from where she had emerged. I had many dreams meeting her where she showed me very mysterious things. She opened up many doors to the magickal world and to the astral plane where her spirits are. I learned to speak with the dead and to travel around a misty world. I met spirits of different types. The suicides, the restless dead, the trapped ones and even some members of the Aghori sect. The misty world is the hotspot of liminal deity. And I experienced and learned so much more. Without her I would be stagnant.

The first dreams I had with Hekate was in a completely dark place. I could hear a group of people bumping around in there with me. They were completely silent and appeared o be sleeping or muted. Then a pair of hands took a gentle hold of me, they lead me out of there and into a new room. When I woke up I had a word in my head. I held onto the word so that I would never forget it – *"Sheol..."*

I dreamt again the next night. This time I entered an apartment, not that large - just a hallway, a room and a kitchen. In the hallway was a woman with black hair, about 30 years old with a mystical smile. She was stunning, wearing an orange sweater and jeans Very modern for a Bronze Age goddess! Her eyes had a faint peculiar glow to them and I knew it was Hekate. Then she was gone, and behind the door stood a very large black dog on its hind legs. It plunged forward and grabbed my neck in its jaws. I closed my eyes in fear as I was certain it was going to bite my head off! It then released my neck and when I opened my eyes the dog was gone and the woman was back. Silently I went into the kitchen and sat down at the table, but she was no longer there. Instead the dog entered the kitchen and rested its head on my lap. I felt a great comfort and companionship with the dog, a psychic, almost telepathic connection. Just me and you loving dog I said, *"why did she just leave me here?"* We waited, and I had a look in the fridge where I found a jar of olives with a note attached. It was a prayer to Hekate. I shared the olives with the dog, and then wrote a note onto the prayer – *"Hekate I wanted to speak to you, but where did you go? I wanted to follow your call! P.S. I ate your olives."* Hekate must have a sense of humour and I since then always offered her olives in my devotional work.

I started the miniature shrine a few years ago. At the time I knew that I wanted to build a better one than the one I had at the time. My first shrine was basically a picture from the internet that had been printed out and put on a wall, with a bookshelf underneath serving as an altar for Hekate. I had some ideas for a new shrine, at first I thought of some form of roadside shrine, like those you get on the side of the road in some parts of the Mediterranean. They are placed where road traffic accidents took place, and have pictures of the deceased and offerings inside. For me these felt very connected to Hekate

Then one day my mother brought home a wooden shrine from the school that she worked at, it was going to be thrown away and she asked me if I could use it. My mother is a very intuitive person and she was very right, of course I could use it! I had to then decide how the shrine was going to look, I knew that I wanted to include as many different aspects of Hekate as possible, to balance her different qualities. Looking for ideas I browsed through the book *Hekate Keys to the Crossroads*, on the cover a painting by Magin Rose, and inside an essay by her. For me her artwork was the most beautiful depiction of Hekate I had seen, it held true magick and power. Magin's image sparked my inspiration and before I knew it I was all over my new project! Therefore I wish to pay her here, a special tribute for inspiring me. She played a *'key'* role indeed in the creation of my shrine, as I painted my own version of Hekate based on her painting!

Figure 55 - Minature Shrine by Henrik Holmdahl

Inner Hekate image on the left, and the door of the shrine on the right.

People have asked me how I made my shrine. For me, the big secret is to ask the shrine to form itself, asking Hekate to help you with your endeavour, then gather the parts. Don't be in a rush, the shrine will create itself organically. I have been keeping mine for years and it keeps reinventing itself! Its a *'master plan'* of sorts, I have no idea what the final form will be. It is also important to always work on the shrine when you feel inspired to do so, to add the items you feel should be there. Go with your intuition, letting the inner voice tell you what to do.

Inspiration is a great tool to work within magick, because it directly connects you with the primordial mind that you need to utilise in witchcraft. What you feel to express can work its way directly from the other realm and over to ours, art is mediumistic. It is like a spell, but you use paint and creativity, creating a type of portal or gateway. You are inviting Hekate to reside there in the image and work through it. Don't let your mind wander while working and painting. Keep it focused at the intent of your work. I prefer to play music while I paint. I play everything from pagan chants to metal and techno, using music that connect you with Hekate, and relaxes you, putting you in a magical mood. You can also burn candles whilst working. The paints, water and tools should all be consecrated as per your traditions' workings.

I used acrylic paint, its water soluble and works very well for this kind of project. For extra power I mixed finely ground herbs and resins to the paint - this then has the effect of magical ink. Likewise the water can also be magically charged, by for example writing an invocation to Hekate in a water soluble ink and then dissolving the words into the water. The herbs should be ground into a very fine dust powder and then sifted, to prevent lumps in the paint. I use a pestle and mortar to grind with and herbs which are traditionally sacred to Hekate. Unfortunately some of these are very toxic to work with and may be difficult to find in some countries, so if you can't find them use what you have. A pinch of dirt from my favourite crossroad is the most powerful ingredient for me anyway, likewise the best time for me to work on the shrine is at midnight or at the dark moon. Sometimes at the waxing moon, on a Wednesday in the hour of Mercury.

On the bottom of the shrine I made a miniature crossroad from said dirt, mixed with resins and sacred herbs, binding it with transparent wood glue. I use this mini crossroad to place offerings on, especially during the winter months. The ground in between is divided in black, white and saffron. All over the sides of the crossroad I wrote her many names in Greek, English and Theban Script. Hekate's hands are holding torches, which can be fitted with miniature candles presenting real flame. If you are going to do that, you are strongly advised to make the back of the shrine from something fireproof!

The image of Hekate was outlined on the back of the shrine, is the same image as the one on the door of the shrine, I simply shrank it to size using a photo editing program. I then printed it out and placed it on top of carbon copy paper to trace it onto the back. With the outline there, it was far easier to paint. I had no previous experience of painting a figure like this, so have confidence, just ask Hekate to help your hand a bit and she will.

The face holds a great part of the spirit in an image, this should be the most important part of the project. The hymn that has given me most inspiration has been the *Orphic Hymn to Hekate*, in which she is depicted as the saffron clad queen. I painted golden sandals on her feet, as she is standing inside a doorway, there is a starry sky around her. I wanted to reflect back the stars in the hair of Magin Rose's Hekate. To the left is the primordial ocean, and the first land being born. The sky is glowing with fire from its birth and above is the full moon. The cave stone on the side of the shrine is an idea from a dream, I tried to reflect back the energy from the dream to the shrine. The stone was made from plaster mixed with herbs then painted to look like stone and the branches was made from bronze wire twined together to look like roots. I covered them with wood glue, mixed with willow tree. Yew or Oak, or even real roots might have been better. Between the *'made'* roots I sometimes put some Aconite as decoration. They are useful to hang things on as well. The idea of hanging things inside the shrine comes from an ancient Greek practice, a concept I added after reading about it in *Greek and Roman Necromancy* by Daniel Ogden. The same book also inspired the decoration on the outside. Inside the shrine hangs a jar and a key. Hekate's dogs have holes in their eyes, and you can place candles behind the shrine to make their eyes glow. The spirits of the dogs can work their way through the flames, so it has both a visual effect and a practical purpose.

The most important tool for working with her should be your heart and your instincts. Don't wait for the right conditions to arrive; she will clear the path for you. Knowledge about Hekate can't be fitted into an book, writing can only provide glimpses of how other people experienced her. If you want to get to know Hekate, then the best way is to say: *"please show me your mysteries"*. I believe she is there for everyone who dare to approach her in a honest way. The gods favour the bold as Ovid once said. Is the fact that you are holding this book right now just coincidence? Is it just chance? That is for you to decide. If you already know her, then we are flames in the same fire.

Figure 56 - The Temple Ruins at Lagina (1)

Figure 57 - The Temple Ruins at Lagina (2)

SACRIFICES WILL BE MADE

A PERSONAL MEETING WITH HEKATE

BY MORGANA SYTHOVE

This story began in 2004, long before its present writing, when I agreed to meet a young Turkish dance student in Utrecht to introduce him to pagan friends at one of the local *"witch cafés"*. We soon became good friends: his background fascinated me, as I hadn't met many people from Turkey until then. He had a greater interest in my work with Wicca and Pagan Federation International but I persisted. Consequently we met, and later started sharing ritual experiences. I noticed that he wanted to forget his own background and concentrate on the West. I understood this, but at the same time knew that he also had something to share.

I mentioned my *"ancient memory"* of Mesopotamia and my near-obsession with Harran (in Southern Turkey near to the Syrian border). He had heard of Harran, and he suggested that I get in touch with a friend of his who knew more about it. During the Christmas period of 2004 I met Atheneris in Amsterdam; she did indeed know a lot about Harran. We kept in contact and in September 2005 we organised a cultural visit to the ancient sanctuary of Hekate at Lagina.

I had hoped to include a visit to Harran but was warned that it wasn't very safe at the time, so we decided to limit this visit to the ancient province of Caria. Bodrum would be our starting point.

Since we were planning a visit to Lagina I started making preparations (or rather Hekate started preparing me!). I tried to research Hekate but found the books and articles difficult to reconcile with my own inner workings. In fact, the more I read the less I understood. One book that did seem to make sense to me was *Hekate in Ancient Greek Religion* by Robert Von Rudloff.

Rudloff describes Hekate in the image of the young maiden, which was more evident in ancient texts than the old hag one associates with Shakespeare's *Macbeth*. I had already encountered the youthful girl bearing two torches who presented me with a long chain of keys. It seemed as though I was being asked to open doors for various people, including myself. It was, however, a visit to Sweden that would subsequently become significant. In May 2005 I gave a workshop at the PFI Sweden conference in Uppsala. The day after a local archaeologist, Kurt, kindly showed a friend and myself the King's Mounds at Gamla Uppsala, but told us that he had a more important site to show us. He led us to what he called a *"cultus house"*. I recognised it as being akin to a hunebed, a Neolithic dolmen found in the Netherlands.

When asked if human remains had been found there he replied yes, but that the deceased was first burnt. Water was then thrown on the burning body causing the bones to shatter; the biggest bone remains were placed in urns and buried in the cultus house. He then showed us a stone pillar that was lying in the grass. He took a small round stone and hit one end of the pillar – it made a dull thud. He hit it again, but this time at the other end where there was a small indentation, and the pillar rang like a bell! Did I know what this meant? It suddenly flashed through my mind that the bodies had passed through fire, water, earth and now air through the vocal calling of spirits.

Having been born with Congenital Hip Dislocation (Dysplasia) and undergone surgery to replace my right hip in 1986, I knew that sooner or later my left hip would require surgery. The hip had been deteriorating slowly, but in July 2005 my hip collapsed and I couldn't walk. I was taken to the emergency department of my local hospital: the advice was immediate surgery. I refused, as I was under care at a hospital in Nijmegen. I asked for crutches, promising I would get in touch with my surgeon straightaway, which I did. A check-up confirmed that it was time for a new hip.

But I wanted to go to Turkey. Hekate was calling... Sacrifices will be made.

And so I did. Making sure that I had a couple of friends nearby to help me if necessary, Flora and I set off to Bodrum, complete with crutches, for two weeks in early September 2005. We met Atheneris there and continued to prepare for the visit to Lagina, and also visited Ephesus and other sites. Atheneris also met the curator of the Bodrum Castle Museum. She came back and couldn't wait to tell me what she had seen: the curator had shown her some artefacts in the cellars. She hurriedly showed me a photo she had taken. It was of a rough stone. Two ears – life size -had been carved into it. In between them was a labrys – the iconic double axe of the Minoans.

I suddenly realised that the labrys wasn't just an axe – it also represented lungs with the vertical shaft representing the windpipe. And I recalled the ringing stone of Uppsala. Here in Bodrum was the pictorial image of the voice of the Gods, Goddesses and Spirits being heard. Significantly, I had been wearing a labrys symbol around my neck for 25 years. Even more significant is the fact that the labrys is the symbol of Caria, the province in which Bodrum is located. The labrys was later exported to Crete and adopted by the priestesses of Knossos. I hadn't understood when one or two local people had said to me – after seeing my labrys - *"you are one of us..."*

I had only been in Bodrum a few days when I started getting diarrhoea. It was the usual problem: different diet, too much sun. Not convenient though - we still had to make the journey to Turgut and Lagina. We met the rest of the delegation and set off into the mountains in our rented minibus.

We arrived in Turgut and met the archaeologists excavating the site. We met the mayor of the village and other dignitaries, attended the festival organised by the villagers called Hekatesia and also visited a site on the processional way between Lagina and Stratoniceia. Rescue archaeology was being carried out there, but I was so ill that I decided not to visit. Later we set off for some lunch. We arrived at a beautiful place in the mountains where you could see the beehives dotted along the way. The restaurant had a small stream flowing through the garden. But I couldn't face lunch... in fact I collapsed and fainted. I remember thinking to Hekate: *"If I have to die, what a beautiful place to go...*" but Atheneris was gently massaging me and calling me back. Later some of the Turkish waiters offered me a bed to lie down on – which I did. Even later Genghis the minibus driver asked me if I wanted to go back to the hostel, which was a good idea. So Flora, Atheneris, Alan and I went back while the others continued on their exploration of other ancient sites in the area.

After a rest Flora suggested that we should go for a walk. She had discovered a small sanctuary above the village. Of course I couldn't get up a mountain, but a walk was possible. We went through the village and ascended slightly to what looked like a park. There some of the village ladies came to us and offered us tea and food. Atheneris explained on my behalf that I was ill but that I would like some tea. An older lady later brought me some herbal tea, which she said would *"help me"*. I have never tasted such bitter tea, although I could also taste honey. The tea did help though, as soon I didn't feel nauseous.

That evening we held a ritual. The moon was full, and hung low in the sky, making the white stones silvery blue. The archaeologists lent us torches to light up the Sanctuary. Struggling over the large blocks of excavated stones using my crutches, I managed to get to the inner part of the Sanctuary. There we made our offerings. Atheneris had warned us "*Sacrifices will be made.*" She took our offering – a pomegranate – and cut it open revealing the tiny fleshy seeds and blood red juice.

As Flora invoked a falling star was observed.

Then John found a key -"*That's for Morgana....*" and he gave it to me.

I had hardly taken it into my hands when I knew what I had to do. A dear friend of mine had cancer – I had planned to do something private for him, but Hekate had different plans. Without revealing what actually happened I knew she was calling him and that she was ready for him. My job was to let him know it was all right. She would be there to guide him.

Afterwards I knew the key had to be returned. Flora said it had to be brought back to the inner sanctum – there on high, she pointed! There was no way I could make it up the steep blocks of stone, but she knew a different way with little steps. She helped me and together we got to the top. I stood, found the place for the key, dropped my crutches and exclaimed that the rite was over.

The following day we were going to visit the Temple of Zeus at Labranda. Genghis the minibus driver saw me the following morning and looked astounded: "*Mama Turk, it's a miracle*!" He couldn't believe how quickly I had recovered and how much better I looked.

The visit to Labranda was amazing too. There, as in Lagina, was another sacred well, with the sacred bees that drank the sacred water. On the notice at the entrance was a list of archaeologists engaged in the excavations there. Imagine my amazement when I saw listed the University of Uppsala, Sweden. I was reminded yet again of the sanctuary or cultus house there and the significance of the labrys. I was also reminded of Zeus who called Hekate the Queen of Heaven.

We returned home a couple of days later where I had to prepare for the hip operation, which I knew would entail a long recovery period. On November 10th I went into hospital. That afternoon our very dear black cat of 17 years, Raven, died. He had been blind for a number of weeks and was gradually losing his way; it was if he was treading another path, as if he was going ahead.

On the 11th of November 2005 I went into surgery in the very early morning, by the evening I was in recovery. The first message I received was not to wish me strength, but instead to inform me that our friend had died of cancer that very day.

Since then my life has continued to change. I lost my job – after 27 years - during my convalescence. I however had two good hips and for the first time in a long time I could walk with both feet on the ground. And walk I did. Hekate has called me on numerous occasions since and shown me that I can find my way and guide people to find theirs. We just have to find the right keys. I know one of those keys will also get me to Harran one day!

The labrys reminds me to listen to the Gods, not just Hekate, very carefully.

What follows are some extracts from a report of the PFI visit to the Ancient Temple of Hekate in Lagina, with photographs of the site taken during the trip.

HEKATESIA AT LAGINA, 2005

Frederic Lamond (Gardnerian Wiccan Elder), who had also joined, us continues the story:

> "(I was)... just in time to join the main party in the minibus to Turgut Village on 16 September, with a visit to an open cast coal mine on the way, where many archaeological artefacts are frequently found. The Hekatesia festival, which has been taking place since 2000, is mostly a multimedia show for the benefit of the inhabitants of neighbouring Turgut village. The Hekatesia is held to inform local people of Hekate and her sanctuary in Ancient Anatolia and to let them know of the progress of the excavations. However this year there was a splendid procession by the students of an Istanbul drama school. This was unfortunately spoiled by a swarm of press photographers following the procession, taking photographs from all angles as it proceeded. The day after the official festival, on the evening of 17 September 2005, our group was allowed to hold a private ceremony in the temple ruins, which in the bright moonlight had a remarkable atmosphere. The place was full of power despite not having been used as a place of Pagan worship for 1600 years. At least this is what the archaeologists told us. The 1000 previous years of continuous worship must have left their mark, or else it is a natural power spot and was chosen for that reason as the location of a temple to Hekate. After linking in a circle we each of us went individually to address our own personal prayers to Hekate, and I felt a very strong personal contact with the Goddess."

The 11km/7 miles long Sacred Road, lined with tombs and starting from the entrance gate, connected Stratoniceia - the political centre - to Lagina Sanctuary - the prominent religious centre of Caria (Karia) dedicated to Hecate. During religious festivals, a splendid ritual procession carried the key of the Temple of Hekate from Lagina to Stratoniceia.

The Lagina Sanctuary, which was a prominent cult centre of the Carians is still famous today and is also known by the name of Leyne. Recent research has revealed that this region was inhabited from the Antique Bronze Age (3000 BCE) to the present. The Kings of the Seleucid dynasty by virtue of great constructional efforts built the Lagina sanctuary as a religious centre, and the city of Stratoniceia, 11km. away, as the political centre. At the Lagina sanctuary there is a propylon (monumental gateway), the interconnecting Sacred Road, an altar (sacrificial and dipping place), peribolos (wall encircling the sanctuary), Doric stoa and the Temple of Hecate. The sanctuary is surrounded by walls of about two metres in height, which also form the back wall of the stoa. The monumental entrance building, with three entrances and an apsis at the western end supported by four Ionian columns, is connected to the stoa with a door. From the monumental entrance gate to the altar, there are ten rows of steps leading to the stone-paved road. The temple, encircled with five rows of steps, located on an Attic Ionian pedestal, with a single row of columns with Corinthian capital, is at the centre of the sanctuary. The temple is pseudo-dipteral with 8x11 columns, and is built in the Corinthian style. The inscriptions at Lagina and on the walls of the Bouleterion at Stratoniceia reveal that those two cities were connected by a Sacred Road and during festivities a splendid ritual procession carried the key of the temple from Lagina to Stratoniceia.

Figure 58 - The Temple Ruins in Moonlight at Lagina (3)

ACKNOWLEDGEMENTS

Photos by Alan & John and published with permission and thanks! Thanks also to Fred Lamond for his report of the visit.

Notes & Bibliography
"*Hekatesia 2005*" For the official report see:
http://www.paganplaza.paganfederation.org/members/newsletters.php?archive=1
Hekate in Ancient Greek Religion by Robert Von Rudloff , Horned Owl Publishing
Hekate Soteira, Sarah Iles Johnston
Hekate: Keys to the Crossroads, Avalonia, Sorita D'Este (Editor)
General information about Pagan Federation International see www.paganfederation.org and
PFI Turkey www.tr.paganfederation.org
Pagan Federation - www.paganfederation.org
Silver Circle – www.silvercircle.org

Figure 59 - Maiden Mother Crone by Emily Carding

The Fortunes of Hekate

By Madre Van der Merwe

O thou that wast before the earth was formed
Fiery celestial Hekate.
O tideless, soundless, boundless, bitter sea,
I am thy priestess, answer unto me.

I don't remember the moment when Hekate first started affecting my life. I think it was in my dreams, waking remembering lights in caves, torches flickering and casting shadows on rock walls. I started having shivers of the *'someone walking over my grave'* variety at particular moments, like when I heard my keys rattle together in my handbag, or when I saw the evening star shining over Table Mountain. With hindsight it is obvious, but at the time it was like a challenge, remember what you already know, see through the mist and find me!

Until Hekate made her presence felt, I had been most profoundly influenced by the writings of Dion Fortune. Mainly her fiction, and the way she portrayed the gods. I loved her borrowing from Apuleius and portraying Isis as the Great Mother. This spoke to my soul and like many before me, (and others since I am sure) I modelled much of my behaviour on her powerful priestess Vivien/Lilith Le Fay Morgan. For me *Sea Priestess* was the primer and *Moon Magic* was the manual, describing processes and giving all that was needed to establish and empower my magical personality.

O radiant Hekate, come to me!
Ruler of heaven, earth and sea.
The hour of the dark moon-tide draws near,
Hear the invoking words, hear and appear
Fiery celestial Hekate!
I am thy priestess, answer unto me.

In true Fortune style I gathered the woods to make the Fire of Azrael. I remember reading somewhere in a Wiccan book that this should be performed on a beach, but was relieved when re-reading my novels to see this was not the case. The Fire of Azrael was performed on the hearth at home, which was definitely preferable.

So the time came, I prepared myself and lit my fire, half expecting and half hoping for messages from Isis, who had been the main focus of my attention when I called on the goddess. This is the only drawback of basing your life on fiction, you have to trust yourself to spot the truth whether it is represented as fact or fantasy. This is also a plus, as it gives you a greater scope to draw on what rings true, and there are some fine writers in the world today restating the ancient myths in a modern setting, giving a vibrancy that can be tuned into and utilised.

The hour of the dark moon draws near;
I hear the invoking words, hear and appear
Chthonia, Enodia, Trioditis
I come unto the holy bliss

When I was skrying in the ashes I got a bit of a shock! Isis had three heads! Then I realised it wasn't Isis, but another goddess, who was talking to me. Even though I had never worked with her, I knew a bit about Hekate. Not only did Apuleius in his second century CE work *Metamorphoses* (*The Golden Ass*) equate her to Isis, but she was also mentioned by Fortune in her novels in the classic chants performed by Le Fay Morgan. And I realised, if Hekate was equated with these other goddesses to Isis, then equally Isis and other goddesses could be equated to Hekate. The reference by Apuleius which had grabbed my attention was not the more common one where lots of goddesses are equated, but the one where he said *"At another time you [Isis] are Proserpina [Hekate], whose howls at night inspire dread, and whose triple form restrains the emergence of ghosts as you keep the entrance to the earth above firmly barred. You wander through diverse groves, and are appeased by various rites"* (Note I was so happy to see the entry on Isis-Hekate in Sorita d'Este's book *Hekate Liminal Rites* – talk about proving a point!).

I am she who ere the earth was formed
Was fiery celestial Hekate
Ruler of the soundless, boundless, bitter sea,
Out of whose deeps life wells eternally.

Of course I asked Hekate how she would like things done. Now I am not suggesting in any way that Hekate is pushy, but she sure has definite ideas about how to do things! Move it to the dark moon, offer me these foods, put your altar on the ground not up in the air, replace the statues with depictions of me, and the list went on! However the contact was so strong and moved me so much that the idea of turning her down never crossed my mind until much later, and by then I laughed at the idea as she had me well and truly hooked on her unique light, laughter and power. One thing I did do which she didn't ask for was to adapt the words Dion Fortune wrote, what I call her *'Ea, Binah, Ge'* chant, so that they focused on Hekate with no other goddesses or Qabalah in there. This essay contains parts of my rewritten Hekate version, with due credit and thanks to Dion Fortune for coming up with her original Isis version. But for me, Hekate is like a spiritual eclipse, everything else becomes a blackness given definition by her twin flames.

I am the flame that burns ever on;
All things in the end shall come to me.
Mine is the kingdom of Nexichthon,
The inner earth, where lead the pathways three.
Who drinks the waters of that hidden well
Shall see the things whereof he dare not tell
Shall tread the shadowy path that leads to me
Kleidouchos, Soteira, Hekate,

Shadows have passed through my life, bad times like everybody has. However since Hekate removed my veil it has been more manageable. Where I might have slipped into depression I now feel melancholy. Where I might have railed against the Fates, I now look for the moment where opportunity presents itself. Because one thing Hekate has taught me and shown me again and again is that there is always a moment where you can turn things around. I think that is the greatest gift she gives, and I will always honour her through my deeds and thoughts, knowing that she is the light in the darkness, through birth, death and rebirth. She is the light in the dusk and the dawn, and hope in the clouds and the storm.

I am the Star that riseth from the sea,
The twilight sea.
all tides are mine and answer unto me
Tides of men's souls and dreams and destiny
Fiery celestial Hekate.

Figure 60 - Table Mountain, Cape Town (South Africa) by Madre van der Merwe

BIBLIOGRAPHY

Apuleius. *The Golden Ass.* Indiana, Indiana University Press, 1962.
D'Este, Sorita, & David Rankine. *Hekate Liminal Rites.* London, Avalonia, 2009
Fortune, Dion. *The Sea Priestess.* New York, Samuel Weiser, 1972.
Fortune Dion. *Moon Magic.* London, Aquarian Press, 1956.

Figure 61 - Gorgon by Izzy Purplespoon

HEKATE: HER SACRED FIRES

UNTOUCHED

ALEISTER CROWLEY, GEMATRIA AND THE GODDESS

BY MICHAEL ELLIS

This is the story of a magickal journey, one which started with a question, raised more questions, and has left me with questions still to answer. It started with the novel *Moonchild* by Aleister Crowley, and a phrase written by the Beast which jarred my senses and caused me to start my quest. The phrase in question was:

> *"Hecate, a thing altogether of hell, barren, hideous and malicious, the queen of death and evil witchcraft."*

This felt wrong to me, so I decided to investigate this goddess who had caused Crowley to write such a negative comment. It seemed to me that she had somehow caused him to have a bad reaction, and there was something not being told here. So my starting place was her name, Hekate. My way of working is to follow the number trail and then follow the book trail. Looking at the Gematria I saw that Hekate's name added to 334 (Εκατη), as did the Greek words for *'passage'* (παρακομιδη) and *'race'* or *'tribe'* (εθνος).

My first thought was of the Orphic Oath, *"I am a child of earth and starry heaven, but my race is of heaven alone."* To me this has always seemed cognate with *"Every man and every woman is a star"* (AL 1.3) in the *Book of the Law*, Crowley's received text. *The Book of the Law* (*Liber Al*) has been my inspiration for many years, never failing me and making me appreciate that to do my will I do not need the personalities, histories or structures of the past. The Orphic Oath was spoken at the entrance to the underworld, and I remembered that Hekate had an association with the underworld, so this seemed significant.

However then like a bolt of lightning the other word struck me! Passage! I should be looking at the passage corresponding to Hekate's name in the *Book of the Law!* I immediately opened my battered copy of *Liber Al* and looked at chapter 3, verse 34 – corresponding to the 334 of her name. What I saw was one of the (for me anyway), key verses of the text:

> *"But your holy place shall be untouched throughout the centuries: though with fire and sword it be burnt down & shattered, yet an invisible house there standeth, and this shall stand until the fall of the Great Equinox; when Hrumachis shall arise and the double-wanded one assume my throne and place. Another prophet shall arise, and bring fresh fever from the skies; another woman shall awake the lust & worship of the Snake; another soul of God and beast shall mingle in the globed priest; another sacrifice shall stain the tomb; another king shall reign; and blessing no longer be poured To the Hawk-headed mystical Lord!"*

My first thought was to check the multiples of 334, as this is one of the first steps for me in looking for significant numerical connections. Sure enough, I found significant links with the number 1336 (4x334), which is the value of the words *'to keep secret'* (κατασιγαω), and *'the prophet'* (ο προφτης). Considering the reference to a prophet in the verse this was an obvious connection. *'To keep secret'* is interesting, as it presents the idea of the elemental axiom of Earth (*to keep silent*), but also the dichotomy that the last thing a prophet does is keep silent! Certainly Crowley did not seem to display the virtue of Earth very often in his life.

So back to Hekate, why did this verse speak to me? Well I have always found that the verses in *Liber Al* have a number of meanings which may be uncovered at different times, and it can be a mistake to try and make the whole of a verse fit, when it might just be parts of it that are significant for a particular key to the cipher you are looking for. The first part of the verse which called to me was *'another woman shall awake the lust & worship of the Snake'*. Hekate is often connected with snakes, being crowned with wild serpents and also with serpents coiled around her. This is seen in a variety of sources, but my favourite reference is in the *Chaldean Oracles*, which describes her as:

> *"the She-Serpent, and the snake-girdled; others calling her on account of her appearance Girt in serpent coils."*

In fact *The Chaldean Oracles* were a real eye-opener, as I had not realised how significant they were in influencing modern magick. The way bits of them have been taken by magical groups like the *Golden Dawn* to provide the words for things like the *Ritual of Opening by Watchtower*, or in the initiation ceremonies. That Hekate is described as Saviour (Soteira) in *The Chaldean Oracles* also matches the tone of this verse of *Liber Al*.

Next I pondered who was the *'double-wanded one'* who would *'assume my throne and place'*. The double wand always makes me think of the caduceus in its twin serpent variety as born by Hermes, the trickster god of magick, who I noted was also often associated with Hekate. Of course in the information age, Hermes could be said to have assumed the throne. But is that the case? I was also conscious of the fact that one of the last verses of *Liber Al* has the line "*I am the Lord of the Double Wand of Power; the wand of the force of Coph Nia*" (AL3.72). Two immediate avenues opened up to my thought process, which were to apply the principle I did with Hekate's name and look for Greek words adding to 372, and to consider the Coph Nia.

The number 372 gives the word for *'power'* or *'bliss'* (ολβος), entirely in keeping with the essence of the verse and the nature of the double wand, so that was promising. Coph Nia is the word that was inserted later by Rose, Crowley's wife, as it was not clearly heard when he was receiving the transmission of *Liber Al*. Rose did not know Hebrew, and so Coph is likely to have been Qoph, giving Qoph Nia. This would then literally be *'the daughter (Nia) of the back of the head (Qoph).'* However Qoph when spelt in full is comprised of itself and the letter Peh, meaning *'mouth'*. Thus it is literally that which is received at the back of the head and spoken through the mouth, i.e. inspiration or prophecy.

Prophecy is particularly associated with Hekate, so the wand of prophecy and power is very appropriate for Hekate. The fact that it is wielded by a Lord did not fit however, so I returned to my earlier premise that perhaps this refers to Hermes, and the pairing of the two of them as was seen at gateways and in some spells. More than ever this has convinced me that it is a mistake to just assume that the pantheon of *Liber Al* is the Egyptian gods mentioned in the text, particularly as Hadit seems to have no existence before Crowley and *Liber Al*. A number of the references through the text could imply other gods, and who is to say they do not, apart from people who want to be shunned as centres of pestilence for discussing the book, like I am doing!

Another part of the verse which jumped out at me was the reference to *'fire and sword'*. I remembered reading in a book on Hekate that the torch and word were both symbols associated with her, and found the reference was actually from an early Christian writer mentioning her in his arguments:

> *"The symbols of Hecate are wax of three colours, white and black and red combined, having a figure of Hecate bearing a scourge, and torch, and sword, with a serpent to be coiled round her"*

So although this may seem somewhat wide-ranging, for me the collection of connections which all sprang together so quickly have provided the inspiration and a doorway into the mysteries of Hekate. Now I am far more interested in Hekate than Egyptian gods, and see in *The Chaldean Oracles* a proto-*Liber Al*, from a time when the world appreciated its gods more. The complex nature of Hekate and her many forms to me encapsulates what is missing from the heart of many modern currents, a completeness that feeds every part of the magician's being.

My focus is now fully on *"the barbarously shouting goddess"* who has captivated not only my heart but my intellect too, setting me alight with flames of passion and flames of knowledge!

FURTHER READING

Barry, Kieran; *The Greek Qabalah: Alphabetic Mysticism and Numerology in the Ancient World;* 1999; Samuel Weiser Inc; Maine

Crowley, Aleister; *The Book of the Law: Liber AL vel LEGIS;* 1976 (received 1904); Samuel Weiser Inc; Maine

D'Este, Sorita (ed); *Hekate Keys to the Crossroads;* 2006; Avalonia; London

D'Este, Sorita, & David Rankine; *Hekate Liminal Rites;* 2009; Avalonia; London

Ronan, Stephen (ed); *The Goddess Hekate;* 1992; Chthonios Books; Hastings

Figure 62 - Tetrahedron by Tara Sanchez

One, two, three...

Where's number four, Timaeus?

By Tara Sanchez

The word initiate derives from the Latin word *initiare*, it means to begin. When I sat down and began to write this, I questioned myself, what could I bring to the equation, what validity was there in me sharing my words. What did I really know of Hekate as an Initiatrix and Guide, I tried writing something clever and witty yet full of academia to validate what I was saying and it came out like trite rubbish, then she said to me, go back to your beginning, so I shall.

I sat there shivering, looking past the person in front of me towards the early morning mist receding slowly backwards across the mill pond, it was late October in the North of England, the last thing I really wanted to be doing was sitting in nothing much but a cotton robe listening to somebody informing me of my magickal inadequacies. Inadequacies I was more than painfully aware of. I'd been expecting this interview for days, each time I stumbled out of bed at 5am for morning meditation, wondering what weird and wonderful evocation the day would bring, I had expected to be pulled aside, my dirty secret revealed, that I was a fraud, an idiot, or worse totally magickally inept without an ounce of talent to my name.

To say I had spent a week totally out of my depth would have been an understatement, discussions and rituals involving entities I'd never heard of, using texts I didn't understand, for purposes beyond my comprehension. Everyone far more experienced than me, seemingly understanding, nodding sagely, and spontaneously coming up with obscure esoteric facts and fantastical sounding anecdotes of past magickal experiences. The odd sometimes impatient looks when I made naive comments, or jokes to cover a deep seated sense of unease that had been growing in my mind as a result of my apparent lack of knowledge and experience. My esteem at that point, it would be safe to say was at an all time low, casting my mind back and looking at it dispassionately I wonder what my life would now be like if my desire to run had actually outweighed my sheer stubborn nature that makes me see a thing through to the bitter end.

"You're a frog you know"

"A what?"

I was brought abruptly back out of my wallowing self pity, realising that I had been doing a good approximation of listening but hadn't heard a thing that had been said, I had basically tuned out at the point where I had been told that all I was good for was working with elementals, something at the time I saw as indicative of my poor abilities, you know, throw her a bone and give her the fairies, make her feel that she has achieved just a little something. An opinion over the years I have subsequently revised drastically but that is another story for another time.

He smiled, *"Your totem, it is a frog; I do not normally tell my pupils what their totems are, it is better they find out on their own, but in your case I feel it is for your protection that you know".* The conversation then meandered around a number of subjects, mostly over my head; frustrated but refusing to show it, I smiled through gritted teeth, and nodded in the right places and made the correct murmuring noises.

"I can help you, but there are some things that you cannot learn from me, it is not my area of expertise, you need to find another teacher, but I don't know of anybody suitable"

Ah here it was, the gentle let down, I had been weighed and measured and had been found wanting. Well so be it, just 24 more hours and I could be out of there, hi-tailing it for the hills never to be seen again.

"I want you to get a statue of the Goddess Heqet"

I stared blankly at my companion, my knowledge of the Egyptian pantheon at that time being pretty much limited to all things Isian care of such authors as Ellen Cannon Reid and Tracy De Regula.

"She is the Egyptian Frog headed goddess of childbirth and fertility, I want you to invoke her into the statue and ask her to provide you with a teacher and a guide".

I agreed verbally, but mentally took note that I would absolutely not be doing any such thing, after all, only a few weeks earlier my companion had suggested I summon Asmodeus and serve him lightly sautéed Bulls testicles and a glass of port, so as to avenge a fairly minor personal slight, that I genuinely felt did not require magick in any way shape or form to deal with, so after politely excusing myself, I spent the remainder of that day quietly counting the hours, the following morning packing my bags and heading home, ready to close the book on this experience, learn from it, move on, preferably as quickly as I possibly could. If only it had been that easy.

I withdrew pretty much entirely from the Magickal community as I knew it at the time; I licked my wounds, contemplated my navel, generally mooched around and tried to start writing a new chapter in my life. But something kept stopping me, something or someone kept dragging me back to that point, sometimes it manifested as a deep husky yet feminine voice whispering to me in the grey time between being awake and asleep, sometimes it was more tangible yet equally obscure, an owl feather at high noon floating down in front of me out of nowhere, no shadow passing over to indicate the presence of its original owner. What did it all mean? I searched and tried to piece it all together, mostly failing miserably.

I started researching this Egyptian Goddess and seemed to be going nowhere fast, I didn't get her, didn't understand why she would be interested in me, and more importantly from my view point at that time, why I should be interested in her. What I did keep coming across were claims that she was somehow connected to the Goddess Hekate, claims which I could not find any substance to, each time I went down that route and reached a dead end, I would sigh with relief, I didn't want *"her"*. At the time, I suppose, it seemed to me it was all rather fashionable to work with Hekate, every witch and their familiar seemed to be doing so at any rate, and often talking about it rather loudly and in an *"Ooo look at me aren't I scary"* kind of way; so although I kept a reserved interest, or was it an interest in me, I never have worked out which came first, I suspect it is a chicken and egg situation; anyway whatever it was, I kept it very quiet and generally tried to ignore it when I could.

Eventually late one night in anger and frustration, I called out to this alien goddess, Heqet, bring me a teacher; bring me a guide, because I am just flailing around in the dark here. I don't know what I was expecting from this heartfelt plea, accompanied by the tearing of hair and the beating of a bared chest, but I certainly wasn't expecting what I got, the distant laughter drifting on the breeze and then nothing but the sound of my own heart beating in my ears.

It started slowly at first, so slowly I barely noticed a thing, in fact, I pretty much convinced myself that nothing was happening at all, and managed to stay that way for ever such a long while. So well did I convince myself of this, that the whole thing rather crept up on me, much like the first fingers of dawn creep gently in heralding a new day, the change from black to midnight blue is almost imperceptible. Hindsight, of course is always twenty/twenty as they say and looking back I can see how obvious it all was, first a discussion on an internet forum, then an article for pagan periodical, then talks at moots and finally magickal workshops and group rituals it slowly and steadily grew. Like Ixion, I was tied, albeit initially unawares, to a wheel spinning round, inexorably drawing closer and closer to my point of origin, this motion like the iynges of ancient time invoking a deity as old as the earth itself, as bright as a flame, and dark as the night.

For a long time I struggled to understand why my Hekate didn't always tally with other people's view of her, particularly the crone aspect, early on in my relationship with her, I had tried to find her origins in the Maiden, Mother, Crone (MMC) concept, hoping perhaps to find a glimmer of "the Old Religion" but it didn't work, in ancient Greece the Gods weren't old (unless they were hiding out in a disguise), they were rarely if ever described as ugly and certainly the early descriptions of Hekate as a maid with bright shining hair couldn't be further from Crowley's vision of her in his novel *Moonchild*, which was the earliest example I found of the Maiden Mother and Crone:

> "And thirdly she is Hecate, a thing altogether of hell, barren, hideous and malicious, the queen of death and evil witchcraft"
>
> ~ Moonchild, Aleister Crowley, 1929

I suppose I had assumed that one day something would click and I would eventually join the ranks of the followers of this supposedly geriatric Goddess, whom from all accounts was either a bit like the aged aunt that always appears at the family get together and everyone avoids because they look fierce, are slightly senile, very wrinkly, possibly smelling a bit overripe, masked with a scent of Tweed; but who is actually rather nice and fun, with a wicked sense of humour, once you get over the stern exterior and the initial distaste; or alternatively downright terrifying who at best would teach me that adrenalin was brown and sticky and worst chew me up and spit me out in bits. That was until the first time I worked with her alone and I realised that the entity I encountered was nothing like the ugly crone creature that I had heard so many people talk of.

Yet ever the perfectionist, it bothered me, I didn't get it, something was wrong, or perhaps I was? The harder I looked the more it slipped away from me. Most magickal practitioners at some point, especially if they are given any level of structured training of a particular type are taught about testing the entities that they work with, and a plan formulated in my mind. The thought of testing a deity made me feel just a little like a precocious and obnoxious teen, demanding that a teacher jumps through hoops before respect is given, but I could see no other option, I don't do belief,

I do knowing. And I had to know, was I dealing with an ancient Goddess or was I being led up the proverbial garden path by something else?

Suffice to say the outcome was a very stern conversation where she forcefully demanded to know, *"Why do you always forget the fourth face"*? And with that, like the good like little occultist that I am, I trotted off to see what I could find and generally slap my forehead in the style of Homer Simpson as for the first time I noticed what had been sitting in front of my face for so long.

If we consider the oft quoted Hesiod, he quite clearly states that, *"Zeus son of Kronos honoured [Hekate] above all, granting her magnificent privileges: a share both of the earth and of the un-draining sea. From the starry heaven too she has a portion of honour, and she is the most honoured by the immortal gods"*. Hesiod would not have considered these attributes as elemental though, considering the discovery of the four elements as we understand them didn't happen for another three hundred years when Empedocles a pre-Socratic philosopher defined the *"roots"* as he called them. Yet here, in the earliest literary reference to her, we see tangible and understandable attributes, earth, air and water; I suppose you could say these are her publicly visible faces that we hear so much about. But these are only three of her four attributes, the fourth being her private face and in many ways hidden in plain sight, the element of fire.

Although not obvious in the *Theogony* of Hesiod, which can be dated roughly to the 8th century BCE by the 7th century and the *Homeric Hymn to Demeter* her association with fire becomes more overt:

> *"Hekate came to meet her, holding a torch in her hands and offering her news"*

The idea of Hekate being associated with fire is not limited to a few obscure fragments either; some of the classical *"all time greats"* attribute a fiery aspect to her nature, it's a pretty exhaustive list that reads like a Who's Who of the classical world, although some are more obvious than others. Sophocles for example, in a fragment of his lost play *Rhizotomi* declares, *"O sun thou lord of light, and thou, sacred fire of Hekate"*.

Euripides character Medea, and possibly the most famous of the Thessalian witches invokes her thus, *"For, by Queen Hecate, whom above all divinities I venerate, my chosen accomplice, to whose presence my central hearth is dedicated"*, an unusual statement for the hearth was normally the remit of Hestia, an interesting conundrum in its own right but discussion of such is beyond the limits of this particular essay; but suffice to say in my opinion it re-enforces her connection with fire.

The Greek Magical Papyri is a veritable treasure trove of fire related Hekate imagery, especially if you are prepared to accept her syncretisation with other deities such as Persephone, Selene and the Babylonian Goddess Erischigal. Of the eighteen papyri fragments that pretty much unarguably refer to Hekate, eight of them have one or more references to her fiery nature. By this point, I was convinced that this triple Goddess undoubtedly had four faces, confusing I know, well it was to me anyway, but I decided to accept this condition and incorporate it into my work with her, hoping that understanding would happen as a consequence of experience rather than book learning, as I could neither visualise it or grasp any deeper meaning other than *"it was"*.

The first inkling occurred when I started to try and understand her role in the Chaldean system as Soteira, these are a collection of fragmented philosophical writings, from a diverse range of authors purporting to knowledge and wisdom passed down from an ancient race of philosophers and magicians. In these fragments Hekate is described in a rather abstract manner:

> *"About the hollows beneath the ribs of her right side there spouts, full-bursting, forth the fountain of the primal soul"*

> *"On the left side of Hecate is a fountain of virtue"*

> *"And from her back, on either side the goddess boundless nature hangs"*

I sat there reading these fragments, and again I pondered the dichotomy of a four faced triple Goddess when my eyes fixed upon a collection of carved Platonic solids lined up along the back of my desk, I had bought them on a whim just a few weeks earlier not really knowing what I wanted them for, actually cursing myself for buying yet more tat to clutter up my temple room. And it came to me, *"unutterable, fire-bodied, light giving, sharply armed"* (PGM VII) My problem you see was that I had been anthropomorphizing, an entirely human condition, one we have used for millennia to explain the unexplainable and make sense of abstract concepts, but to truly understand her I needed to take away whole idea of humanity being made in the likeness of deity, remove her human body, and make her *"fire-bodied"*.

I needed to visualise her as a Tetrahedron, a Platonic solid, one of the purest geometric forms and surprise, surprise, associated with the element of fire. It is effectively a three sided pyramid. Twist it, turn it, flip it over, from a birds eye view, there will always be three visible faces, no more, no less. As I mentioned earlier, it makes sense to me that the public and readily accessible faces are associated with earth, air and water and this is how she is most often viewed, but how you approach her and the lessons she will teach are wholly dependent upon your own particular view point, and that is something you as a magickal practitioner have the ability to influence and change; if you're rooted in earth and look only at this face, you will only see her as chthonic, the terrible Goddess arising from the cave under Mt. Averne beckoning Aneas forth, but if you look from above you may see any combination of three of the four elements depending upon which vertices you look from.

I meditate on this concept regularly, and there's just one combination I have yet to manage, but there is no humanly possible way to see four faces in their totality together, I can come close by closing my eyes and holding that little carved Platonic solid in my hands and imagining the shape as a wire frame rather than a solid, but even then the element is obscured, not pure, for you are viewing the fourth element *"through"* the others, earth of fire, air of fire and water of fire. Perhaps one day she will teach me to see all the faces un-obscured, to quote (and bastardize) the poet John Gillespie Magee, perhaps she will one day teach me *"to slip the surly bonds of Earth, Put out my hand and touch the Face of God"*.

BIBLIOGRAPHY

Triumph of the Moon, Hutton R. Oxford University Press, Oxford UK, 1999
Moonchild, Crowley, A. Mandrake Press, 1929 (later impressions by Red Wheel/Wieser)
Theogony, Hesiod, Trans Dorothea Wenda, Penguin Books, London England, 1973
The Homeric Hymns, Trans Jules Cashford, Penguin Classics, London England, 2003
Magic in Greek and Latin literature J.E. Lowe, Blackwell, Oxford England, 1929 (currently available as a reprint by Kessinger Publishing)
Medea, Euripides, Trans Phillip Vellacott, Penguin Classics, London England 1963
The Greek Magical Papyri in Translation, Edited by Hans Deiter Betz, University of Chicago Press, 1992
Chaldean Oracles, G.R.S. Mead, Kessinger Publishing, 1993.

Figure 63 -Lunar Shrine by MDL

HEKATE WEARS TARTAN!

BY DAVID RANKINE

Much of the old magic may be found hidden in plain view if you but look in the right places. And those right places are often old histories and works of folklore. A case in point which grew from a seed to a precious fruit was a reference I found in Franck's 1658 work *Northern Memoirs* when Sorita d'Este and I were researching our book *Visions of the Cailleach* (2009). In the Notes at the back of the book there is a reference to *'Old Chanery, hung about with charms'* – surely an intriguing reference to any practitioner of the magical arts? There, as bold as the stag on the hill, was a stunning statement which hinted at so much more:

> *"Nicneven, the Hecate of Scottish necromancy, is thus introduced:-*
>
> *Nicneven and her nymphs, in number anew,*
>
> *With charms from Caitness, and Chanrie in Ross.*
>
> *If the witches of Chanrie possesses, as is intimated, the power of compelling grampuses [killer whales] to come ashore, their skill must, in such a situation, have been of great use to their town-folks."*

This initial find led me on a crooked path of research to the Capon Tree. And did Hekate hang the Golden Fleece there in the Highlands for the brave of heart or pure of spirit to find? Yes, I believe in some ways she did!

The reference to Nicneven and her nymphs comes from an earlier 1585 work, *The Flyting of Montgomery and Polwart*. Flyting was a verbal contest of insults, often given in verse, between two poets in medieval Scotland. This tradition has an ancient history, and may be found in many cultures around the world. Interestingly it was often used as a prelude to physical battle between warriors, including in ancient Greece, where we find Hekate. Whilst discussing the classic epic the *Iliad*, Hilary Mackie observed:

> *"In short, Achaeans are proficient at blame, while Trojans perform praise poetry."*

Nicneven is Nic-neven, or Nic-Nevis, i.e. the *'daughter of Nevis'*. She is the traditional Queen of the Fairies whose hall is the otherworldly realm under the earth, in this case beneath Ben Nevis, the highest mountain in Scotland. So how does this connect to Hekate, you might ask? Well Hekate also turns up in connection to witches in this Flyting:

> *"On ane thre headit hecate in haist pair they cryit:"*

(On a three-headed Hecate in haste there they cried)

The reference to the triformis Hekate in this text associated with witches was quite stunning. This is even more so when you see the content of the proceeding invocation, which is effectively what is described in the text. Even though they are found in an insult contest, what is particularly striking is the way that classical Hekate has been placed firmly in the context of Scottish witchcraft practices and folklore. Thus she is invoked:

> *"By the height of the heavens and by the howness [pit] of hell,*
>
> *By the winds and the weirds and the Charlewaine [Ursa Major]*
>
> *By the Horns [Ursa Minor], the Handstaff [Orion's Sword] and the King's Ell [Orion's Belt],*
>
> *By thunder, by fyreflaughts [lightning flashes], by drought and by rain,*
>
> *By the poles and the planets and the signes all twell [twelve],*
>
> *By the mirkness [darkness] of the moon – let mirkness remain –*
>
> *By the elements all that our craft can compel,*
>
> *By the fiends infernal, and the Furies in pain"*

The inclusion of the Great Bear (Ursa Major) with Hekate is very intriguing, when the charm connecting them in the *Greek Magical Papyri* is recalled (PGM VII.686-702). However the fact that a number of constellations are listed emphasises her stellar nature and recalls her mother, the star goddess Asteria. The inclusion of the planets and zodiacal signs, the elements, heaven and hell as well as the other major stars hints at a more cosmic Hekate, not simply the witch goddess.

I speculate that this Flyting was the source for Shakespeare placing Hekate in Scotland for his *Macbeth*, written some twenty years later in the period 1603-7, particularly as Hekate refers to charms twice in her speech in Act IV, a piece which is far more interesting and inspirational than the witches chant that has been so popularised. The declaration in *Macbeth* that *"witchcraft celebrates pale Hecate's offerings"* and *"black Hecate's summons"* may well have influenced the later use of her name to describe the head of a covine in the nineteenth century as chronicled by Scott.

Well returning to that original quote, where Nicneven was linked to Hekate, I realised that the reference to orcas (grampuses) was an echo of the description of one of Hekate's powers in the *Theogony*, that of aiding fishermen, where it stated:

> *"and to those whose business is in the grey discomfortable sea, and who pray to Hekate and the loud-crashing Earth-Shaker, easily the glorious goddess gives great catch, and easily she takes it away as soon as seen, if so she will."*

Another major factor of note with Nicneven is that she is a giantess. In Scotland and the other Celtic lands it was common for the gods to be described as giants, and this continued into folklore, with the Old Ones often surviving in local legends, sleeping in the landscape or in the wild shadows waiting for the call of the ivory horn and the silver pipe. Back in Greek literature, Hekate was described by Lucian in his *Philopseudes* as being a giantess who stamps her foot on the ground causing a vast chasm to the underworld which she jumps into, and where the hero sees dead relatives at the bottom before it closes again.

Returning to Nicneven as the queen of the fairies, this can be seen as akin to Hekate as queen of the restless spirits who haunt the crossroads, particularly when we remember that the fairy queen told Thomas the Rhymer:

"This road leads to heaven, and this roads leads to hell,

And this road leads to elfame, where thee and I must go."

Clearly Nicneven had Thomas at the three-way crossroads, and by taking him to Elfame she was initiating him. She is fulfilling the same role as Hekate, Initiating Queen of the Crossroads. She is also taking him to the paradisiacal beauty of Elfame, which is akin to the Elysian Fields of the Greek otherworld, which is ruled by Hekate! Of course the otherworld can be the place of death as well for many, and this is emphasised by the initial reference to necromancy. Walter Scott in Letter V of his *Letters on Demonology and Witchcraft* (1830) described the head of a Scottish covine of witches practising necromancy as both the Hekate and the Nicneven at different times, significantly using the terms interchangeably.

The connection between Hekate and fairies may be found earlier than this however, in William Warner's epic work *Albion's England* (1586). Here Hekate as queen of hell or the otherworld is directly linked with fairies and elves, who are implied as her servants, making her the fairy queen:

"Saw Hecat new canonized the Sourantisse of hell,

And Pluto bad it holliday for all which there did dwell …

The Elves, and Fairies, taking fists, did hop a merrie Round:"

So as with many other parts of the world, Hekate made her mark and has continued to dwell in the local Scottish landscapes of myths and folklore.

BIBLIOGRAPHY

Betz, Hans Dieter (ed). *The Greek Magical Papyri in Translation.* Chicago, University of Chicago Press, 1992

D'Este, Sorita and David Rankine. *Visions of the Cailleach.* London, Avalonia, 2009

Evelyn-White, Hugh G. (Trans). *The Hesiod of Theogony.* Stilwell, Digireads, 2008 (originally 1914)

Fowler, H.W. & F.G. (trans). *The Works of Lucian of Samosata Volume III.* Oxford, The Clarendon Press, 1905

Franck, Richard. *Northern Memoirs.* Edinburgh, Archibald Constable & Co, 1821 (reprinted from 1658).

Mackie, Hilary Susan. *Talking Trojan: Speech and Community in the Iliad.* Maryland, Rowman & Littlefield, 1996

Scott, Walter. *Letters on Demonology and Witchcraft.* Nuvision, 2005 (originally 1830)

Shakespeare, William. *Macbeth (The Annotated Shakespeare).* Yale University Press, 2005 (originally 1603-7)

Stevenson, George (ed). *The Poems of Alexander Montgomorie and Other Pieces from Laing MS 447.* Edinburgh, Edinburgh University, 1910.

Warner, William. *Albion's England.* Chalmers English Poets, 1810 (originally 1586)

Figure 64 - Hekate by Sara Croft

ANCIENT RITES, MODERN TIMES

HOW ANCIENT SOURCES INSPIRE MODERN DAY MAGIC

BY YURI ROBBERS

I was first introduced to Hekate in grammar school. We learned about classical mythology, and translated many of the tales from Latin and Greek for ourselves. Hekate appealed to me, more than to most of my classmates. The makings of a young witch perhaps? She was, therefore, a logical choice for me when in my own spiritual path I started working with deities and performing magic. In my own practice since I work with various deities, since I am a panentheist and haven't dedicated myself to one specific deity. When I work with Hekate it tends to be especially at Full Moon, Dark Moon and Samhain. And if classical sources can help me, I will of course make use of them gladly.

Sometimes I encounter her in pathworkings or visualisations, or I enlist her help in inviting the spirits of the dead to my Samhain supper. And other times I call upon her to aid me in the casting of a spell. For these purposes, I tend to write custom-made texts. It is my experience that it often helps, and never hurts to put serious effort into any magical work, and writing a new invocation, pathworking or spell is part of that effort for me. I do re-use some parts or make use of ancient sources, since the power of repetition in ritual should not be underestimated, but I always endeavour to include something new.

I, for example, turned to Hekate when my eyesight started to fail, with the following incantation:

> *With the waxing of the Moon*
> *And the waning of the Sun*
> *With the Bay-leaves strewn*
> *And the crimson wool spun*
> *Grant me this dark night*
> *Oh Great Hekate so bright*
> *The returning of my sight*
> *So that I may again see Thy light!*

When Hekate appears in my rituals, she does not always appear in the same guise. Despite popular iconography I do not often see her in any triple or threefold manifestation: far more often she appears as a single woman, but her appearance can be completely different. Usually she looks like a lithe young virgin or young woman, whereas sometimes, though rarely, she appears as a stooped old hag. She is generally long-haired, and almost always wears a cloak, though often she is naked under that cloak, whereas at other times she wears clothes. Often she is accompanied by at least one, but more commonly two or three dogs. Sometimes I have seen her with two extremely bright torches. In rare cases did she persistently appear to my inner eye with the Moon behind her in a phase that did not match the one in the physical world.

Hekate is a grand, many-faceted and powerful Goddess. When working with her, I have found that the old cliché of having to expect the unexpected is very true. The strangest things may happen, but she never fails to impress me, and she does seem inclined to come to the aid of humans when asked sufficiently nicely. I hope to work with her for many more years to come.

Our knowledge of the role Hekate played in people's lives is limited. It comes mainly from four sources:

- Temples, statues and altars
- Mythological stories
- Literary sources
- Actual remains of rituals and spells, such as curse tablets

Of course even combined these four sources cannot give us a complete picture, but we can glean a lot from them, and they can give sufficient inspiration for our own rituals and spells.

TEMPLES, STATUES AND ALTARS

Hekate was often venerated at altars that are, by their location, or by association, related to death, demons and the underworld: places like graveyards or sites of violent death. As ruler of these realms, it was in her power to have the dead return to haunt the living, to scare them, and to cause nightmares, madness and epilepsy. At the same time, she was often seen as protector, since she could command the spirits to leave certain people alone, or even send dead souls to protect the living. She was also considered instrumental in all acts of necromancy, such as communing with the dead, or even raising them.

She was also honoured at three way crossroads. Perhaps the fact that she is often depicted as three women dates from the older practice of having a mask face each of the three roads meeting at a crossroads. This is only conjecture, but of all the existing theories it is the one I find most appealing. Other possible explanations for her triplicity are the fact that she rules the three realms: land, sea and sky, or the three major provinces of human life: birth, health and death.

Since Hekate was also sometimes considered to be the Mistress of the Underworld, along with Persephone, She was often venerated near suspected entrances to the underworld. Here especially she was often seen in her aspect of a huge black dog, or accompanied by dogs – sometimes even the Hell-hound Kerberos himself. At such places important temples to Hekate were built. Of course she had temples elsewhere too, but some of her most important ones are at liminal places like this: where the underworld is near or, maybe the veil between the worlds is thin. At such places also were the Mysteries of Hekate most commonly celebrated.

MYTHOLOGICAL STORIES

Mythology portrays Hekate as one of the oldest deities of the pantheon, and one of the most independent characters. Her ways are those of the night and the underworld, and she is the Goddess of the Moon, revered by the moon-conjuring witches of Thessaly and famous sorceresses like Medea and Circe. She stands at doorways such as birth and death, and initiation. She rules sickness and health, sanity and madness. She leads a ghostly retinue and can set the dead against the living, or make the dead serve the living. She is important for cursing and protecting, and she is the Phosphoros, the bringer of light. This might refer to the moon, but more likely the two torches she is invariably depicted with in this role, refer to the Evening Star and the Morning Star, both the Planet Venus: the brightest object in the sky after the Sun and the Moon.

LITERARY SOURCES

Various literary sources speak of Hekate. She occurs in prose, poetry and plays. Sometimes literature recounting the old mythological tales, but sometimes she occurs in tragedies as well. Of course, as in modern times, literary sources sometimes sacrifice part of the truth in order to tell a better story, or tell a story in a better way, but much can still be gleaned from them. Examples of literary sources which speak of Hekate include:

- The second Idyll from the *Pharmakeutria* of Theokritos, with a vivid description of how one Simaetha curses her deceitful lover Delphis, with the help of Hekate.
- The *Hymn to Hekate* from the *Theogony* of Hesiod, which describes the powers of Hekate and her ancient origins.
- Medea working magic as described in the *Metamorphoses* of Ovid, where a magical working under supervision of Hekate is described in some detail.

For those readers unfamiliar with the above texts, I include here my translation of the Second Idyll of the *Pharmakeutria* of Theokritos as an example, and will let the text speak for itself.

> *"Where are my bay-leaves? Bring them to me, Thestylis [slave-girl]? And where are my magical tools? Clothe the bowl in the choicest crimson wool so that I may bind a spell upon my beloved, who is so hard on me. He has not visited me for 12 days, the bastard, and has no clue whether I am dead or alive. Nay, he has not knocked but once on my door, so cruel is he! I'm certain Eros and Aphrodite have taken his fickle fancy elsewhere. Tomorrow I shall go to Timagetus' wrestling school to see him, and I shall reproach him for treating me thusly; but now I will bind him with fire spells. Nay, shine bright, O Moon, for to thee, Goddess, will I softly chant, and to Hekate of the underworld, before whom even the dogs stand shivering, as she comes over the graves of the dead and the dark blood. Hail, grim Hekate, and to further my ends attend to me, and make these drugs of mine as potent as those of Circe and Medea, or even the golden-haired Perimeda.*
>
> *My magic wheel [a four spoked wheel with a rope tied through the axle], draw to my house the man I love!*
>
> *First let hulled barley seeds smoulder on the fire. Nay, throw them on Thestylis! You poor fool, whither have your wits taken wing? Am I to be*

mocked even by thee then, feeble wench? Throw them on, while you say repeatedly: "I throw the bones of Delphis".

My magic wheel, draw to my house the man I love!

Delphis wreaked havoc on me, and I for Delphis burn the bay. And as the bay-leaves crackle loudly in the fire and alight all of a sudden, and when no longer even the ashes of them remain to be seen, so may Delphis's flesh waste in the flame.

My magic wheel, draw to my house the man I love!

And now I will burn the bran. Oh thou, Artemis, who hast the power to move Hell's adamant, and aught else as stubborn – Thestylis, the dogs are howling all over the town; the Goddess is at the crossroads! Quick! Clash the Bronze!

My magic wheel, draw to my house the man I love!

Lo, still is the sea, and stiller yet the breezes. But not so still is the torment in my breast: all on fire am I for him who has made of me, alas and alack, instead of a virtuous maiden not a wife but a wretched thing.

My magic wheel, draw to my house the man I love!

As, aided by the Goddess, I melt this wax, so will Delphis of Myndus waste away with love straight away. And as by Aphrodite's power this brass rhomb is turned, so may he turn about my door.

My magic wheel, draw to my house the man I love!

Thrice do I give thee libations, Lady, and thrice cry thusly: "Whether it be a woman who lies with him now, or whether it be a man, may he forget them as quickly and cleanly as once, or so men say, Theseus forgot in Dia the fair-haired Ariadne."

My magic wheel, draw to my house the man I love!

Coltsfoot is a herb from Arcady, and all the foals and swiftest of the mares upon the hills run to it in a mad frenzy. Thusly may I see Delphis, and may he come from his beloved wrestling school towards my house like one of those maddened horses.

My magic wheel, draw to my house the man I love!

This fringe of a cloak that Delphis lost I will shred now and cast into the cruel flames. O, torturing Eros, why hast thou clung to me like a leech from a bog and drained all the dark blood from my body?

My magic wheel, draw to my house the man I love!

I will crush a lizard, to be used in an evil potion I can bring him tomorrow. But for now, Thestylis, take these magic herbs and knead them over his threshold while it is still dark, and while doing so whisper: "I knead the bones of Delphis".

My magic wheel, draw to my house the man I love!

Now that I have been left alone, from what moment on shall I lament my love? Whence shall I begin? Who brought this curse upon me? Eubulus' daughter, our Anaxo, went to the grove of Artemis, bearing a basket, and in honour of that Goddess, many a wild beast was paraded about Her that day. A lioness was among them.

Mark, Lady Moon, whence came my love.

And Theumaridas' Thracian nurse, now dead and gone, but who used to dwell at my door, had begged and besought me to come and see a show. And I, unhappy wretched girl, went with her. I wore a soft, long linen dress, with Clearista's finest stole over it.

Mark, Lady Moon, whence came my love.

And when I had progressed about halfway already on the road, where Lycon bides, I saw Delphis and Eudamippus walking together. More golden than Helicryse were their beards, and their chests more beautiful than thou, O Moon, for they had recently left their labour at the wrestling school.

Mark, Lady Moon, whence came my love.

I saw, and madness seized me, and my hapless heart was aflame. My looks faded away. No eyes had I thereafter for that show, nor do I have any recollection of how ever I got home again. Instead, some parching fever shook me, and ten days and ten nights I lay upon my bed.

Mark, Lady Moon, whence came my love.

And all the time my skin turned as pale as the Smoke Tree, and all my hair was falling from my head, and naught but skin and bones was left of me. And to whose house did I not go, and which hag's did I pass over, of those that possessed the skill of magical charms? But it was no easy matter, and time was flying by.

Mark, Lady Moon, whence came my love.

And so I told my maid the truth of the matter: "Come, Thestylis, find me some remedy for this dreadful ailment. The Myndian, alas and alack, possesses me body and soul. Nay, go thou forth and keep watch by Timagetus' wrestling school, for there it is where he bides and loves to sit.

Mark, Lady Moon, whence came my love.

And when thou art sure that he is alone, sign to him secretly and say "Simaetha bids thee come." and lead him hither." So did I say. And she went and brought the supple-skinned Delphis to my house, and no sooner was I aware of his light-footed step across the threshold of my door –

Mark, Lady Moon, whence came my love.

Or I turned chillier than snow from head to toe, and from my brow – like the damp dew – started a sweat. Nor could I speak a word, nay, not so much as babies who whimper in their sleep, calling to their dear mother, but all of my fair body turned as stiff as a doll's.

Mark, Lady Moon, whence came my love.

After a glance at me my untrue lover fixed his eyes upon the floor, while sitting down on the couch, and spoke: "Truly, Simaetha, with thy summons to this house thou didst outrun my coming by no more than I recently outran the charming Philinus.

Mark, Lady Moon, whence came my love.

For I would have come anyway, by sweet Eros, at early nightfall. With two or three friends, bearing before me apples of Dionysos, and on my brow the white poplar, holy plant of Herakles, wreathed all around me with crimson bands.

Mark, Lady Moon, whence came my love.

And if you would have received me, it would have been most pleasant, for I am regarded as athletic and beautiful among the young men. And if only I had kissed your pretty lips, I would have slept soundly. If instead you had tried to thrust me out and barred your door against me, then truly I would have brought axes and torches against you.

Mark, Lady Moon, whence came my love.

But things being as they are, my thanks are first and foremost due to Cypris, I say, and secondly after her, my lady, thou. For thou hast caught me from the flame, all but consumed, by summoning me hither to thine house. And it is true indeed: Love does often kindle a blaze hotter than the forge of Hephaestus at Lipara.

Mark, Lady Moon, whence came my love.

And with dire madness he may scare any maiden from her bower, or any bride to desert her husband's bed before it turned cold." Thusly he spoke, and I, always too easily won, took him by his hand and pulled him down onto the soft couch. And swiftly body warmed to body, and faces burned hotter than before, and sweetly we whispered. And to keep the tale from being too long in the telling, dear Moon, all was accomplished, and we both came, as we desired. There was no fault he could find with me, nor I with him, till yesterday. But today, when the steeds of the rose-fingered Dawn were bearing her swiftly up into the sky from the ocean, the mother of our flute player Philista and her brother Melixo came to me; and she spoke of many things. Of how Delphis was in love. Whether it was a woman or a man for whom he was gripped with desire, She could not tell for certain. But she did say that he kept on calling for unmixed wine and toasting to Eros, and that in the end he went off swiftly and said he would crown that dwelling with garlands.

This was the tale my gossip told me, and she is no liar! For verily: in times before had he visited me three or even four times a day, and often he would leave his Dorian oil flask with me. But now twelve days have passed since I have so much as seen him. Must he not have found his delight elsewhere and have forgotten about me?

Now, with my love magic will I bind him. If then he shall vex me still – so help me the Fates – he will beat upon the gates of Hades. Such evil drugs, I swear, I keep in a box for him. I learned the lore from an Assyrian stranger, o queen. But bid thy farewells, my Lady, and turn thy steeds towards the ocean. I shall no longer bear my longing as I have endured it until now. Moon on thy gleaming throne, I bid thee farewell, and farewell also to thee, o stars, that follow the chariot of the quiet night!

REMAINS OF RITUALS AND SPELLS

There are two good sources of ritual and magical remains of Hekate. First of all, there are her temples and the compounds of her mysteries. Many an effigy or beseechment has been found here. The biggest category seems to be of people who have come to Hekate's temples to ask her to stop torturing them with her curses. As Terry Pratchett says: *"Everyone eventually comes to a witch, in some cases to ask her to stop."* This was obviously already true in ancient times. Many people felt that Hekate was responsible for things that did not go well in their lives, or when they were tortured by spirits (real or imagined) or their own memories. They would often bring rich sacrifices to her altars. Another large category consists of women who have asked for help in childbirth, or for starting their flow of milk leaving countless little statues and written wishes. Then there are the gifts of those who felt their own death approaching or who came on behalf of a dying or recently deceased friend or relative. The final category of note is the gifts and wishes from people who sought the divinatory powers of Hekate to aid them in whichever way.

Forks in the road – places where three roads meet – are especially sacred to Hekate, and often had statues or images of her (sometimes along with a statue of Hermes, another chthonic deity). It was quite common for people to perform spells or sacrifices at such places, usually at night, and especially when the moon was full or dark. The most common types of such spells were the swearing of oaths in her name, and the fabrication of so-called curse tablets (καταδεσμοι in Greek or *defixiones* in Latin). These curse tablets were made from lead, and contained a written curse of someone. These curses tended to be very elaborate and specific, and usually had to do with one of three main areas of life: love, money and sports. Here is an example of an actual curse tablet, found near Athens and probably dating from around 400 BCE, to show how elaborate these curses usually are:

> *O triple Hekate, great goddess of mortality, moon and magic, curse Philippos of the Quarter of Pottery, my opponent in tomorrow's long distance run, so that he may be struck blind, and not see his way, so that his nostrils may be blocked and his ability to breathe reduced, so that his heart will thump loudly and make him worry about dying, so that his skin erupts with a rash and pustules so that he cannot bear the light of the sun on it and he cannot go without stopping to scratch for more than a few steps, so that his bladder becomes infected, causing him to have to stop in order to piss very often, so that his thighs have cramps, and refuse to move quickly, so that his kneecaps break and make it impossible for him to stand up, so that his ankles are twisted and he cannot stand or walk, and so that his feet swell up to thrice their size and become unusable to him. This I, Theophilos son of Arissteides [spelling error?], ask of thee, so that I may be the winner of tomorrow's run. And I will sacrifice to thee the blood of three dogs, should the victory be mine.*

Obviously no half measures! A curse tablet like this is fairly typical of those that were made frequently over a huge area and throughout many centuries.

To conclude, I will leave you with this, my translation of Hesiods' *Theogony*, the *Hymn to Hekate*:

> *She is the one who is honoured most by all the immortal gods themselves! Because when one of the humans on earth asks the gods a favour and honours them with solemn sacrifices according to tradition, they call upon Hekate – and a great honour will be bestowed upon this human, without reticence, if she graciously accepts their prayer. Yes, she may even give him riches: this also lieth within her power. For lo, hers was the right to partake in each and every privilege bestowed upon the children of Gaia and Ouranos.*

> *Never has Zeus, son of Kronos, harmed her, and never has he taken anything that she was given in the Age of Titans, the gods of yore; still does she own what was bestowed upon her at the time of the original division.*

> *She is, however, an only child, but the esteem she is held in is none the less for it, nor any privilege or honour on the earth, in the sea or in the sky; yes, she receives even more, for Zeus himself pays her homage. Overwhelmingly does she give to any she chooseth her aid and her help: is a court of justice instated, then she sits with the honourable kings; is a meeting in progress, then whosoever she chooseth shall shine above all others; are arms being taken up for battle in a man-annihilating war, then this goddess giveth protection to whomever she chooseth, giveth in her benevolence the victory to him as well, and enjoys letting him achieve glory.*

> *She has the power, when people go to compete or fight over prices, to give her aid whenever and to whomsoever she chooseth. Should he win by force, then he will carry the coveted price homeward, happy and without trouble, where his parents shall share in his glory!*

> *She has the power to help whichever of the horsemen she chooses.*

Also upon those, who work the grey, grim seas tortuously, praying for help to Hekate and the thundering causer of earthquakes, does she bestow good catches without trouble, yet she takes catches as well, even when they were already visible...

She has the power to multiply, together with Hermes, cattle: herds of cows or tribes of wide-wandering goats, flocks of woolly sheep – an it tickles her fancy, she doth make them fertile and large when they are small, but she maketh large ones small as well.

Therefore didst she, even though she is her mother's only child, receive precedence and honour in the midst of all the eternal Gods.

Wet nurse did Kronos' son Zeus make her, of children who beheld after her the brilliant light of the far and wide radiating Eos. Thus did she become their wet nurse, and these were her privileges.

ACKNOWLEDGEMENTS

I am grateful to, in alphabetical order, Amaranth Feuth, Siward Tacoma, Jaap Toorenaar and Anne van Zilfhout for providing me with some hard to find literary and scientific sources. Thank you also to Morgana.

BIBLIOGRAPHY

Berg, W. (1974) *Hekate: Greek or Anatolian?*, in: *Numen* 21: 128-40.

Boedeker, D. (1983) *Hecate: a Transfunctional Goddess in the Theogony?* In: *Transactions of the American Philological Association* 113: 79-93.

Burkert, W. (1985) *Greek Religion.* English ed. Cambridge.

Clay, J.S. (1984) *The Hekate of the Theogony.* In: *Greek, Roman, and Byzantine Studies* 25: 27-38.

Edwards, C.M. (1986) *The Running Maiden from Eleusis and the early Classical Image of Hekate.* In: *American Journal of Archaeology* 90: 307-18.

Farnell, L.R. (1896-1909) *The Cults of the Greek States.* 5 vols. Oxford.

Fullerton, M.D. (1986) *Hekate Epipyrgidia.* In: *Archaologischer Anzeiger*: 669-75.

Halbertsma, R & Mol, L. (1995) *Beeldhouwkunst uit Hellas en Rome.* Leiden

Heckenbach P. (1912) *Pauly's Realencyclopedie der Klassischen.* Altertumswissen-schaft, p. 2769-2782.

Hordern, J.H. (2002) *Love Magic and Purification in Sophron,* PSI 1214a, and *Theocritus' Pharmakeutria, Classical Quarterly* 52: 164-173.

Johnston, S.I. (1990) *Hekate Soteira.* Atlanta.

Kraus, T. (1960) *Hekate*, Heidelberg.

Laumoinier, A. (1958) *Les Cultes Indigènes en Carie*, 344ff., Paris.

Marquardt, P.A. (1981) *A Portrait of Hecate.* In: *American Journal of Philology*102: 243-60.

Moormann, E.M. & Uitterhoeve, W. (2007) *Van Alexander tot Zeus*, Amsterdam

Nillson, M.P. (1955-1967) *Geschichte der Griechischen Religion I-II*, München.

Petersen, E. (1880-1881) *Die dreigestaltigen Hekate 1-2*.

Schober, A. (1933) *Fries des Hekateions von Lagina*, in: *IstForschung 2*, Vienna.

West, M.L., ed. 1966. *Hesiod: Theogony.* Oxford

von Willamowitz-Möllendorf, U. (1931) *Die Glaube der Hellenen I-II*, Berlin.

Figure 65 - Crystal Ball by MDL

Figure 66 - Shrine by MDL

A Goddess for all seasons

By Amelia Ounsted

The blending of work with Hekate in a Wiccan framework is something that I've been working on for some years. I spoke on this subject at *Witchfest International* (London) in November 2006 and ideas have continued to evolve since then. My personal devotion to Hekate coincided with my discovery of Wicca, which I wrote about in my contribution to *Hekate Keys to the Crossroads*.

One of the first Sabbats I celebrated was Samhain and quite appropriately we worked with Hekate. However the next Sabbat was Yule and I wanted to work with Hekate. And come Imbolc...Well. I'm sure it's no surprise that I wanted to work with Hekate again! Almost ten years later, as a Wiccan High Priestess running my own initiatory coven, I find that these two passions of Wicca and Hekate continue to compliment and enrich each other.

This enthusiasm for Hekate made me wonder if it was possible to work with Hekate at each Sabbat without changing either Hekate's nature and attributes or the meanings of the Sabbats. This article suggests aspects of Hekate that you can work with at the Sabbats – based on the Wiccan Wheel of the year – and argues that She is relevant to all of them. When discussing working with Hekate and the Sabbats I will also cover some general information about these festivals, so as to make clear Her relevance to them. It is not so much a practical *'how to'* guide as a meditation upon the many aspects of Hekate and how they relate to the Sabbats.

In discussing the ways in which you can work with Hekate through each Sabbat you will see that often there is more than one aspect of Hekate to consider each time. This is not just because Hekate is so multi-faceted, but because each Sabbat has more than one theme associated with it. The Sabbats on the Wheel of the Year are not one dimensional. It can be easy to slip into this pattern of looking at only one aspect but I would encourage creativity. What we do should reflect the changing seasons and the spiral of light to dark to light and life to death and rebirth, but if you look closely at these patterns and traditions you will find a plethora of ideas for each Sabbat, and of course for working with Hekate at them. Indeed, this article can really only touch the surface of how you might work with Hekate at each Sabbat. By working with different aspects of Her at different times of the year we can increase our understand of Her.

Even if you are not Wiccan the structure of the Sabbats – 8 season festivals placed roughly six weeks apart throughout the year – is a useful one to use. Arguably all Sabbats mark a liminal time as each one marks a transitional stage throughout the year and therefore within us and on that basis alone Hekate is an appropriate Goddess to work with, however, as we will see there is more to Her than the liminal.

WINTER SOLSTICE

The festival of the Winter Solstice takes place (usually) on 21st December. It marks the time of year of the shortest day and is opposite the Summer Solstice on the Wheel. At Winter Solstice we focus on the fact that this is the darkest night of the year. It is a time for internal contemplation. We might come across our own *"dark night of the soul"*; a time to face our inner demons, fears and doubts that dwell within depths of our unconscious. Working with these dark aspects of ourselves we can invoke a darker aspect of Hekate by looking at her Chthonic aspect. Chthonic means *'of the earth'* (and by extension, the underworld), and the festival of Winter Solstice is also associated with the element of Earth. Chthonic deities in Greek religion were worshiped at altars close to the ground, so if you want to work with Hekate in this aspect setting up an altar on the floor (or if not practical on a low table or first shelf of a bookcase) would be appropriate. We can regard Hekate as a guardian of the unconscious, just as She guards the entrance of the underworld. She is mistress of all that lives in the hidden part of the psyche. She holds the key that unlocks the door to the way down, and She also bears the torch that illuminates both the treasures and the terrors of the underworld. One way to Her wisdom is to descend into the underworld of our unconscious. This confrontation and acceptance of the darkness is necessary for us to understand ourselves, our motivations and to confront the unconscious fears that hold us back.

Winter Solstice is also the time when we celebrate the rebirth of the Sun. The sun has been dying since he reached his peak at the summer solstice and on the darkest night we say that he has *'died'*. Yet this is not a linear path for we see that death is necessarily followed by life and renewal and darkness is followed by light. Paradoxically, the death of the sun also marks the death of the darkness. Although it may not seem so after the Winter Solstice the days get longer and we turn once more to the light. So after we have followed Hekate into the darkness and contemplated the depths of our souls we must also seek the rebirth of light and life within us. It would seem obvious in this celebration of returning light to invoke Hekate as Phosphoros, the torch bearer. Yet there is another aspect of Hekate that often gets over looked but would be very relevant to this time of year, that of Hekate Kourotrophos (*'Child's Nurse'*), a title that was specifically applied to those who govern childbirth. Torches, one of Hekate's key identifiers in art, are a common attribute of Birth-Goddesses. Hekate's association with child birth is a later addition to her attributes (from 5th century BCE onwards) whereas Her torches are part of Her iconography from much earlier so it's unlikely that a role in childbirth is the reason for Her torches. However, the role of Child's Nurse is appropriate for Hekate as a Goddess of the transitions. At the liminal time of the Winter Solstice the Child of Promise (identified with the Sun) is about to be reborn, and birth is one of the major transitional points in life. So we can see Hekate as a midwife, not just of the returning sun but whose torches of purification burn away the darkness of the psyche and enable our own rebirth.

IMBOLC:

Imbolc is most often associated with a goddess who, needless to say, is not Hekate, but Brigid/Bride. But that shouldn't stop us! It's interesting to look at comparisons between Bride and Hekate at this time. Bride's festival as a Saint (and arguably a continuation of her worship as a Goddess in Ireland) is at the same time as Imbolc. In Christian mythology Bride is the nurse/foster mother of Jesus (retaining her own virginity and purity whilst allowing her a mothering aspect) and Hekate, as I have just mentioned, also has a role of nurse. The role of midwife is pertinent to the season as this is also the time of the birth of spring lambs. Hekate is generally portrayed in classical art and literature a maiden goddess and is very rarely paired with any other God in the Greek pantheon (although She is said to have had sex with Zeus but this seems to be the case with almost every female Greek deity). She is said to have given birth to Scylla, Medea and Circe and there is a possible mention of her having sex with Hermes (but she is described as being a maiden prior to this encounter). That said, her maidenly aspect is prominent and we should also remember that in Wiccan myth the wheel of the year reflects the life cycle of the goddess and god – at Imbolc, the Goddess is firmly in her role as maiden.

The alternative name for Imbolc, is Candlemas. This is the name for the Christian festival also known as the Purification of the Virgin Mary. The idea of purification again harks back to the purifying fire of Hekate's torches and their connection with birth. At Imbolc the High Priestess sometimes wears a crown of lights and we are reminded of the phrase in Hesiod *'Hekate of the bright headband'*. Thus Hekate's torches and her role as a bringer of light are again emphasised. Once again Her significance as a light in the darkness is appropriate.

The very name, Candlemas suggests the candles or torches that used to be lit on cakes made to honour Hekate. It's worth mentioning the role of Hekate's suppers in this context. These were meals held in honour of Hekate and left at the cross roads on the last day of the month. Aristophanes says: *"Hekate can tell us whether it isn't better to be poor or hungry. She says that rich people send her supper every month whereas poor people snatch it away when it has hardly been put down."*

Imbolc can be regarded as the time when we are hibernating in preparation for the spring to come. Part of this time of sleep and darkness has already been covered in Yule but we can also use this time to be aware of our dreams as a way to access our unconscious. Euripides calls Hekate the bringer of dreams and in one version of Her history She is referred to as the daughter of Nox (night) Guardian of the unconscious.

SPRING EQUINOX:

The Spring Equinox is a time of equal balance between light and dark. More so even than Imbolc this is the time of new beginnings. We have meditated and contemplated throughout the dark times of the year (for anyone who has ever suffered through an English February knows how false the idea of lengthening days and spring seems at that time). At Spring Equinox, however, we can see the bright promise of the sun fulfilled with the yellow daffodils, and the crocus which bloom at this time are a most appropriate offering to Hekate, for saffron is sacred to Her. Hekate can also be honoured in Her Chthonic aspect as the dark mother who holds within her the seeds of new life and new beginnings and by whose light they have now come into fruition.

Spring Equinox also marks the time when we look at the myth of Demeter and Persephone and contemplate the mysteries of Eleusis. The Eleusinian mysteries took place in Ancient Greece from around 1500 BCE and were centred around the myth of Demeter and Persephone. This myth is often understood to be a metaphor for the cycle of the seasons; Persephone is kidnapped by Hades, Lord of the Underworld sending her Mother Demeter into such a rage and grief that she turns the earth barren until her daughter is returned to her, bringing with her the renewal of life. Hekate's role in this myth is twofold. Firstly She – together with the sun god Helios – is the only one to hear the abduction of Persephone. Secondly She (and/or Hermes) goes into the underworld to broker a deal with Hades and guide Persephone back to her mother. Although we don't know exactly what part Hekate played in the mysteries we do know that She, together with Hermes, was present at the entrance of the complex and it therefore seems likely that She acted as a guide to the initiate.

Invoke Hekate in her Propolos (*'Guide'*) aspect and meditate on Her leading Persephone from the Underworld. Hekate is the one who hears Persephone's cry for help and alerts others to her plight. So can we call upon Her to guide and support us at this time when our quest for balance within ourselves can require some painful soul searching and transformation. We have undergone our period of soul searching in the winter months when we have resided in the underworld and we are now prepared to move forward. Hekate as the guide can be invoked to show us the way.

The time of balance can also be likened to a cross road with paths open before us. These paths can be unknown and it can be frightening to feel that we have to walk them, but we can work with Hekate not just as the guide, but also remembering Her role as companion. She did not just lead Persephone out of the underworld, but *'and from that moment she was forever at her side'*. It is worth noting that Hekate is said to be *"tender hearted"* and thus, although we have to make the journey along the spiral path we do not have to do so without guidance and we do not have to do so alone.

On a lighter note, eggs are associated with this Sabbat and they also have strong associations with Hekate so they should definitely be on you shrine or altar at this time.

BELTANE:

Finding a way to work with Hekate at Beltane initially presented a huge problem for me. In the wheel of the year the one thing that seems to describe Beltane for most people is sex. The symbolism of the maypole and the broomstick, both symbols of this festival, are suffused with sexual imagery and it is at this time that the Goddess and the God consummate their passion. Hekate has strong connections with the Goddess Artemis, herself so fiercely virginal that she killed men who saw her naked and even killed those of her maidens who had the misfortune to be raped because they failed to keep themselves pure. Although there are no such myths directly associated with Hekate she is, as I noted earlier in comparing her with Brigid, most often described as a maiden with few sexual attributes ascribed to her. Girls who had died before they were married were said to go to Hekate. In Lagina home of her most important shrine, Hekate believed to have been served by Eunuchs, in this she is linked as a companion to Cybele whose male followers used to ceremonially castrate themselves and whose son and lover Attis was also castrated and killed (although he was resurrected!) There is evidence linking Hekate to love and magick in particular. In Theocritus' *Idylls 2* the narrator invokes Hekate to return her lover to her. However, since Hekate is invoked as *"Queen of Terrors"* and the narrator declares *"As this wax image melts to the Goddesses laughter/ So let my lover melt in love once more/ As this bronze blade whirls with all my power/ Let him roll and twist in pain about my door/ Turn magick wheel and force my lover home" (R.Hutton trans.);* this is perhaps not the best manner in which to celebrate a festival dedicated to love and pleasure!

However, to regard Beltane as a Sabbat solely about sexual love is to limit the deeper meaning of the festival. Yes, this is an important part of Beltane, however perhaps the power of Hekate's connection to this festival is that she forces us to look beyond the surface and find the deeper meaning. For Beltane is as much about the fertility and transformation as symbolised by the sexual act as it is about the act itself. When considering Beltane and Hekate, a good place to start is with the colours associated with the Sabbat – red, white and green. These traditionally are seen as the red of menstrual blood (which as seen as the fertilising power of the woman), the white of semen and the green representing the life that came from their combining. These attributions come from the Alchemical texts and writings of the middle ages and earlier. Hekate is mentioned in the Egyptian inspired esoteric writings with Hermes Trismegistus and thus connected with Alchemy. It is worth remembering that the transformation of lead into gold by the Alchemists was seeking to transform the base person into the adept master. Therefore in working with Hekate (and perhaps in partnership with Hermes who after all is one of the few Gods she is supposed to have taken as a lover) at Beltane we can work on the transformation of ourselves and creating fertility and growth within our lives through the balancing of the masculine and feminine energies within ourselves.

Finally, we can consider another traditional aspect of Beltane in relation to Hekate. At Beltane (as at Samhain) the veils between the worlds of men and the other world are said to be thinnest. Whereas at Samhain that thinness is said to bring the worlds of the dead closer to us, at Beltane it is the world of the Faery. These are not necessarily the pretty flower faeries at the bottom of the garden. These fae, or Sidhe are those beings who take men away to their caverns under the hill for hundreds of years, who turn the milk sour and lead unwary travellers astray. At the very best, Beltane is a time when the fae are known to cause mischief. Hecate can be invoked to protect against these beings in her aspects as Apotropaios (averter of evil) for she can guard against unseen spiritual foes. It is worth noting that despite the fact that Apotropaios means averter of evil the Fae are not evil as we understand it, rather they are amoral beings. For those of you who do wish to work with the Faery at this time you can invoke Hekate in her aspect of Propylaia. Propylaia means *'The one before the gate'* and statues of Hekate Propylaia were found at the entrances of temples and of common peoples homes for she was a guardian of entrance ways – effectively she protects the entrances and exits, the places of transition. Thus when working with the Fae at Beltane it would be appropriate to invoke her to stand at the gate between the worlds, offering protection from what is beyond a boundary, and keeping the entrance open to ensure safe return.

SUMMER SOLSTICE:

The Summer Solstice marks the longest day of the year, when the night is at its shortest. We celebrate the strength and wealth symbolised by the warmth and power of the sun at his height. Once again, it might not be immediately obvious how we might work with Hekate who seems to have such strong connections to the darkness. I think it's important, if we can, to work with and understand these deities that we work with from a place of balance. Very rarely (if ever) are they one dimensional and often they have qualities that balance each other. Thus Hekate, Queen of the Restless dead is also a goddess of life and abundance, of spiritual wealth and transformation.

At the Summer Solstice we can focus of Hekate Phosphoros whose twin torches are no longer the light in the darkness but are now the light itself. Its worth remembering that   Hekate is described as having a bright headband or a shining light about her head, that her feet are described as ruddy (another solar colour which also reflects the blood of life) and she is also described as wearing saffron coloured garments. Thus she is a shining goddess of at the height of summer whose fires and radiance burn away all negativity and illuminate the gifts that we have received.

As such we can work with Hekate as Soteira (Saviour or world soul). This aspect of Hekate is found in the so-called *Chaldean Oracles*. The *Chaldean Oracles* are fragmentary texts from Alexandria in 2nd century CE and they describe Hekate as the mediating World-Soul. The *Oracles* speak of *"The life-producing bosom of Hecate, that Living Flame which clothes itself in Matter to manifest Existence"*. Even in the *Oracles* Hekate serves as the point of balance on the liminal. In this case she is the barrier or perhaps membrane would be a more accurate word, between two fires, the fire of intellect and the material fire that creates the Universe. As such she mediates all divine influence on the lower realm i.e. the Earth.

Hekate Soteira can be a hard one to understand and She can be so all encompassing that it can be difficult to visualise or understand all of the qualities she possesses in this role. For those of you familiar with Norse mythology it can help to see her as something akin to Ygdrassil the world tree that holds up the world and provides a conduit between the three worlds. Hekate Soteira performs this function but she is envisioned as a living flame rather than a tree. This image also makes a nice connection between this later Chaldean Hekate and the Hekate of Hesiod's writing who rules Earth and Sea and Sky. Thus Hekate Soteira as the soul of the world is the force that gives life and light to all living this. As such when we take our ease and enjoy the earthly pleasures as part of our summer solstice celebrations we are enjoying the pleasures provide by Hekate Soteira. For in the mysteries of the *Chaldean Oracles* She not only lights the way from the underworld, but She could restore the initiate and lead them refreshed and reinvigorated to the world of life.

LAMMAS:

Lammas (usually 1st August) is the first of three harvest festivals celebrated on the Wheel of the Year. As the harvest of grain this is the time in the journey of the God when he is cut down, sacrificed so he may be born again as the child of promise at the Winter Solstice. It is the Sabbat at which we prepare to reap the seeds that we have sown at Imbolc/Spring Equinox and we recognise that to do we must sometimes be prepared to make a sacrifice. In much the same way that we might really want that new job but we must sacrifice our old one to get it (and the pay packet for a more stimulating role or ease of travel and so on).

Think about making a sacrifice to Hekate as part of your devotion; perhaps giving up something that you like, in order for her to bestow her blessings. This is also a time when we can give thanks for our personal harvest from the year. If our Harvest is not quite what we hoped for it is worth remembering the words of Hesiod: *"For to this day, whenever any one of men on earth offers rich sacrifices and prays for favour according to custom, he calls upon Hekate. Great honour comes full easily to him whose prayers the goddess receives favourably, and she bestows wealth upon him; for the power surely is with her".* We can make offerings to Her to encourage our own harvest. I would not recommend the sacrifices of sheep or dogs which were common in Greece, but we know that eggs, honey and garlic are all acceptable sacrifices to the goddess. We could also consider using the bounty of the harvest to prepare a meal for friends in the manner of a Hekate supper. For me the strain of cooking is quite enough of a sacrifice as it is (as eating the results may be for others!). As Hekate suppers were arguably a form of charitable giving we may wish to make a financial sacrifice as well.

At this time of fruitful harvest we can see Hekate as the dark mother who separates the wheat from the chaff and cuts away that which is unnecessary from our lives. If we have the courage we can work with Hekate as the goddess of transformation. This act of transformation whilst painful is reward in itself as we must transform and change in order to grow. This act of transformation was something that devotes of the ancient Mysteries at Eleusis appeared to have been striving for. A tomb stone of one initiate suggests that after death she would be transformed into Hekate herself.

Lammas is also a traditional time for fairs where people would meet to display and sell the wealth that the harvest had brought them. At these fairs as well it was common to play games and this often forms a part of our festivities when we celebrate Lammas today. It is worth remembering Hesiod's point about Hekate in relation to games and sports: *"Good is she also when men contend at the games, for there too the goddess is with them and profits them: and he who by might and strength gets the victory wins the rich prize easily with joy, and brings glory to his parents."* In August is frequently a time for summer holidays so it would be appropriate to invoke Hekate in her role as protector of travellers when you embark on your journey.

AUTUMN EQUINOX:

The Autumn Equinox is the second point of balance, of equal day and night in the year. Whereas at the Spring Equinox we were looking forward to the returning light, and planting our seeds for the harvest we are now preparing to enter the dark half of the year. This is the second harvest we will reap, that of fruit and we are reminded of the pomegranate of Persephone the seeds of which bind her to the underworld. For this is the time when we celebrate Persephone's return to the underworld and Hekate accompanies her on her dark journey back to the realm of Hades. We can once again invoke Hekate as Propolos the guide who will be with us as we prepare to enter the darkness. For this is the time of endings and the start of our journey into the dark realms where we turn from working on the material world around us and start to work on our own personal development.

At this time we can also work with Hekate Kleidouchos ('*Key holder*'). The bearing of a key often symbolised the ability to open and close the gates between heaven, earth and other realms (such as that of Hades). As the keeper of the keys that unlock the doors of our subconscious She can help us understand what aspects of ourselves we need to improve or change in order to obtain the balance within ourselves that is the focus of this Sabbat. Her keys unlock other doors as well and if you practice Magick you can certainly ask Hekate to unlock other doors that are keeping you from achieving your goals on the material plane!

The time of the Autumn Equinox is also the time of the Harvest moon, when the moon is closest to the Earth (around 23rd September). It is therefore appropriate to work with Hekate as a lunar deity. Although she is often described as a Moon Goddess in modern pagan literature Hekate's role as a moon goddess comes from Roman times (5th century BCE onwards) and seems to stem from her relationship with Artemis. In the *Greek Magickal Papyri* Hekate is also identified with Selene and the moon. It is not just on the full moon that we can work with Hekate in her lunar aspects. The Greek calendar was a lunar one and they made offerings to Hekate on the first of the month, that is to say the new moon.

In considering Hekate as a goddess of the moon we can also think about her aspect of ruler of the seas (which is often over looked) for the Moon rules the tides of the sea. Hesiod says: *"and to those whose business is in the grey discomfortable sea, and who pray to Hecate and the loud-crashing Earth-Shaker (Poseidon), easily the glorious goddess gives great catch, and easily she takes it away as soon as seen, if so she will."* Thus we can at any time we find ourselves near the ocean acknowledge Hekate as Pelagia, of the sea and as such a ruler of the fate and tides of mankind.

SAMHAIN:

At Samhain we take stock of the year which has passed and draw our energies inwards as we prepare for the long winter months ahead. Samhain is the time when the veils between the worlds are thinnest and the world of the dead encroaches on the world of the living. The darker aspects of Hekate are highlighted and where we can find *"blood bathed Hekate … From whom dogs cower as she wanders through the graves"*. Therefore at Samhain we see Hekate Prytania – Invincible Queen of the Dead who can be honoured in the dark and wild places. This is also where the aspect of her as Apotropaios (averter of evil) comes into its own. She offers protection from dark spirits that roam the night, a role is probably directly related to the role of Queen of the Dead on the grounds that *"she who sends the ghost can also ward against it"*.

You can also work with her as Hekate Enodia (Goddess of Crossroads). The Cross roads were thought to be supernatural places where magick can be worked and spirits encountered, for better or worse. In Greek literature they are the site for Kathartic (purification) and apotropaic (banishment) rituals. Hekate is associated with these liminal places, often residing at sacred three-way cross roads, so we are reminded of Her popular image as Trivia or three formed.

This might be a time to work with animal headed Hekate or with the energies of the animals that are associated with Her. Some of the animals associated with Hekate can also be connected to Her role as Queen of the Dead. The animal that is arguably the most associated with Hekate is the dog and it was thought that She could be summoned up from the darkness with long howls. There is an old belief that the souls of the unburied dead could appear as dogs and the dogs howl was believed to be a harbinger of death. Hekate is sometime identified with being the creator of the three headed dog Kerberos, who guards the entrance to Hades. The appearance of black, howling dogs at night was an ominous herald of her presence and their barking announced her approach. Virgil wrote *"Then earth began to bellow, trees began to dance, and howling dogs in glimmering light advance, ere Hekate came"*. On a less fearsome note, dogs were also associated with deities like Hekate who watched over childbirth and the dog is also well known as a guardian of the house, standing watch at the front door, fearsome to those beyond but caring to those within.

The other animal commonly connected to Hekate is the snake. A common belief was that the dead could appear in the form of snakes. As Hekate Chthonia, she is described as *"all entwined with fearsome serpents and leaves of oak"* and *"entwining herself in coils of serpents"*. We should also remember that the serpent with its shedding of its skin is a symbol of rebirth.

Now is the time to remember that She is the mistress of magick and a great aid to witches with spells and divination. The thinness between the worlds at Samhain makes it easier for us to see what is to come. At this time we can work with Hekate Hesperides, of the evening star. Hekate's mother, Asteria, governed the stars and knew the secrets of reading them. When Asteria abandoned Earth Hekate was said to take on a lot of her mother's attributes and therefore Hekate can be used for the divination of the stars or astrology.

Samhain or Halloween is the time most associated in modern times with witchcraft and there's no denying that Hekate has always been special to Witches. Aristophanes states that a person could purchase the services of a *"woman witch"* from Thessaly to *'draw down the moon,'* or create an eclipse. Two of the most famous witches in history, Medea and Circe invoked Hekate in their magic and indeed in some stories She is their mother. Her magick is mentioned in the *Greek Magical Papyri* and She was prevalent in curse tablets. Hekate can be invoked for any form of magick or witchcraft but thinking specifically about Samhain we can also consider the root of the word of the Thessalian witches, *Pharmakis* which suggests herbs. Hekate taught Medea herbs – in fact when Jason and Medea arrive at Thessaly it is the herbs she carries that are supposed to have taught the people of Thessaly witchcraft. Thus all herb magick is sacred to her (another reason why incense is an appropriate offering). Since a lot of the herbs sacred to Hekate are hallucinogenic any magic or work involving trance or other altered states of consciousness is also appropriate.

As I hope I have demonstrated there are more aspects to Hekate than can possibly be covered in one article or worked with in a single years' round. I also feel that it's important to be open to what Hekate has to teach you Herself. In the work that I have done with Her in connection with the Sabbats I have sometimes been surprised at the aspects of Hekate that She has revealed to me but it is this personal connection with Hekate and Her way of teaching that makes the work so enriching and rewarding.

Figure 67 - Forest Shrine by MDL

THE CALL

From the Beginning, I have been here.
All-encompassing, ever-present,
loving yet distant and unknowable:
I am Nyx. I am Chaos.
I am the Beginning of All.

I sing: Mother of Night, of Infinity;
the Dance of the Stars;
The Endless Waltz of the Galaxies;
the Death Spiral of Black Holes.
I AM ALL – singularity and unlimited possibility.
I am Sweet Loving in the Unfathomable Depths of Time.
I exploded and birthed all that is.
The Goddesses are My Daughters.
The Stars are My Daughters.
Every woman who has ever lived is also My Daughter...
for what are you if not Star Stuff?
You, too, are celestial children of the Cosmos,
formed from the embers of giant stars that died to give you life.
In your cells sings the Music of the Universe.
Do you hear it?
Can you open your ears and listen to a sound that pounds through you
as surely and undeniably as your own heartbeat?

My hand is always out to you to bring you back into the Cosmic Dance.
I am She Who is the Soul of the Cosmos. I am Oldest of the Old, yet I am a Maiden.
I hold Power in all realms and spread My Blessings to the Lost, the Frightened, the Wronged, as well as the
Strong Amazon who whispers My Name as she rides under a Full Moon. I am with you.
I am calling to you.
Say My Name...

Dare it! Do it! Call to Me!!!   HEKATE!

By Tinnekke Bebout

Figure 68 -Raven by Emily Carding

RAVENS

By Jen Ricci

It's funny how they were dancing all around
In the almighty day of my anointment
As I met you my dearest as you made me yours
In soul and spirit
The ravens called and I turned
In threes they talked with their eyes to speak
About you, my beloved Hecate, who have been to me
Kind and generous, my Queen.
Yet I will serve you.
The three birds just watched and stood
As I bowed and again swore allegiance
This time fully conscious in my body and soul
I remember my Goddess as you called me the first time
And you bestowed with that knowledge and power
And the eternal youth of my soul in return.
I will serve you faithfully.
The very clouds came down to haunt this day
That seemed to me as bright as it should be
It was indeed as my mind reached what it should have
Power bestowed to me
Oh Hecate help me
Protect me, my Goddess...

This poem is a much more recent one than the one I wrote on that fateful night, a long time back: I was twelve. One evening, I sat transfixed in my room, the light of the full moon illuminating the furniture faintly through the open window...the magic silence of the countryside the only presence.

I looked at the moon and something powerful and beautiful hit me, and I had to put it on paper: I subsequently won a prize with that poem.

Not a conscious one, but that evening was a turning point, a milestone for me: because I believe, you see, that we don't choose our goddess or god, I believe they choose us. It's certainly the case for me: she circled and circled around me, until I finally recognised her and swore allegiance and loyalty to her, the great Hekate. Only when I promised I would honour her she showed me the thread that had run through my life and how she had always been there for me, following me step by step, protecting me, making sure no serious harm would come to me. I am ever so grateful for this.

The Hekate I know is the compassionate goddess, I know nothing of that other terrible face they say she has: I believe she shows her wrath only with good reason, and I never gave her any reason to. She loves a pure heart: she might not be one for hugs and fluffiness, but be sure that her word is as good as cast in iron.

When I willingly embraced her, many years after that night, where some kind of mystery to do with the subtle power of the moon was shown to me, she knowingly smiled to me, as if I were the prodigal child who had finally come back home.

As soon as I was home, things started going surprisingly well for me: lots of business coming in, lots of new and interesting friends, my spells having sudden and amazing results... and she nodded. I can't help but feel that I've been recruited... and that she's been patiently on my case for quite a long while...

The day I made the decision of becoming one of her brood, I was walking in a park, holding a book on Hekate, and I said in my mind: *"Yes, this is the way forward, I'll have an altar prepared for you Hekate. I promise."*

Suddenly, the unmistakable feeling of being watched. It was very very strong: my intuition never lies.

I was in the middle of a huge park, not a tree in sight, just grass, and more grass and more grass. Yet, I was being watched... instinctively I turned and behind me there were three –her number- huge ravens, at equal distance, staring at me...I had to laugh. Ok, I thought, ok Hekate, I get it: you are on my case, you want to make sure I know you are...I also had a dog with me.

Coincidence? I have stopped believing in coincidences a long time ago... too many to believe they are casual...too many turning points due to a *'coincidence'*.

I am a follower *'in training'*: this is very clear to me, that something is being prepared for me to do, for which she will need my skill and knowledge, which I am still acquiring.

I work, day by day, following a direction that comes to me in bits and pieces, through people, news, things I get to know by chance...

What I found truly amazing is how many doors have suddenly opened for me when I made the conscious decision of embracing and being part of her world.

I don't honour her within a group, I am a solitary witch and my connection to her is very private, although I have no problems at all with talking about it to people.

I notice that the average person is unsettled by the darkness and mystery that surrounds this beautiful goddess... I find that darkness protects, and that the truth is in what is not seen... I have a small altar in my home dedicated to her. I work with animals in between other things and like all witches I have a strong connection to nature: dogs though are for me like a bridge to Hekate's ways and world.

Do you wonder why she likes dogs and wolves so much? Because they are extremely just animals. Their society is one ruled by simple rules... animals cannot be evil, they can only become vicious if mistreated, they become insane when denied their needs.

Figure 69 - Light Shrine by MDL

FROM THE SHADOWS

That night, a shadow came from the dark and turned solid
I fought until there was no fight left in me,
I screamed until I could no longer breathe
Damp earth in my mouth, in my nostrils
And the shadow-man's hot breath
Darkness above, and fear – I was alone, with him
I turned my face away

Hekate, help me
You heard, and you came.

His hands no longer held me down, the weight of his body lifted
His voice that had spoken vile things now stammering, confused He ran
I was free.
...
You stepped from the shadows into the world of mortals and saved me.

Hekate, My love and my thanks I lay at your feet.

EXTRACT FROM A VOTIVE THANK YOU

BY ANON, 2010

Figure 70 - Chthonic Shrine by MDL

DAYS FOR THE DEAD, AND LIVING

BY PETRA SCHOLLEM

If asked I would probably have to say that Magick has always been a part of my life, though might have been in denial for much of my earlier life, it is thanks to an encounter with Hekate that it is now firmly a part of my everyday consciousness. I live in Mexico, with my husband and our 4 children, though I am originally from the north of England, where as a teenager I dabbled, as many did in the 1970's, with a bit of Witchcraft, and many other attempts at being alternative, with varied levels of success, and certainly none of it was long lasted.

My husband's family is Mexican and have many curious beliefs and customs, which they reconcile with their Catholic religious tradition, the best known and perhaps most significant of their festivals is *Los Dias De Los Muertos* or the *Day of the Dead*, which is a national holiday in Mexico and coincides with the Catholic *All Saints Day* on November 1st. It is a special day for people to gather with friends and family to pay respect to their ancestors. This is of course very near to the Celtic Pagan Samhain festival, but the two are not the same, though many of the same themes are present and can be seen in both and I believe that the Pagan festival has borrowed quite significantly from this Mexican festival, just as the commercial Halloween has. Instead the roots of *Los Dias De Los Muertos* is believed to be in an ancient Aztec festival which is ruled over by the Goddess Mictecacihuatl.

Mictecacihuatl is the Goddess of the dead, the Queen of the Underworld who rules there with her husband, the God Mictlantecuhtli whose cult members were believed to have engaged in the eating of human flesh, that is cannibalism! He is one of the principle Gods of the Aztec tradition. Mictecacihuatl watches over the bones of the dead, so she is naturally the Goddess associated with *Los Dias De Los Muertos*.

As my fascination grew with the traditions of the ancient Aztec people, so did my need to learn more about the traditions of my own ancestors who came from all over Europe. My interest in particular at the time was with trying to find out more about Wicca, a tradition which I had explored a little bit when I had my *'phase'* during my teens, but had often thought about over the years. Searching through various internet sites I found a page with information on the Goddess Hekate, who was described as a Goddess of Witchcraft and as Queen of the Dead. My senses was heightened, I needed to find out more! So books were ordered and websites trawled with what information I could find, until those precious books arrived from the United States by post. Then things really started to happen.

I found myself holding a copy of the book *Hekate Keys to the Crossroads* which helped me tremendously in understanding Hekate through the experiences of others being recounted, as well as through the concise overview of the various roles of the Goddess Hekate given in the introduction. That book really changed my life and it is also the reason that I decided that I had to share my experiences in this collection, as I feel that it is a way of thanking the contributors to *Keys to the Crossroads* for the wonderful things they brought into my life.

The essay *Working with Hekate* by Harry Barron in particular struck a cord with me when I first read the book. He starts by saying *"Hekate is alive and talks to you in dreams..."* and goes on to recount his own introduction to Hekate. What resonated with me so much about this was that I had been having dreams ever since the first time I attended the first *Los Dias De Los Muertos* of a woman beckoning me to her. At first I thought this might be the spirit of one of my husband's ancestors, but the woman of my visions did not at all fit the description of any of his ancestors! My thoughts turned towards *Santa Muerte* who is venerated here during the *Los Dias De Los Muertos* too, even though the Catholic Church condemns it.

She was tall, maybe as tall as 6 foot and athletic in build with long raven black tresses, some of which hung plaited on her shoulders. Her eyes shone with a special spark, like she knew something, a magical knowledge which was there as a challenge for me to discover. Around her neck was a gold key on a red string. Behind her an expanse of stars. There was a stillness about her that I cannot readily put into words, yet at the same time there was a feeling of union, a feeling of completion. Her face was that of a young woman, maybe in her late twenties, early thirties, a classical beauty with a wildness to it, and in my dream it shifted from being human to being half cow, then wolf and then something like a goat, before turning back into a human shape again. It was a very vivid dream!

One by one reading through those essays I found clues which made me realise that the dream vision I had was one of the Goddess Hekate. But why? Why would a Greek Goddess show herself to me in Mexico? What did she have to do with *Los Dias de los Muertos?* And rather more importantly, why did I have this vision?

As the months went by I found myself reading more and more about the history of the Goddess Hekate, several books, websites and much personal correspondence with Sorita d'Este helped me to gain a good understanding of Hekate and her role in the mysteries of the ancient world. Likewise, reading and re-reading the essays in *Keys to the Crossroads* really helped me to gain an understanding of the connection people felt with Hekate and the experiences they had, which gave me pointers for when I finally started my own work with the Goddess Hekate in the weeks leading up to *Los Dias De Los Muertos*. Hekate was a Goddess of the Dead, she was also the Guide in Darkness and a Goddess held the keys to the Underworld. More importantly I learnt that she was associated with the untimely dead, that is people who died unnatural deaths through murder or suicide for example. This was interesting, because a number of people in my husband's family had been killed in a violent attack some years earlier, and my own mother had committed suicide as a result of depression caused by years of abuse suffered at the hands of my controlling father.

By then I instinctively understood what it was I was meant to do. *Los Dias De Los Muertos* is about remembering the dead, honouring our ancestors through whose sacrifices we are able to be here today. For those attending the *Los Dias De Los Muertos* festival and who honour their ancestors in this way, their ancestry is often of mixed European and Aztec descent, something which was very true of my husband and his family, as well as for our own children! So whilst Mictecacihuatl, the Aztec Goddess of the Dead might be relevant as a Goddess for the spirits of the Aztec ancestral spirits, a European Goddess would make a lot more sense for the spirits of our European ancestors. My own ancestors came from all over Europe, and the worship of the Goddess Hekate travelled to many parts of Europe, she was a Goddess that at least some of my own ancestors might well have known and worshipped!

I had learnt about Hekate Suppers, which are in their way not much different from the shrines made for the departed ancestors, when we put images of them together with their favourite food out for them on the night, often with candles. Hekate Suppers are instead left at a crossroads for Hekate at the New Moon each month, together with the sweepings from the house when you clean it to ensure that there are no restless spirits in the house. The sweepings are taken to the crossroads, with cakes and candles, so at the New Moon preceding *Los Dias De Los Muertos* I performed this rite and left the food at a quiet crossroads, with two small candles and all the sweepings from my house. When I got home I created a shrine onto which I placed just one image of the Goddess, also with two candles ~ one red and one black ~ and a small bowl of seeds as offerings. This would become my shrine for the festival at the start of November.

In the days which followed I spent time each day tending that shrine, adding flowers and more candles, burning incense and making further offerings. I read out hymns to Hekate which I found in *Keys to the Crossroads* and found myself developing a very close bond with her. I realised that my role was to be that of a guide, someone who would help Hekate to guide the souls of the restless dead to where they belong. I had little experience of mediumship, mostly gained from watching others perform séances, here in Mexico many people are *'sensitive'* to such things and it is not unusual for people to discuss such things openly in my husband's family, indeed one of his aunts are considered to be a very gifted medium and I decided to talk to her and ask her to teach me what I needed to know. I learned a lot from her and she also taught me more about *Sante Muerte* whom I had considered as having a possible link to my vision. It would seem that this *'saint'* who was so despised by the Church but loved by the criminals and those who honoured the old ways of their ancestors had a lot of characteristics in common with Hekate. Something which I think is worth mentioning is that she is often depicted as holding different objects in her hands, including items like a scythe with which she is said to be able to cut the silver thread which binds us to life. Like Hekate she is the *Señora de la Noche,* meaning the *Lady of the Night* and people often invoke her to protect them during the darkness of night; something which Hekate is also invoked for as she is the protector! These might be mere coincidences, or could hint at the idea that it is a different guise of the Goddess whom the Hellenes called Hekate, maybe just maybe she is a Goddess of many names and faces, just like the Triple Image of her hints at?

That year and each year since, I have done workings with Hekate to find and guide many dozens of souls to where they belong. Its been a journey of great sadness at times and one of great joy when the task has been completed and had a happy ending. For me Hekate is a compassionate and joyful Goddess, she is not a dreadful Queen of horrors as she is often described. The Hekate I know and love is one who reaches out and who is forgiving, for me she is the soul of the world through whom we can reach a greater understanding of ourselves and our fellow human beings – I have There is no doubt that she is demanding, but she gives more than she ever takes.

Dedicated to all the contributors to Hekate Keys to the Crossroads.

Figure 71 - Hekate's Art by Vlasta Mijac

HEKATE'S ART

Who knows who is she...
Is she a green or a blue
or aquamarine
as alike a deep side
of the sea dark blue
or only asleep
as alike a muse
into deep side
of the horizon
from sunset
violet mixed
by turquoise
into the light
slowly glittering of the stars
into the mind...

by the darkness of hidden ages

BY VLASTA MIJAC

WISE GRANDMOTHER HEKATE CRONE

WISE GRANDMOTHER HEKATE

BY NIKKI CULLEN

I was born in Queens, New York, in the United States in the 1970's. A mother to three beautiful children who I believe are the reason I breathe and have saved me in some ways. I am Welsh, Italian and Spanish and possibly some Native American Indian thrown in there somewhere I hear but really will never know for sure as being that my mother was adopted. Born to a pagan mother and catholic father and yes they made it work. I grew up with your basic knowledge of catholic teachings while attending after school religious education and attending catholic school from 7th grade to the completion of high school.

But it was at home where I learned that there is more to a religion then just all the constant babbles from so called religious educators. Since I was a toddler I could hear and see things others couldn't. It was my mother, who practiced the old Celtic tradition of the Goddess Craft, who taught me how to deal with this *'gift'*. I learned about herbs for medicinal purposes as well as magical. I learned about the power of intent. I learned the power of words. I was taught about the Sabbats and Esbats. The power of the moon and her phases and so on.

Since I was a little girl I felt most comfortable the presence of nature. Trees, grass, dirt, flowers forests, it is where I felt most alive and I guess magical. I was taught how sacred nature is and how to commune with it. My first meditation was at age 7. I was taken to Forest Park. Not very large in comparison to other forests of the world but for Queens, It went on forever, especially when you're that little. There are some places there still hidden for some. There was a large open patch of area surrounded by trees. I sat on the ground, put my hand to the ground and waited eyes closed in silence except for summer breezes and birds. I felt a slow heat pulsing sensation from the ground, a heartbeat (Gaia) then my own heartbeat I could hear. It then meshes into one steady rhythm, loud to my ears and it was at that moment I knew we are all connected. I will never forget it. Getting older and entering adulthood I started to study different goddess and occult teachings other than the Celtic ones. I also started to, perhaps you can say, take my learning to a slightly darker place.

Out of all the goddess energies I have had the pleasure to work with, I am always drawn to her ~ Hecate. To me I have always seen her as Crone. I see her as a grandmother type figure. Although not like the typical grandmother one would see in traditional families. She is tall, veiled in the dark colours of night. She wears the sacred triple aspect symbol of maiden, mother, crone, in silver around her neck. She is sacred and she is wisdom.

She is dark which is where sometimes I'm most comfortable to be.

Throughout my spiritual journeys, starting in childhood, most pagan based religions talked of love and light which is fine, however they never really explored the darker aspect of one-self and sometimes I was made to feel that it was wrong to have such dark moods. That anger, depression or hatred I had for some was wrong.

I went to do some searching. Then, I found her or perhaps she found me. I kept hearing her name, in stories, in passing and the name stayed in my head until one day I searched for it on the internet, I was 19 at the time. I came across an amazing website that taught me so much. What surprised me most was *"Hecate dark, Hecate crone"*. Through invoking her and learning more and more about her it was then that I learned that through the dark one will find the light. Through the dark one can heal. I learned that anger can be destructive but it can also fuel you to do good. I always seemed to have a fire within and just didn't know how or where to direct it. I was going through a dark phase in my life and change was made.

I still do on occasion go through these moods of doubt, anger and some depression but through Hecate, my ancient and ever wise grandmother, I will turn to. I had a dream of Hecate once, when I was 19. I had my first child and was going through a bit of a hard time transitioning. Not so much a hard time being a mother, that came naturally enough. I was having a hard time letting go of some things and with any transition of change comes conflict in one's own head.

Letting go of what you were to embrace the new, a changed you.

After a particular kind of unsatisfactory day I went to bed a little extra frustrated with myself. It was here, in my dreams, where I had visions of her. I was in a forest at night with a full moon with the most beautiful darkest blue sky you ever seen. I was coming out through the trees approaching a pool of water that reflected the moon. The moon looked particularly large and white. I was staring into the pool and at me. A hand touched my shoulder, I turned to see her, standing there. Exactly as I envisioned her to be.

She didn't smile, she was serious and to the point. She told me that...

> *YOU once were Maiden, YOU ARE NOW MOTHER and you have a very long way to go before you are Crone.*

As she spoke this to me her face changed to each phase of life she spoke of as did my reflection of self in the pool did as well. It was understood.

She showed me what I once was, what am I now and what I should focus on and that I have a long way to journey before I can really not only at the end of my life but before I can achieve wisdom. I will always be learning. There was such strength in those words that when I woke I felt better, motivated refreshed and anew sense of being and of who I was. I believe she intervened to give me a kick in the pants to realize I was sacred as a mother and not to take that lightly.... Yes, I believe sometimes we have to sit in the dark for awhile.

Figure 72 - Hekate by Sara Croft

THE WOMAN AND THE TRAVELLER

(Honouring a different face of Hekate)

A woman sits on a mossy log
In the twilight beside a branching path.
She caresses the golden horn of a unicorn
Laid with love and trust upon Her lap.

Serenely She gazes at the beast
And hearing a footstep, looks up smiling.
A traveller stops short - indecision apparent.
Which way? Left? Right? Ahead?

As the night deepens the traveller turns back.
"Wait!" the woman slowly rises.
In the palm of Her hand is a globe of flame.
"The night is never as dark as you suppose."

She tosses the globe into the air.
It soars high and hangs above the treetops -
A glistening moon suspended in the velvet sky.
All ways are illuminated and inviting.

The traveller smiles her gratitude,
Stepping out with confidence upon her chosen path.
Glancing back, she can see the long way she has come.
This makes the way ahead seem possible to achieve.

The woman sits upon the mossy log
In the moonlight beside a branching path.
She caresses the golden horn of a unicorn
Laid with love and trust upon Her lap.

Momma White Cougar

Figure 73 - Serpent Shrine by Lezley Forster

SHE IS I AND I AM SHE

BY LEZLEY FORSTER

THE PAST

Hekate – you who stride the wild and untamed places
I call you
From the mountain tops
From the darkest pits of the sea
From the veil of the stars
And the depths of the forest

I call you
From your dance amongst the stones and the caves
From the dead's own tombs
From the places of dread and shadow

I call you!
Rise up from your earthen womb, entwined in leaf and vine and root Hear the song of
your wolves resonate about you
And feel the serpents writhe beneath your feet
You who art Mistress of all those beasts that walk and crawl

Waken Lady of Hades!
You who are the great vessel that contains the secrets of initiation, the mysteries of
rebirth and the words of power that echo in the darkest caverns of our souls
You, primeval passion, cloaked in the darkness of the moon
Darkness that the light cannot touch

You, Hekate Chthonia, Goddess of the Underworld
Bestow upon us your wisdom
Answer our prayers and our darkest desires
Enable us all to stand between the worlds
For the great doors are barred and shut
And it is you who holds the keys to that great realm.
Let us brave of heart and strong of spirit gain audience

Hekate I call upon you to join us!
Hail Hekate!

My favourite part of honouring Hekate was to write. I often felt inspired at odd moments, when I would have to grab pen and paper, or interrupt work to capture the words going around in my head. There was a connection, an opening of the void, of stepping into the shadows between the worlds.

When I wrote the invocation above, it was nothing more than that, an invocation, words and spirit intermingling for a ritual, to draw the energy of the goddess. I had no idea that it would be the key to the start of a different relationship with her. As I stood before the altar, my words my offering, I realised that I was doing more than invoking, I was linked to the divine energy, I could feel it coursing throughout my entire body. I struggled to speak, to stand. Sheer determination got me through that short invocation, though it felt as though it lasted a lifetime. I was fully enveloped, I stood within a vortex of power, something had stepped through into the physical. I was shaken.

Returning home that evening I could think of nothing else but the sensations, the feelings I had experienced. I had felt the touch of divinity, I had stood with my goddess and she had shown her true face and power.

When performing oracles or drawing down of the moon for Hekate, this bond strengthened. I could see her clearly, the link and bond growing stronger. The connection easier to maintain, I felt as if I had lost part of myself and it was replaced by a flame, a glowing jewel that burned deep within. It was in these moments that I began to realise that I had truly given myself to her and she would always be there.

Many things have changed over the years since these moments and Hekate has indeed been by my side though the wonderful and the bleak and dark.

In group working, there was ritual, pieces put together, altars, tools, representations. There was a power in working with people that you trusted and an energy that exists nowhere else but in the centre of that. But, eventually group working became difficult, I felt it no longer fit me or the way I wished to work. I had to bid a sad farewell and walk my own path as things were changing. I needed to realise my own strength and power, I had to be my own teacher and not rely on others. I took tentative steps towards defining my own path, my own tradition as it were, building on the foundation that had already been laid, working magic into my everyday life, strengthening my will to achieve results. Through meditation and intuition and the wisdom of Hekate, I have learned to let go and simply be.

No research, no dependence on the religions and the worships of the past, Hekate for the modern world that exists now. I can look back with interest but I have found that, for me, Hekate is a goddess of the here and now. I am a 21st century woman and this is how she speaks to me. That she seems to speak to so many and has done throughout the centuries, shows that she is there for anyone who is willing to look, no matter how they work or the path they are on. Spend time developing a personal relationship with her, research but also be brave enough to stretch your wings and let her show you herself.

This took years, not months and is not for the faint hearted. Grounding and developing a foundation of knowledge first but easy to step between the worlds when I wished. I hide facets of myself from the world, as we all do but have now found it beneficial to be more honest with myself and be more confident in my own skin in all areas of my life. With self-healing, meditation, drumming screaming dancing, I start to ask again for what I want, guidance on what I want to be and what the gods and spirit want of me. I have paid with tears, sweat and blood once more but Hekate has become more of a sister than a god to me. Is that arrogant, precocious? No, some things just are, just become part of our lives.

I am the altar, the tools, the paper, the book, the ritual. My body embodies the elements, my mind constructs my working space, my voice calls into the void, across worlds. Sweat, tears and blood my offerings. Open the mind, hear her words, shout them out, though there may be only yourself to hear. She speaks through me and I struggle to concentrate on her words. I may use a drum, create a heart beat that you can hear echoed in the earth, deep in the earth, giving voice to song, to sounds, to screams. Embrace the feeling of ecstasy, of being everywhere and nowhere. I send out a prayer, a song, a dance. In return she comes to me, magic is performed, wishes sent on breath, physical manifestations.

An invocation by the river, a prayer underneath a tree, a walking meditation across the wilds of the moor, a poem in time with a drumbeat. This is where Hekate lives. My Hekate, my goddess, my teacher, my sister, holder of the keys to the deep dark caverns of my spirit. It is about the now, not the past, not the future. What can I do now? Where am I now? Gather strength and wisdom. Put down the books, dance under the light of a full moon and contemplate during the dark!

A RITUAL

I work with Hekate mainly on the dark of the moon, for this is when her call is strongest. Before the ritual I may wish to prepare some devotional or magical work. I use my body as paper and write and draw upon it with a knife to draw blood, or with henna, pencil, or the creation of temporary tattoos. Words, pictures, sigils. These drawn images might be removed immediately after my working is done or they will remain on my body as reminder of Hekate for several days and become part of a devotional period.

My temple room is blacked out on these occasions so that no light enters the room. I will put on music and I will perform breath work to centre and open myself up, visualise energy emanating from myself and filling the room. I will then turn off the light and sit in the darkness. I visualise drawing the dark moon down before me. I will use this as a doorway, stepping through this to meet her.

After this will step back through and send the moon back to the sky. I will then meditate upon the images and messages or the work that was performed. Sometimes I will have my drum to hand to softly beat a rhythm, creating a light trance.

I then pull my energy inwards again, change my breathing to centre myself and come back into reality.

I have had times over the years where my spiritual development and work has come to a grinding halt or I am unsure of where to go next. Life interferes and a magical life is not always practical. With the relationship built up with Hekate, she has allowed me this space. She knows with me when to stand back, when to give me the opportunity to explore other work, letting me fail, letting me find myself again. When this is work done she is there to remind me and push me and in those instances she will not be ignored!

Hekate - of the earth, of the underworld, keybearer, lightbringer.

There is so much more but it is too private to share. That side of our practices that are ours alone. Here I wish to show that Hekate is a goddess like no other, there are no boundaries, no rules but you can develop a deep and lasting relationship with her that could last lifetimes. She showed herself to me 11 years ago. I had no idea who she was but I understood what the vision meant. I knew I would meet people who would give me that knowledge of her. Little did I know where it would take me.

THE PRESENT

Where she steps, I step
I am priestess, daughter, goddess
Her divine flame burns deep in my soul
Do you see it?
Do you feel it?

When I am drowning in the darkness
She is there
When my walls crumble and the floor has fallen away beneath me
She is there
When I am screaming in the night
She is there
When caught in a web of fear and disbelief
Her whispers in my ear
Her presence towering behind me
The feel of a hand brushing my cheek
Strength, power, self-belief flood me

I have her, I am hers, she is I and I am she

I tread my own path
I rise above

I have her, I am hers, she is I and I am she

No fakery, no frippery, not tools, no games
She is here and forever will be
Even when I have doubted
When I have faltered
She is here and forever will be

I have her, I am hers, she is I and I am she

Draw the dark moon downwards
Step into a world beyond knowing
Through the veil, through the shadows
With everything stripped away, facing the mirror
Forced to open eyes to the bare truth
She is here and forever will be

Teacher, mother, Goddess divine
When I have cried tears of happiness
When my heart fills with ecstasy and unbridled joy
Sharing my secrets with my love in the darkness
In the beauty of the woods and the meadows
Hearing my laughter
She is here and forever will be

I have her, I am hers, she is I and I am she

Figure 74 - Moon and Sun by Aedos Alala

From the silence I speak
The Mistress of day and night
Your voice ringing out
The fires consuming the offering you made
A labour of love
Standing proudly on my altar stone
I am the Mistress of this hearth

From the darkness I whisper
The Moon in my left hand
The Sun in my right
I bring balance and understanding
I bring knowledge
Union of the knowledge of the past.
I am the Mistress of your Mind.

Aedos Alala, Turkey, 2010

Figure 75 - Three by Magin Rose

HEKATE: STAR AND CENTRE

Bright and Shining One
Lady of Torches
Gentle guide, Searing flame
Starlight wanderer
Riding the night sky
Raise your voices in her name
Star at the centre, flaming circumference
Hekate Phosphoros

In your praise
Treasure of deep Earth
Queen of the Underworld
Mistress of Darkness and souls of the dead
Pythoness, Seeress
Dancing the pathways
Driving us deeper, Lady of Dread.
Star at the centre, flaming circumference
Hekate Chthonia

In your praise
Lady of the Cosmos
Soul of the whole world
Axis Mundi, Towering Queen
Crowned in the Heavens
Arms all encompassing
Saviour of all things, Seen and Unseen
Star at the centre, flaming circumference
Hekate Soteira

In your praise
Radiant Goddess
Standing at the gateway
Guarding the threshold, You hold the key
Seas washing over us
Earth keep and nurture us
Reaching for the starlit sky, you set us free.
Star at the centre, Flaming circumference
Hekate Propolos
You set us free.

By Magin Rose

(WRITTEN IN 2007)

Glossary of Terms

Aigina: Greek island which had a Hekate temple and celebrated her mysteries, said to have been founded by Orpheus..

Anatolia: Ancient kingdom of what is now most of Turkey.

Angel: A spiritual being which acts as a messenger for a particular deity. Commonly depicted as a winged human in form.

Antaia: *'Sender of Nocturnal Visions'*, a title of Hekate.

Apollo: Greek god of music, healing and prophecy, son of Zeus and Leto, and twin of Artemis.

Apotropaic: *'Evil-averting'*, a term often used for amulets and banishing or protective rites. Apotropaios or 'Averter of Evil' is a title of Hekate.

Argos: Greek island which had a Hekate temple.

Artemis: Greek Virgin Huntress goddess, daughter of Zeus and Leto, twin sister of Apollo. From C5th BCE she was conflated at times with Hekate. The temple at Ephesus was dedicated to her as Artemis of Ephesus.

Asteria: Greek Stellar Titan goddess of astrology and dream prophecy, mother of Hekate.

Baubo: Old woman in the Eleusinian Mysteries sometimes equated with Hekate.

Bendis: Thracian lunar goddess and mother of Sabazius. Conflated with Hekate from mid-C5th BCE.

Bona Dea: Roman healing goddess who was conflated with Hekate from C2nd CE.

Brimo: Title given to Hekate, also used by Demeter and Persephone, and as a password in the Orphic Mysteries.

Byzantium: Modern-day Istanbul, centre of the Byzantine Empire and location of a Hekate shrine following her saving the city from invasion in the C4th BCE.

Caria: Ancient kingdom on what is now the west coast of Turkey.

Chaldean Oracles: A fragmentary collection of 226 verses from C2nd CE which portrays a Theurgical worldview with Hekate as the Cosmic Soul.

Charities: Three Greek goddesses of beauty, grace and festive mirth, sometimes depicted with triple Hekate on Hekataions.

Chthonic: *'Of the earth'*, a name given to gods associated with the earth and the underworld, sometimes with the title Chthonia, e.g. Hekate Chthonia and Hermes Chthonia.

Crossroads: In relation to Hekate this is specifically a meeting of three roads (i.e. a Y shape), said to be particularly frequented by the restless dead and sacred to her as a liminal place.

Cyrene: Greek colony in modern-day Libya which had a Hekate temple.

Daimon: Supernatural being usually seen as being higher than man but lower than the gods, e.g. a demi-god or ghost of a hero, though at times also applied to old gods.

Defixiones: Binding curse tablets, usually made of lead and used in Greco-Roman times, containing a request to Hekate and/or other Chthonic deities for aid.

Deipnon: *'Hekate Supper'*, a feast offered to Hekate at the crossroads on the New Moon.

Demeter: Greek Grain goddess, mother of Persephone and sister of Zeus. She was said to have established the Eleusinian Mysteries.

Diana: Roman virgin huntress goddess, who was conflated with Artemis, and subsequently with Hekate. Viewed as the goddess of witchcraft from the early Middle Ages onwards.

Dionysos: Greek god of Wine and Ecstasy, absorbed into the Olympian pantheon as the twice-born son of Zeus, though initially of unknown origin. Often conflated with the Thracian god Sabazius.

Eleusinian Mysteries: A Mystery Religion based at Eleusis, which was a powerful religious centre in the ancient world.

Enodia: *'Of the Roads'*, a title of Hekate derived from the Thessalian road goddess she subsumed.

Ereschigal: Babylonian underworld goddess who was conflated with Hekate around C3rd/4th CE.

Greek Magical Papyri: A collection of magical charms and rites dating from C2nd BCE – C5th CE, which blend Egyptian, Gnostic, Greek and Hebrew material and techniques.

Hades: Greek Underworld god, brother of Zeus and Poseidon. He abducted his niece Persephone to be his bride and end his loneliness. The Romans equated him to him Pluto.

Hekataion: a pillar surrounded by three Hekate figures (triformis). Small versions were placed at doorways to houses, and larger ones at crossroads.

Helios: Greek solar god, brother of Selene. He was conflated with Apollo, and sometimes associated with Hekate.

Hermes: Greek Messenger god, son of Zeus and Maya. He was often associated with Hekate, and together often shown with Kybele.

Hypostasis: The essential or manifest reality of something, as opposed to simplyits attributes.

Iakkhos: Greek god associated with the Eleusinian Mysteries and sometimes conflated with Dionysos.

Isis: Egyptian Mother goddess of magic, who became seen as a universal goddess, and who was conflated with Hekate for a period from C2nd CE.

Iynx: May be either (1) a type of angel who serves Hekate, or (2) another name for the Strophalos, (3) a wheel-based charm for love magic, originally sacred to the Greek love goddess Aphrodite.

Janus: Roman threshold god, conflated with Zeus/Jupiter and sometimes paired with Hekate.

Kali: Indian goddess of time and destruction, often depicted with multiple arms, and equated by some with Hekate.

Kleidouchos: *'Key-bearer'*, a title of Hekate, particularly with regard to the inner sanctuaries of temples. She was also said to bear the keys to the Elysian Fields in the underworld.

Kore: *'Maiden'*, a title usually applied to Persephone, but occasionally to Hekate, as in the *Greek Magical Papyri*.

Kourotrophos: *'Child's Nurse'*, a title of Hekate and some other Greek goddesses.

Kronos: Greek Titan god of time, husband of Rhea and father of Zeus, who deposed him.

Kundalini: Fire Serpent power said to reside dormant at the base of the spine in every person.

Kybele (Cybele): Phrygian and Anatolian Mother goddess whose worship became popular in Greece and Rome as the Magna Mater (Great Mother). Conflated with the goddess Rhea and also sometimes with Hekate.

Lagina: City in Caria where the last great Hellenic temple was built – to Hekate, in the C2nd CE.

Lampades: Torch-bearing nymphs who follow Hekate as part of her retinue.

Lilith: Sumerian goddess, demonised into the baby-killing serpent temptress in Hebrew and Christian texts.

Lucifer: Fallen archangel/god celebrated in the *Aradia* and the Luciferian tradition as the lord of light and liberator.

Luna: Roman moon goddess, conflated with Selene, and subsequently with Hekate and Diana.

Melinoe: Form of Hekate celebrated in the Orphic Mysteries.

Minoan Snake Goddess: Name given to two figures found in Knossos from c. 1500 BCE who may have links to the origins of Hekate.

Moirai: The three Greek Fates, representing inevitable destiny.

Nemesis: Greek vengeance goddess who was sometimes conflated with Hekate after C3rd CE.

Nike: Greek victory goddess, often depicted winged and bearing a wreath.

Noes: Intelligence or mind (Greek).

Ouranian: *'Heavenly'*, a name given to gods associated with the sky, also including the Olympian gods.

Orphic Mysteries: A Mystery Religion said to have been founded by the legendary musician Orpheus, and centred on Dionysos.

Persephone (Proserpina): Greek Spring goddess and Underworld Queen, daughter of Zeus and Demeter. Her abduction by Hades and subsequent division of the year between the earth and the underworld formed the basis of the *Homeric Hymn to Demeter* and the Eleusinian Mysteries. The Romans equated her to Prosperpina.

Perses: Obscure Titan god whose name means *'destroyer'*, father of Hekate.

Phosphoros: *'Light-bearer'*, a title of Hekate regarding her twin torches.

Phrygia: Ancient kingdom, that was part of Anatolia, and which was absorbed into Greece, in what is now central and western Turkey.

Poseidon: Greek Sea god, brother of Hades and Zeus, sometimes associated with Hekate.

Propolos: *'Guide'*, a title given to Hekate in her role escorting Persephone to and from the underworld.

Propylaia: *'Before the Gate'*, a title given to Hekate as guardian of entranceways.

Restless Dead: A name given to those who souls did not go to the underworld, usually through failure to conduct the proper funerary rites, or because they had committed suicide.

Rhea: Greek Titan Mother goddess, mother of Zeus, Hades, Poseidon, Demeter and others. She was conflated with Kybele, and Hekate in the *Chaldean Oracles*.

Sabazius: Thracian god known as the Rider God, son of Bendis, sometimes conflated with Dionysos.

Samothrace: Greek island noted as a centre of Hekate worship, with reference to initiations taking place in the Zerynthian cave there.

Selene: Greek lunar goddess, sister of Helios, conflated with Artemis and Hekate from around C1st BCE.

Selinus: Location of a temple to Demeter, Persephone and Hekate on the island of Sicily.

Soteira: *'Saviour'*, a title of Hekate in the *Chaldean Oracles*, also sometimes applied to Zeus.

Strophalos: A tool, likened to a spinning top, used in Theurgy for drawing down energy and beings, including gods.

Thessaly: Ancient kingdom in northern Greece, particularly associated with witchcraft by later Greek writers.

Theurgia: A spiritual system of magic focusing on perfecting the self through inner union with the gods.

Thrace: Ancient kingdom around the river Danube comprising what would now be south-eastern Bulgaria, north-eastern Greece and the European part of Turkey.

Triformis: *'three-formed'*, a title given to Hekate when depicted as three-bodied.

Trioditis: *'of the three roads'*, a title given to Hekate in respect of her role as guardian of the crossroads.

Zagreus: first form of the god Dionysos, before being killed and reborn. Celebrated in the Orphic Mysteries.

IDENTIFYING SYMBOLS OF HEKATE

Although Hekate has a propensity for turning up in dream, visions and meditations, she is not unique in this. So how can you identify Hekate or her omens and auguries? The following table comprises symbols which are specifically associated with Hekate. A key to identifying Hekate's presence can be the build-up of these symbols in events in your life. One symbol may be random, two may be coincidence (or from another deity who shares some of the same symbols), but five or six? Then you are reaching a critical mass which equates to a psychic knock on the door!

Animals	Black Lamb, Bull, Dogs (especially black), Dragon, Fish, Goat, Horse, Hydra, Lion, Mullet, Serpent, Wolf
Colours	Black, Red, White
Minerals	Bronze, Gold, Iron, Lapis Lazuli, Lead, Lodestone, Meteorite
Plants	Aconite, Ebony, Garlic, Mandrake, Oak, Saffron, Yew
Symbols	Crossroads (three-way), Crescent, Dagger, Dark Moon, Fire, Golden Sceptre, Headband, Herald's Wand, Keys, Lamp, New Moon, Sandal (bronze or gold), Torch, Twin Torches, Whip

THE RITE OF THE HER SACRED FIRES

WRITTEN BY SORITA D'ESTE

This rite was written as an act of gratitude and thanks to the Goddess Hekate for her inspiration, help and guidance through the compilation of this project.

This rite is intended for use on the Full Moon, Thursday 27th of May 2010 by all those who wish to honour the Goddess Hekate and dedicate themselves towards a greater understanding of Her Mysteries, this date coincides with the release of this book. It is included here so that those who wish to perform it in future at the Full Moon for the purpose of honouring the Goddess Hekate and to dedicate themselves to learning more about her mysteries will be able to do so.

The ceremony can be performed by itself, or as part of a longer ceremony, with or without a *"formal"* ritual space – that is up to individual choice. It is preferable (though not obligatory) that the wording and actions of the ceremony as presented below should be kept the same and remain unaltered, though if for spiritual, magical or personal reasons you need or wish to change some of it, you are hereby given permission to do so with the proviso that you do not alter in any way the purpose of the ceremony.

Preparation:

Find a quiet place where you will be able to perform the rite undisturbed. You will need a candle (or another form of devotional fire, such as a lamp or hearth fire) and something with which to light it. You may wish to consecrate the candle, or other materials you will be using in keeping with your usual tradition of working, otherwise please simply ensure that it is clean.

Prelude:

Make yourself comfortable, breathe deeply and find your point of balance, a balance of mind and soul and body, which will present you proud and beautiful to the world. Breathe deeply and find your voice, the voice with which you will speak words of true and pure intent. Breathe deeply and call upon the freedom within your heart so that you will be able to express yourself with purity of intent and with strength of desire.

Place both your hands on your heart (three heartbeats), your forefinger and middle finger of your dominant hand to your lips (three heartbeats), and then to your brow (three heartbeats). Now enclose your thumbs within both your hands (in fists) and raise both your arms to the heavens.

Open your hands and with palm upwards in your left hand, bring your right arm to your side palm facing downwards and invoke the Goddess.

Invocation:

I invoke thee, Great Mistress of the Heaven, Earth and Sea,

By your mysteries of Night and Day,

By the Light of the Moon and the Shadow of the Sun

I invoke thee, Mistress of life, death and rebirth

Emerge now from the shadow realm to feed my soul and enlighten my mind,

Triple-formed Mistress of the three ways

I entreat thee, Key-bearing Mistress of the Nightwandering Souls

To bring forth your wisdom from amongst the stars

To bring down your starfire from the darkness between,

Creatrix of Light!

Goddess of the Shadow Realms! Light-bearing queen!

Whisper now your secrets!

Fire-bringer! Earthly-one! Queen of Heaven!

[Raise both hands with palms facing upwards to the heavens (three heartbeats) and then touch the ground palms downwards]

[Sit before the candle and prepare to light it]

[Take three deep breaths and allow your senses to awaken]

Say:

Hekate, companion and guide to the mysteries

I light this sacred fire in your honour, [light fire]

Its light uniting the stars and stones, the heavens and the earth,

With this fire I express my desire for a greater understanding of your mysteries

Askei Kataskei Erōn Oreōn Iōr Mega Samnyēr Baui (3 times) Phobantia Semnē,

Great Hekate, who spins the web of the stars and governs the spiral of life

Guide me through towards pathways of understanding,

From Crossroad to Crossroad,

The Torchbearers and the Keybearers of your mysteries,

will always find one another,

Now sit and watch the flame flicker and dance, allow yourself to focus on the different colours in the flame, the yellows and reds, the blues and whites, and the black. If you wish you may decide to spend some time meditating on the flame, skrying for visions or omens. Likewise, you may wish to extinguish it and keep the candle - let your true self radiate brightly its beautiful mysteries from this day on forth, the flame of the fires of Hekate burns on in your heart!

I banish now the shadows of doubt from my mind,

Infused by the silence and warmth of our union

I feel your golden radiance within my heart

And the glory of knowledge on my brow,

I am a student of your mysteries.

Extinguish the flame, then place both your hands on your heart (three heartbeats), your forefinger and middle finger of your dominant hand to your lips (three heartbeats), and then to your brow (three heartbeats).

Open your palms reaching towards the heaven, then reach down and touch the Earth.

POSTSCRIPT TO THE SECOND EDITION:

Whilst it will never be possible to know exactly how many people joined in the rite on the 27th of May 2010, the support and fellowship between those who have heard the call of the Goddess Hekate was illustrated time and time again. Numerous magical and spiritual traditions were represented, including those of Druidry, Wicca, Traditional Witchcraft, Ceremonial Magick, Goddess Spirituality, Thelema, Chaos Magick, Threskeia, Root Magick, Hellenic, Odinism, Santeria, Candomble, Voodoo, Hinduism, Buddhism, The Grimoire Tradition and I am even aware of a few mystical Christians and a Discordian.

Taking into account factors such as the number of times the PDF for the ritual was downloaded, how many people committed in one of the online groups to doing it and also the feedback received afterwards, we can now make a conservative estimate that there were around 3000 people who participated and lit a flame for Hekate on the day, in up to 69 countries spanning all six the inhabited continents of the world. Many individuals, groups and Covens have adopted The Rite as a regular part of their practice and are performing it on the Full Moon of every month and many more have expressed a desire that the The Rite of Her Sacred Fires should continue to be performed each year on the Full Moon of May, internationally by those who hear Her call and have a desire to further their understanding of Her mysteries. This will continue to build communities and help to connect people with a passion for Hekate and as such is something I am 100% in favour of.

As a direct result of the enthusiasm and overwhelming support from all parts of the world for the *Rite of Her Sacred Fires* an organisation has now been set up, simply known as **The Covenant of Hekate** through which I hope to encourage the further exploration of the Mysteries of Hekate around the world into the 21st century and maybe, even beyond. More information can be found at **www.hekatecovenant.com** or by writing to *The Covenant of Hekate, c/o BM Avalonia, London, WC1N 3XX, United Kingdom.*

Figure 76 - Altar from the Rites of Her Sacred Fires,
27th May 2010 by MDL

A study of the rituals, magic and symbols of the
torch-bearing Triple Goddess of the Crossroads
Sorita d'Este & David Rankine

196 pages, ISBN 978-1905297238 (2009)

Hekate Liminal Rites

A Study of the Rituals, Magic and Symbols of the torch-bearing Triple Goddess of the Crossroads
By Sorita d'Este and David Rankine

Wherever you look, be it in the texts of Ancient Greece and Rome, Byzantium or the Renaissance, the *Greek Magical Papyri* or the *Chaldean Oracles*, you will find Hekate. The magical whir of the strophalos and the barbarous words of the *voces magicae* carry her message, the *defixiones*, love spells and charms all provide us with examples of the magic done in her name. She was also associated with the magic of death, including necromancy and reanimations, as well as prophetic dreams, nightmares, healing herbs and poisons.

The sorcery of Medea and Circe, the witchcraft of the women of Thessaly, the writings of philosophers such as Hesiod and Porphyry all provide glimpses into the world of those who honoured her. Her magical powers were considered so great that even King Solomon became associated with her, she was incorporated into Jewish magic, and merged with other goddesses include Artemis, Selene, Bendis and the Egyptian Isis. Whilst for some she was the Witch Goddess, for others she was the ruler of angels and daimons, who made predictions about Jesus and Christianity.

156 pages, ISBN 978-1905297092 (2006)

Hekate : Keys to the Crossroads

A collection of personal essays, invocations, rituals, recipes and artwork from modern Witches, Priestesses and Priests who work with Hekate, the Ancient Greek Goddess of Witchcraft, Magick and Sorcery.
Edited by Sorita d'Este (Various Contributors)

Hekate is one of the most fascinating Goddesses of the Ancient World. Loved, feared, hated and worshipped by people throughout history, the Witch Goddess of the Crossroads, facing three-ways, with her three faces, remains an image of power and awe in the modern world today, amongst those who understand and respect her power.

In three parts – Hekate's History Myths and Powers; Hekate's Witches and Recipes, Rites and Rituals.

Combining the best of research with a wide range of experiences this compact volume opens doorways to many of Hekate's realms. It is a unique journey – enchanting, funny, scary, magickal and daring, challenging and informative. Whether you find yourself agreeing or disagreeing with the perceptions with the perceptions you will find within, one thing is certain: there is always more to learn and experience when it comes to Hekate.

Available from
www.avaloniabooks.co.uk

Lightning Source UK Ltd.
Milton Keynes UK
UKOW07f2324240815

257473UK00004B/69/P